M000116237

Ready-to-Go Lessons

Grade 2

About This Book

Your friends at *The Mailbox*® have done it again! We've combined four previously published books from the Lifesaver Lessons® series for Grade 2 *(Language Arts, Math, Science,* and *Social Studies)* into one comprehensive edition. This new compilation—*Ready-to-Go Lessons, Grade 2*—offers everything you need in one book to supplement all four curriculum areas for your grade level.

What Are Ready-to-Go Lessons?

Just as the name implies, this book includes well-planned, easy-to-implement, curriculum-based lessons that are ready to go in minutes. Each lesson contains a complete materials list, step-by-step instructions, a reproducible activity or pattern, and several extension activities.

How Do I Use a Ready-to-Go Lesson?

Each lesson is designed to decrease your preparation time and increase the amount of quality teaching time with your students. These lessons are great for introducing or reinforcing language arts, math, science, and social studies concepts. They'll even come in handy if you're planning for a substitute, as each lesson is planned and written for you and the materials can be easily gathered in advance. After completing each lesson as described, try one or more of the fun-filled extension activities that are included with each lesson.

What Materials Will I Need?

We've tried to make each lesson as easy to implement as possible, so most of the materials can be easily found right in your classroom. Be sure to read each materials list prior to the activity, as some supplies might need to be gathered from your school library or supply room.

Table of Contents

Ready-to-Go Lessons

Grade 2

Managing Editor: Scott Lyons
Contributing Writers: Kathy Bateman, Darcy Brown, Rebecca Brudwick, Elizabeth Chappell, Amy Erickson, Heather Godwin, Cynthia Holcomb, Lisa James, Susie Kapaun, Martha Kelly, Jaunita L. Krueger, Pam Kucks, Karen Leiviska, Laura Mihalenko, Melanie Miller, Vicki Mockaitis, Sharon Murphy, Valerie Wood Smith
Copy Editors: Sylvan Allen, Karen Brewer Grossman, Karen L. Huffman, Amy Kirtley-Hill, Debbie Shoffner
Cover Artist: Nick Greenwood
Art Coordinator: Rebecca Saunders
Artists: Pam Crane, Theresa Lewis Goode, Nick Greenwood, Clevel Harris, Ivy L. Koonce, Sheila Krill, Clint Moore, Greg D. Rieves, Rebecca Saunders, Barry Slate, Stuart Smith, Donna K. Teal
Typesetters: Lynette Dickerson, Mark Rainey

President, The Mailbox Book Company™: Joseph C. Bucci
Director of Book Planning and Development: Chris Poindexter
Book Development Managers: Elizabeth H. Lindsay, Thad McLaurin, Susan Walker
Curriculum Director: Karen P. Shelton
Traffic Manager: Lisa K. Pitts
Librarian: Dorothy C. McKinney
Editorial and Freelance Management: Karen A. Brudnak
Editorial Training: Irving P. Crump
Editorial Assistants: Terrie Head, Hope Rodgers, Jan E. Witcher

www.themailbox.com

©2002 The Education Center, Inc.
All rights reserved.
ISBN #1-56234-517-6

Manufactured in the United States
10 9 8 7 6 5 4 3 2 1

Poppin' Good Sounds

Get your class poppin' with a tasty decoding review.

Skill: Decoding the digraph *oo*

Estimated Lesson Time: 30 minutes

Teacher Preparation:
Duplicate page 7 for each student.

Materials:
1 copy of page 7 per student

Teacher Reference:

Digraph *oo* as in *good*		Digraph *oo* as in *food*	
book	hook	bloom	school
brook	look	boom	scoop
cook	nook	boost	shoot
cookies	shook	fool	smooth
crook	stood	hoot	spoon
foot	took	moon	stool
hood	wood	noon	too
hoof	wool	pool	tool
		room	zoo

Introducing The Lesson:

Tell students to become detectives as they examine a list of words. On the board, write the following list: "school, foot, loop, hood, moon, book." Ask students if they notice something the words have in common. Verify that each word contains the digraph *oo*. Now challenge students to find a way to sort the list into two groups. After several sorting suggestions, confirm that one way to sort the list is to divide the words into the short sound of *oo* (as in *foot*) or the long sound of *oo* (as in *school*).

Steps:

1. Ask students to brainstorm other words to add to the two categories. If desired, keep the list on the board for students' reference as they complete the reproducible activity.

2. Distribute a copy of page 7 to each student.

3. Provide time for students to complete the reproducible.

4. Challenge students to complete the Bonus Box activity.

Patterns
Use with the activities on page 8.

©The Education Center, Inc.   ©The Education Center, Inc.

Poppin' Good Sounds

Read each sentence.
Write the words in dark letters on the correct popcorn popper.
The first one is done for you.

oo
as in
good

1. **good**
2.
3.
4.
5.
6.

oo
as in
food

1. **food**
2.
3.
4.
5.
6.

1. Popcorn is a **good food** for snacking.

2. You can **cook** popcorn in the microwave.

3. Some people **choose** to add butter to it.

4. **Scoop** a handful of this tasty snack.

5. **Look** at each piece carefully.

6. Can you find a piece shaped like a **balloon**?

7. There's one shaped like a flower, **too**.

8. I **took** some popcorn to the park.

9. I put some at the **foot** of a tree.

10. I **stood** still as a squirrel found the popcorn.

11. I will make more popcorn **soon**.

Bonus Box: Do you like popcorn? On the back of this page, tell why or why not.

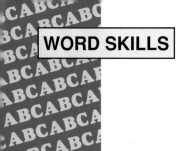

How To Extend The Lesson:

• Use the popcorn art on page 6 to duplicate two pieces of popcorn for each student. Instruct the student to write a word containing one of the *oo* sounds on each pattern. Display the completed patterns on a bulletin board for a delicious vocabulary display.

• Supply each student with an index card (or a copy of the popcorn pattern on page 6) and several kernels of unpopped corn. Instruct the student to copy a list of *oo* words from the board onto his card, gluing a kernel of popcorn in place of each letter *o*.

• Help students learn more about this tasty treat by reading aloud *The Popcorn Book* by Tomie dePaola (Scholastic Inc., 1978). Then pop up a batch for students to enjoy as you review facts from the book.

• Lead your class in a corny cooking activity using the recipe below.

Peanut Butter-Honey Popcorn
(serves 15–20)

You'll need:

1/4 cup butter or margarine	pan
1/4 cup honey	hot plate
1/2 cup smooth peanut butter	spoon
10 cups popped corn	large bowl
measuring cups	access to a refrigerator

Put the butter in the pan and set it on the hot plate. Let the butter melt; then add the honey and peanut butter. Heat and mix the ingredients until creamy. Put the popped corn in a mixing bowl and pour the peanut-butter mixture over the corn; then toss to coat. Put the peanut butter-honey popcorn in the refrigerator for 20 to 30 minutes. Gently use a spoon to separate the popcorn. Eat and enjoy!

Caterpillar Cravings

*Let students wiggle their way to success
as they classify long-vowel combinations.*

Skill: Determining vowel combinations

Estimated Lesson Time: 30 minutes

Teacher Preparation:
Duplicate page 11 for each student.

Materials:
1 copy of page 11 per student

Teacher Reference:
Vowel Combinations

<u>ai</u>	<u>ea</u> (long *a* sound)	need	high	crow
aim	break	queen	light	flow
chain	steak	seed	might	mow
fail	great	sheet	night	row
jail		sneeze	right	slow
paid	<u>ea</u> (long *e* sound)	sweet	sigh	throw
paint	deal	three	sight	
mail	easy	tree	tight	<u>uy</u> (long *i* sound)
rain	flea	week		buy
snail	leak		<u>oa</u>	guy
train	mean	<u>ei</u> (long *a* sound)	boat	
	peak	eight	coat	<u>y</u> (long *i* sound)
<u>ay</u>	squeal	freight	float	by
clay	teach	neigh	load	cry
gray	tea	rein	road	fly
lay	pea	sleigh	roam	my
may		vein	soak	spy
play	<u>ee</u>		toad	try
stay	free	<u>igh</u>		why
tray	green	bright	<u>ow</u>	
		fight	blow	

Introducing The Lesson:

Tell students that they will be visited by some very particular caterpillars. Each caterpillar craves only the things that contain the long-vowel sound that is found in its name. Draw a simple sketch of four different caterpillars on the board and label them "Jane," "Steve," "Ida," and "Joe." Ask the class to brainstorm for things each caterpillar might like. Remind students to choose foods, objects, or games that have the same vowel sound as the caterpillar's name. As students respond, write their suggestions under the corresponding caterpillar.

Steps:

1. Discuss with the class the different spellings for each vowel sound on the list.

2. Distribute a copy of page 11 to each student.

3. Allow time for each student to complete the reproducible activity.

4. Challenge students to complete the Bonus Box activity.

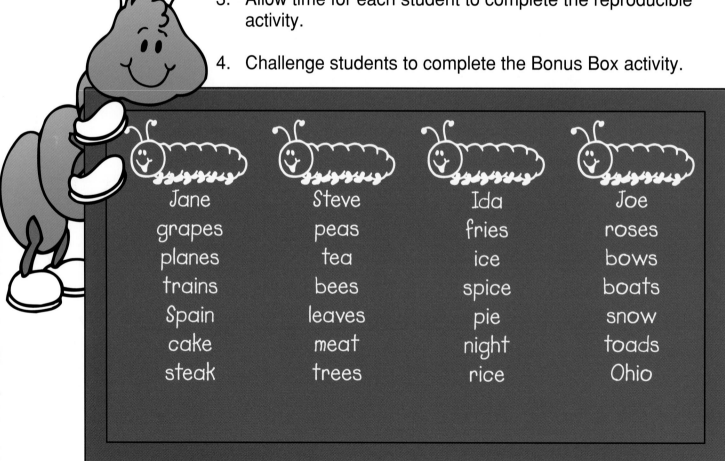

Jane	Steve	Ida	Joe
grapes	peas	fries	roses
planes	tea	ice	bows
trains	bees	spice	boats
Spain	leaves	pie	snow
cake	meat	night	toads
steak	trees	rice	Ohio

Caterpillar Cravings

Read each word in the box.
Write the word on a segment of the caterpillar with the matching vowel sound.

be	rain
buy	right
day	road
eight	seed
fly	snow
hope	steak
nice	team
piece	toe

long *a*

long *e*

long *i*

long *o*

Bonus Box: Add one more segment to each caterpillar. Write a word with the correct vowel sound in each new segment.

How To Extend The Lesson:

- Give each student a 12" x 18" sheet of white construction paper and show him how to fold it into four equal sections. In each section, have the student draw a caterpillar and label it with a vowel sound. Then have the student list information about the caterpillars, using the designated vowel sounds in his responses. For example, information about the long *a* caterpillar could include that his name is Avery, he comes from Maine, he likes to skate, he prefers to eat grapes, and he has a pet snake.

- Have students use pages from their library books to search for words with specific vowel sounds. Instruct students to write down each word they find on a copy of the pattern below. Ask student volunteers to share their lists with the class as you write responses on the board. If desired, discuss the different patterns that create the same vowel sound.

- Ask students to group themselves according to the first vowel sound in their names. After discussing the result, have them regroup by using their middle or last names.

- Assign a vowel sound for the day. Have each student draw a picture containing objects that feature that vowel sound. Provide time for students to share their drawings with the class.

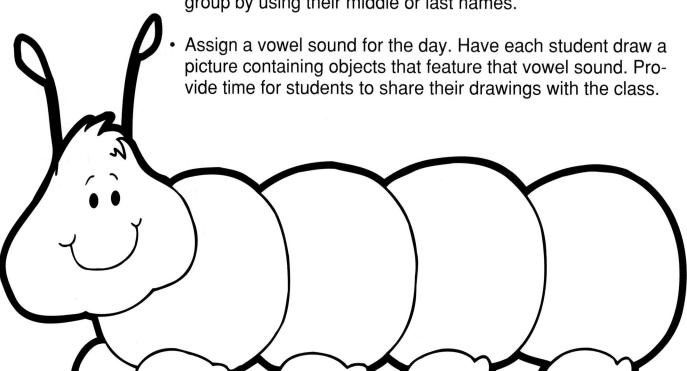

Way-Out Word Birds

Students will take flight with this skills review that pairs up beginning blends with word endings.

Skill: Decoding three-letter blends

Estimated Lesson Time: 30 minutes

Teacher Preparation:
Duplicate page 15 for each student.

Materials:
1 copy of page 15 per student
scissors
glue

Teacher Reference:
Additional Three-Letter Blends

spl-	*squ-*	*shr-*	*thr-*
splash	square	shrank	thread
split	squiggle	shrimp	three
splotch	squint	shred	threw
splinter	squid	shrill	thrill
splurge	squish	shrink	throat
	squeeze	shrub	throne
			throw

Introducing The Lesson:

Make a sketch of an owl on the chalkboard and write the sentence "The screech owl will scramble for straw in the spring" beside it. Tell students to listen for the beginning sound of each word as the class reads the sentence together. Focus attention on the blend in the word *scramble.* Ask students to think of other words that begin with the *scr* sound. Record their responses on the board. Repeat the procedure for the blends *spr* and *str*. Tell students that they will be working with these three blends to complete a reproducible page.

Steps:

1. Distribute a copy of page 15, scissors, and glue to each student.

2. Provide time for students to complete the page.

3. Challenge students to complete the Bonus Box activity.

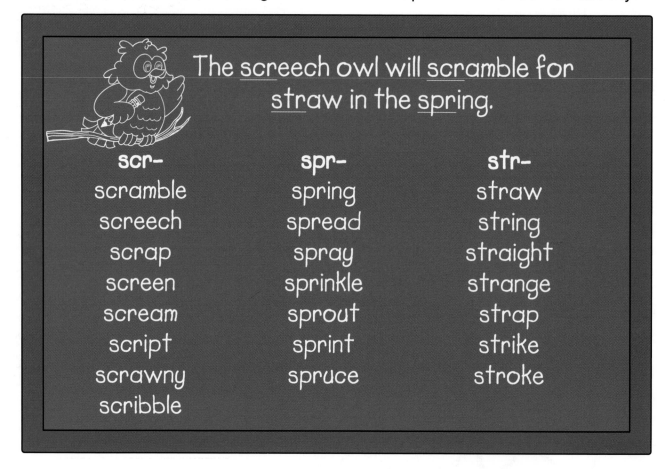

The screech owl will scramble for straw in the spring.

scr-	spr-	str-
scramble	spring	straw
screech	spread	string
scrap	spray	straight
screen	sprinkle	strange
scream	sprout	strap
script	sprint	strike
scrawny	spruce	stroke
scribble		

Way-Out Word Birds

Complete the word on each bird with the letters *scr, spr,* or *str.*
Cut out each bird.
Glue it in the matching nest.

Bonus Box: Choose one word from each nest. Write a sentence with each word on another sheet of paper.

How To Extend The Lesson:

- Place students in small groups for a brainstorming session on blends. Provide each group with a different colored marker and a sheet of chart paper labeled with a different blend. Allow each group a predetermined amount of time to brainstorm for words containing the blend. After the allotted time, have each group switch chart papers with another group. Using the same colored marker, each group continues to add words to the list. After each group has had an opportunity to add to every chart paper, explore the resulting lists with the class.

- Save leftover reproducibles for a blend activity for partners. Pair students and provide the partners with several unused reproducibles. Have the pair locate and circle words that contain a certain blend. Then have the students write each word they discover on a word bank to be displayed in the classroom.

- Challenge students to look for blends in literature. Place a supply of blank index cards in your reading center or on your library shelf. When a student comes across a blend in her independent reading, she writes the word on one side of the index card and illustrates it on the other side. Encourage students to use these cards in partner flash-card practice.

- Encourage students to compose and illustrate tongue twisters using beginning blends. Compile the tongue twisters and illustrations into a class book for students to enjoy.

The clumsy clown closed his closet.
The tremendous troll tripped over a tree.
Spray the spreading sprout in the spring.
The shriveled shrimp shrank by a shrub.
The scrawny scarecrow scratched the
   screen.

Something's Fishy!

Get into the swim of things with this review of word meanings.

Skill: Determining synonyms and antonyms

Estimated Lesson Time: 30 minutes

Teacher Preparation:

Duplicate page 19 for each student

Materials:

1 copy of page 19 per student
scissors
glue

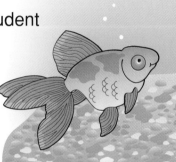

Teacher Reference:

Synonyms

Synonyms are words of similar meaning.

afraid—scared	home—house
alike—same	incorrect—wrong
angry—mad	jump—leap
begin—start	keep—save
below—under	late—tardy
correct—right	look—see
cry—weep	loud—noisy
easy—simple	neat—tidy
end—finish	odd—strange
fast—quick	rip—tear
find—discover	road—street
friend—pal	shout—yell
glad—happy	skinny—thin
grin—smile	small—tiny
hard—difficult	story—tale
	throw—toss

Antonyms

Antonyms are words of opposite meaning.

above—below	fat—thin
add—subtract	float—sink
alike—different	forget—remember
asleep—awake	found—lost
backward—forward	frown—smile
bad—good	happy—sad
begin—finish	left—right
clean—dirty	lose—win
close—open	mean—nice
cold—hot	noisy—quiet
cry—laugh	over—under
day—night	play—work
down—up	right—wrong
dry—wet	rough—smooth
early—late	sour—sweet
fast—slow	tame—wild
false—true	whisper—yell

Introducing The Lesson:

Draw sketches of a small fish and a large fish on the board. Ask students if they know what the phrase "telling a fish story" means. Explain that when someone catches a fish, he sometimes exaggerates how large his catch was. When people exaggerate, we call it telling a fish story. Ask students to think of different ways to express a *large* size. Record words such as *big, huge, jumbo,* and *gigantic* on the board. Reinforce that these words are similar in meaning and are called *synonyms.* Repeat the activity using the word *small.* Record responses on the board. Explain that the synonyms for small are opposites of those for the word large. Reinforce that words that are opposite in meaning are called *antonyms.*

Steps:

1. Distribute a copy of page 19 to each student.

2. Provide time for students to complete the reproducible activity.

3. Challenge students to complete the Bonus Box activity.

large	small
big	little
huge	tiny
jumbo	slight
enormous	petite
gigantic	puny
hefty	dinky

Something's Fishy!

Cut out each fish.
Read the word pair on the fish.
Glue the fish in the correct fishbowl.

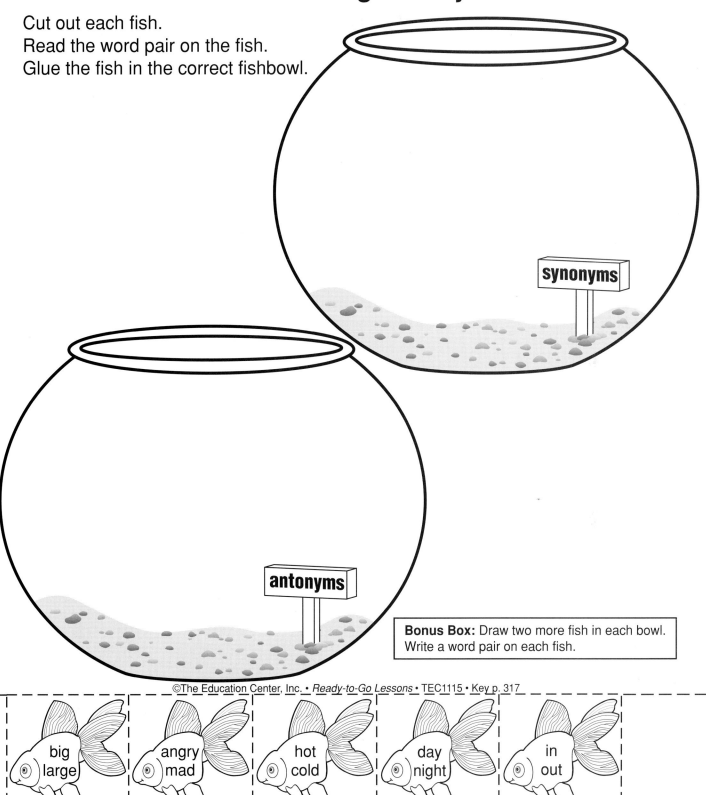

synonyms

antonyms

Bonus Box: Draw two more fish in each bowl.
Write a word pair on each fish.

©The Education Center, Inc. • *Ready-to-Go Lessons* • TEC1115 • Key p. 317

big large

angry mad

hot cold

day night

in out

happy glad

quick fast

open close

kind nice

up down

How To Extend The Lesson:

- Obtain two small glass fishbowls. Use a marker to label one bowl "antonyms" and the other "synonyms." Place the bowls in a center along with a supply of fish-shaped cutouts (see the patterns below). When a student thinks of a pair of synonyms or antonyms, he writes them on a cutout and stores the cutout in the appropriate bowl. Review the contents of each bowl with the class at the end of every week.

- Write several synonym (or antonym) pairs on the chalkboard in a scattered arrangement. Select a student to come to the board and circle two of the words that create a synonym (or an antonym) pair. (To check her work, the student asks the class for verification). If her answer is correct, the student calls a new player to the board. If the answer is incorrect, she erases the circles before calling the next player.

- Write a word of the week on the board. As students think of an antonym or synonym for the word, invite them to write it under the featured word. Remind students to indicate whether their words have the same or opposite meaning as the featured word.

- Prepare a fishy feast for students by filling a clean fishbowl with blue-colored gelatin. Before the gelatin is completely set, stir in a package of jellied fish candies. Serve each student a portion of the mixture in a clear plastic cup. After they eat the treats, ask students to come up with a list of synonyms for "delicious"!

Fish Patterns

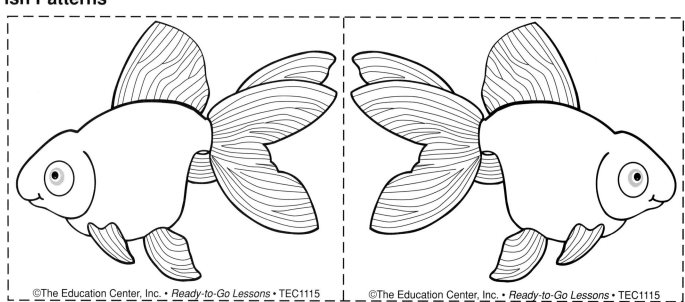

Shortcut Spelling

Introduce contractions as a shortcut to writing.

Skill: Using contractions

Estimated Lesson Time: 40 minutes

Teacher Preparation:
Duplicate page 23 for each student.

Materials:
1 copy of page 23 per student

Teacher Reference:

Contractions

A contraction is a shortened form of a single word or word pair. An apostrophe is used to show where a letter or letters have been omitted to create the shortened form.

words with "am"	
I am	I'm

words with "are"	
they are	they're
we are	we're
you are	you're

words with "has"	
he has	he's
it has	it's
she has	she's
what has	what's
where has	where's
who has	who's

words with "have"	
I have	I've
they have	they've
we have	we've
you have	you've

words with "is"	
he is	he's
it is	it's
she is	she's
that is	that's
there is	there's
what is	what's
where is	where's
who is	who's

words with "not"	
are not	aren't
cannot	can't
could not	couldn't
did not	didn't
do not	don't
does not	doesn't
had not	hadn't
has not	hasn't
have not	haven't
is not	isn't
must not	mustn't
should not	shouldn't

was not	wasn't
were not	weren't
will not	won't
would not	wouldn't

words with "us"	
let us	let's

words with "will"	
he will	he'll
I will	I'll
she will	she'll
they will	they'll
we will	we'll
you will	you'll

words with "would"	
he would	he'd
I would	I'd
she would	she'd
they would	they'd
who would	who'd
you would	you'd

Introducing The Lesson:

Ask students, "What is a shortcut?" Listen to responses, and summarize that shortcuts provide a way to complete a task in a shorter amount of time, or with less work involved. Introduce contractions as a shortcut to writing. Show students how the meaning of two words can be written as one when contractions are used.

Steps:

1. Write several contraction word pairs on the board and show students how two words are combined to form a contraction.

2. Have students brainstorm a list of contractions while you record correct responses on the board.

3. Provide each student with a copy of page 23.

4. Challenge students to complete the Bonus Box activity.

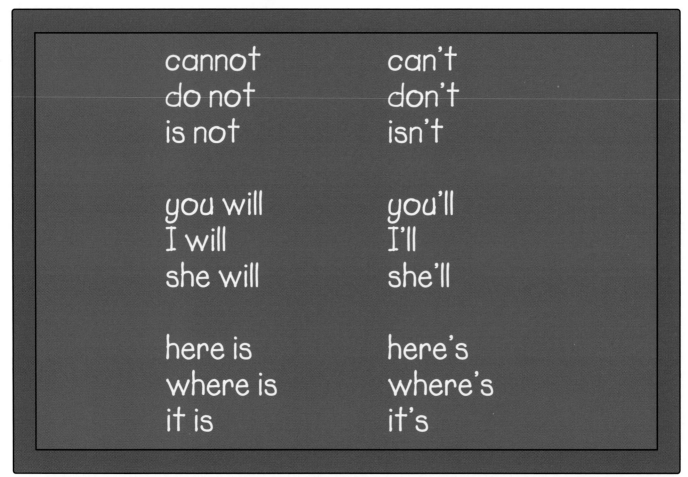

cannot	can't
do not	don't
is not	isn't
you will	you'll
I will	I'll
she will	she'll
here is	here's
where is	where's
it is	it's

Shortcut Spelling

Read the letter from Sherry Shortcut.
Follow the directions to find the contractions.
The first one is done for you.

Dear Friend,

   My name's Sherry Shortcut. I look for shorter ways to do things. It's fun and it saves time. I don't like to clean my room, so I use a shortcut. I pick up my toys after I play. I wouldn't leave them on the floor. I'd have to pick them up later if I did that.

   Sometimes I use a shortcut for writing. It's called using *contractions*. Can you find and circle all the contractions I've used? You'll find ten of them in this letter.

   When you've found them, write each contraction below. Then write the two words each one stands for. You're going to know a lot about contractions!

                                        Your friend,
                                        Sherry Shortcut

---

1. *name's*_____ = *name*_____ *is*_____

2. _____ = _____ _____

3. _____ = _____ _____

4. _____ = _____ _____

5. _____ = _____ _____

6. _____ = _____ _____

7. _____ = _____ _____

8. _____ = _____ _____

9. _____ = _____ _____

10. _____ = _____ _____

Bonus Box: Choose three contractions. On the back of this page, write a sentence with each contraction.

How To Extend The Lesson:

- Provide magazines and newspapers for a contraction hunt. Students find and circle as many contractions as possible, then write the two words that make up the contraction on a sheet of paper.

- Have the class brainstorm pairs of words that can form contractions. Spray a small amount of shaving cream on each child's desk and have each child practice writing contractions from the word list in the shaving cream.

- Supply each student with a baggie filled with alphabet-shaped cereal and pasta. Students use the letters to spell contractions. (Use elbow macaroni for the apostrophes.) Have students glue the words to individual index cards. Pair students with a partner to review the words on the cards for correct spelling.

- Create a contraction center with copies of the patterns below. Program a contraction on each race car and the two words forming the contraction on the wheels. Place the programmed pieces in a center. A student visits the center to match a pair of wheels to each contraction car. Program the back of each car for self-checking.

Car Patterns

©The Education Center, Inc.

©The Education Center, Inc. • *Ready-to-Go Lessons* • TEC1115

Cacklin' Compounds

*Create "egg-citement" over compounds
as students scramble to build words.*

Skill: Recognizing compound words

Estimated Lesson Time: 30 minutes

Teacher Preparation:

1. Duplicate page 27 for each student.
2. Program each of a class supply of index cards with a word that can be used as part of a compound word. If desired, duplicate copies of the chicken pattern on page 26 to use in place of index cards.

Materials:

1 copy of page 27 per student
programmed index cards or chicken patterns

Teacher Reference:

Compound Words

airplane	doghouse	handshake	peanut	somebody
barnyard	dollhouse	homework	playground	something
baseball	doorbell	indoor	policeman	strawberry
bathtub	downstairs	keyboard	popcorn	suitcase
bedroom	fingernail	ladybug	rainbow	sunlight
beehive	firecracker	lighthouse	railroad	sunshine
birdbath	flashlight	mailbox	sailboat	teamwork
birdhouse	football	newspaper	sandpaper	teapot
butterfly	goldfish	nobody	seahorse	toothbrush
chalkboard	grandparents	notebook	scarecrow	underline
cowboy	grasshopper	outside	sidewalk	watermelon
cupcake	groundhog	paintbrush	skateboard	weekend
daydream	hairbrush	pancake	snowflake	
daylight	haircut	patchwork	snowman	

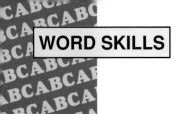
Introducing The Lesson:

Tell your students that they are going to visit a henhouse to hatch some compound words. Write "henhouse" on the board and explain that it is an example of a compound word. Ask students to find the two words that joined together to form the compound. Then distribute a programmed index card to each student. Explain that each student will use the word on her card to create a compound word. The student writes the compound word on the board under the word *henhouse* and draws an egg shape around it.

Steps:

1. Allow time for each student to write a compound word on the board. Discuss the resulting list with the class, redirecting any incorrect responses.

2. Distribute a copy of page 27 to each student.

3. Provide time for students to complete the reproducible.

4. Challenge students to complete the Bonus Box activity.

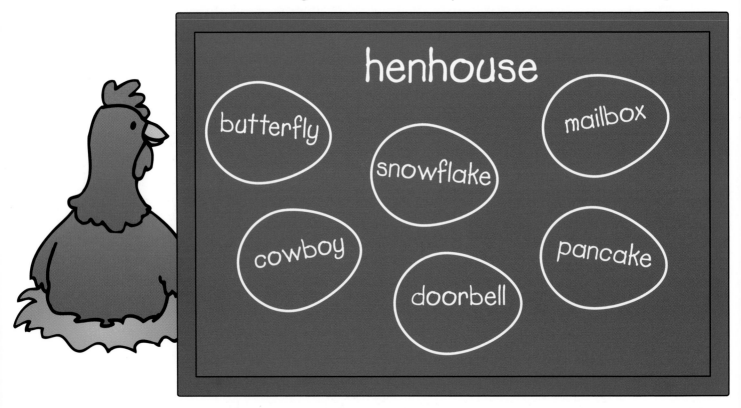

Name _____

Cacklin' Compounds

Read the word list on each chicken.
Make two compound words from each list.
Write your answers under the nests.

1.
bell
door
knob
1. _____
2. _____

2.
ground
house
play
1. _____
2. _____

3.
fish
gold
star
1. _____
2. _____

4.
rise
shine
sun
1. _____
2. _____

5.
ball
flake
snow
1. _____
2. _____

Bonus Box: Think of things in your house that have compound names. Make a list of them on the back of this paper.

©The Education Center, Inc. • *Ready-to-Go Lessons* • TEC1115 • Key p. 317

How To Extend The Lesson:

- Place students in small groups. Assign each group a word such as *fish, sun, snow,* or *bird.* Challenge the groups to think of as many compounds as possible using their words. If desired, have them write their responses on cutouts in the shape of their assigned word.

- Have the class brainstorm for objects in the classroom that have compound names. Begin the list with the word *classroom.*

- Post the weekly menu in an easily accessible place. Have students find as many compound words as possible on the menu. If desired, have students use a highlighting pen to mark the compound words they find.

- Write a compound word on each of several index cards. Cut each card apart to resemble two puzzle pieces. Make sure each piece contains an entire word. Store the pieces in a resealable bag and place it in a center. Students use the pieces to join words together to make compounds, and check their answers by interlocking the pieces.

- Provide a supply of old magazines for students to look through in search of compound words. When a student locates a compound, he cuts out the word and glues it on an index card. Store the cards in a center for students to use as flash cards, for alphabetizing practice, and for other language activities.

Patterns

Stocking The Shelves

Old Mother Hubbard went to the cupboard...for a review of alphabetizing skills! Help students stock up with practice in alphabetizing words to the second letter.

Skill: Alphabetizing to the second letter

Estimated Lesson Time: 30 minutes

Teacher Preparation:

1. Duplicate page 31 for each student.
2. Gather a class supply of index cards. Program pairs of cards with the same letter of the alphabet.

Materials:

1 copy of page 31 per student
scissors
glue
programmed index cards

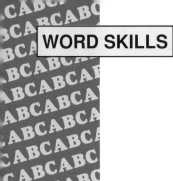

Introducing The Lesson:

Ask for a show of hands from students who have been to the grocery store with their parents. Tell students to think of an item in the grocery store that begins with the letter on the index cards you are going to distribute. Hand each student a card and allow her time to think of an item. Then ask for each student's response and record it on the board. Tell students that before these items can be placed on "shelves," they must be arranged in alphabetical order.

Steps:

1. Draw a simple shelf sketch on the board. Ask students to determine which of the items on the board would come first in alphabetical order. Since there will be two words that begin with the same letter, it will be necessary for students to look at the second letter of the words.

2. When students have determined which item comes first, write the name of the item on the shelf you have sketched. Continue this procedure with the other items listed on the board.

3. After students have practiced alphabetizing to the second letter, distribute a copy of page 31 to each student.

4. Allow time for students to complete the activity.

5. Challenge students to complete the Bonus Box activity.

Stocking The Shelves

Cut out the boxes.
Place the boxes on the shelf in ABC order.
Glue each box to the shelf.

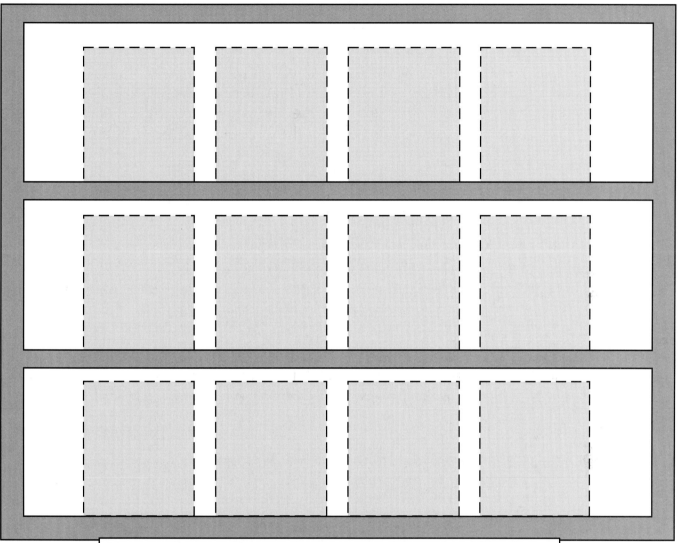

Bonus Box: What would you buy at the grocery store? Write the names of five items you would buy. Write them in ABC order.

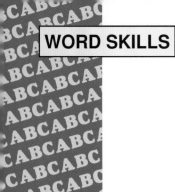

How To Extend The Lesson:

• Have students create a new set of items to go on the shelves. Provide each student with a blank pattern of boxes the same size as those found on the reproducible. Instruct him to program each box with a grocery-store item. Select a dozen of the boxes to use with a new copy of the reproducible.

• Instead of their putting groceries on the shelves, have students create a set of toys to put away. Program a set of boxes with toy items for students to arrange alphabetically on the shelves.

• Provide an actual shelf for students to use as they alphabetize a set of books, a collection of canned food, an assortment of classroom items, or a set of blocks programmed with the students' names.

• Use the school lunch menu to reinforce alphabetizing. Each day have students list the items on the menu in ABC order.

• For a quick alphabetizing activity, instruct each student to select five crayons from her supply box. Have her arrange them in ABC order. Have a partner check her work before the student returns the crayons to the box.

• Use the award pattern to reward students' efforts with alphabetizing practice.

Amazing!
Bravo!
Congratulations!

Your alphabetizing skills deserve a round of applause!

Busy Bookworms

Inch your way to success as these bookworms head for practice with dictionary guide words.

Skill: Using dictionary guide words

Estimated Lesson Time: 30 minutes

Teacher Preparation:

1. Duplicate page 35 for each student.
2. Prepare an overhead transparency of a dictionary page. If desired, use the sample on page 34.

Materials:

1 copy of page 35 per student
prepared overhead transparency
scissors
glue

sail—village
sail
sugar
table
tiger
train
umbrella
uncle
village

apple—drum
apple
bee
boat
candy
cotton
deer
doll
drum

oak—rice
oak
orange
package
pie
queen
quilt
rain
rice

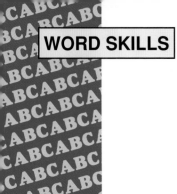

Introducing The Lesson:

Tell students that you are feeling very loquacious today. Write the word on the board. Ask students if they know what the word *loquacious* means. Then ask them how they could find the meaning. Confirm that a dictionary is a good place to find word meanings. Display a dictionary page copied onto an overhead transparency.

Steps:

1. Ask students if they think the word *loquacious* will be on the dictionary page. Have them explain their answers.

2. Point to the guide words on the transparency and inform students that all the words on the page will come between those words in alphabetical order. If desired, point out several words on the transparency and have students confirm their place in alphabetical order.

3. Distribute a copy of page 35 to each student.

4. Instruct students to complete the reproducible without being loquacious, or talkative, as they work.

5. Challenge students to complete the Bonus Box activity.

ladder—lunch

ladder (lá-der) *n* a structure with steps used for climbing up or down
lake (lāk) *n* an inland body of water
leaf (lēf) *n* an outgrowth from a plant stem
lemon (lé-mən) *n* a pale yellow fruit
lift (lift) *v* to raise from a lower to a higher position
lizard (lí-zərd) *n* a member of the reptile family
loom (lüm) *n* a machine for weaving threads into cloth
loquacious (lō-kwā´-shəs) *adj* very talkative
lullaby (lé-lə-bī) *n* a song used to quiet chidren or lull them to sleep
lunch (lənch) *n* a light meal eaten in the middle of the day

Busy Bookworms

Cut apart each bookworm.
Place each bookworm on the page with the correct guide words.
Glue the bookworms in alphabetical order.

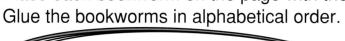

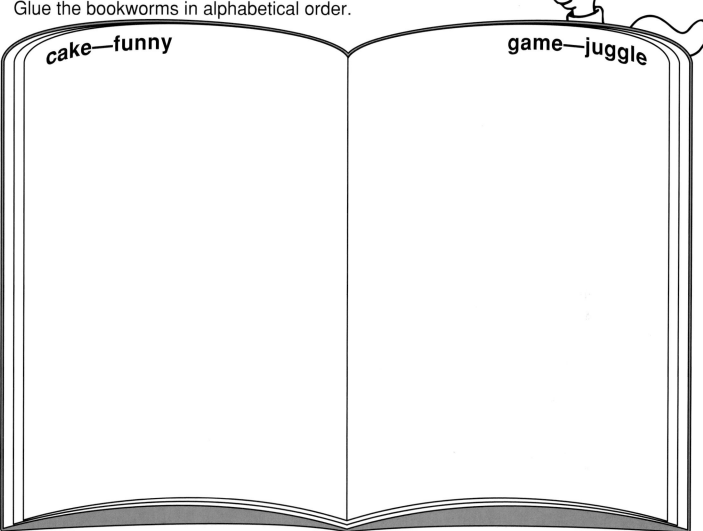

cake—funny

game—juggle

Bonus Box: Draw two more bookworms on each page. On each bookworm, write a word that could be found on the page.

insect

fish

ice

joke

horse

desk

cowboy

candy

grape

farm

eagle

doll

hero

jelly

How To Extend The Lesson:

- Draw a page featuring a pair of guide words on the board. Have students think of ten words that could be found on the page.

- Create a center activity with plastic cups and craft sticks. Label each plastic cup with a pair of guide words. Program several craft sticks with words that fall between the guide words and label them for self-checking. Students visit the center and sort the craft sticks into the appropriate cups, then check their answers.

- Challenge your class with a list of unfamiliar words. Display a list of three or four words on the chalkboard each morning and place several dictionaries on the chalk rails. Students who have a few minutes of extra time during the day can locate the words in the dictionary. At the end of the day, ask student volunteers to define the words.

- Expand on the concept of guide words by explaining that the dictionary can be divided into three sections: The beginning *(A to G)*, the middle *(H to Q)*, and the end *(R to Z)*. Create a display similar to the one pictured below and mount it on a bulletin board, making certain that a pocket is formed behind each section. Provide an assortment of word cards. A student sorts each card into the appropriate section. If desired, program the back of each card for self-checking.

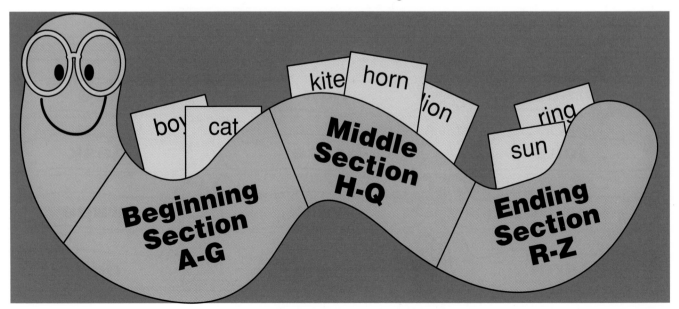

Come To Order!

Students will sharpen sequencing skills as they describe the steps of a favorite activity.

Skill: Sequencing

Estimated Lesson Time: 30 minutes

Teacher Preparation:
1. Duplicate page 39 for each student.
2. Gather the materials listed below.

Materials:
1 copy of page 39 per student
crayons
class supply of drawing paper

Teacher Reference:
Possible sequencing topics:

- making a bed
- brushing teeth
- feeding a pet
- getting dressed
- playing a game

- making a sandwich
- packing a lunch
- wrapping a present
- planting a seed
- washing hair

Introducing The Lesson:

Distribute a sheet of drawing paper and crayons to each student. Ask the students to draw and color a picture of a favorite activity. Provide time for students to complete their drawings; then have them share the pictures with the class.

Steps:

1. After each student has had the opportunity to share his picture, ask the class to think about the sequence of the steps they performed in the drawing activity. List responses on the board as students name steps such as organizing materials, thinking about a subject to draw, sketching in pencil, coloring the picture, and showing the picture to the class. After students generate the list, have them organize it in sequential order.

2. Ask students to look at the picture they have drawn and think about the order in which they perform the activity they have illustrated. Tell students to think of three important steps necessary to perform the activity.

3. Distribute page 39 to each student.

4. Provide time for each student to describe the sequence of his activity.

5. Challenge students to complete the Bonus Box activity.

1. I got out my supplies.

2. I thought about what to draw.

3. I drew the picture in pencil.

4. I colored the picture.

5. I showed the picture to the class.

Come To Order!

Name a favorite activity.
Draw a picture showing how to do each step.
Then write the steps to the activity in order.

first

next

last

The activity is _____.

This happens first:

_____

_____.

This happens next:

_____

_____.

This happens last:

_____

_____.

Bonus Box: On the back of this page, list the order of events in your school day.

How To Extend The Lesson:

- Use the current holiday for a lesson on sequencing. Have students describe the steps for decorating a Christmas tree, making a Valentine's Day card, or decorating an Easter egg. Encourage students to make an illustration of the final product.

- Use the calendar to reinforce the sequence of events. At the end of each day, have students describe an event that happened during the day. Make a note of the event on the calendar. At the end of each week, have students write a summary of the week telling what happened first, what happened next, what happened after that, what happened then, and what happened last.

- For a look at sequencing in reverse, read the story *The Day Jimmy's Boa Ate The Wash* by Trinka H. Noble (Puffin Books, 1992). Then have your students try to describe the events of a day in reverse order.

- Incorporate a writing lesson with the sequencing review. Have students list the steps of making a simple snack such as a cheese sandwich, or peanut butter and crackers. After listing the steps, have students compose a paragraph telling how to make the snack. Then provide the ingredients for the snack and have students prepare it according to the directions in their paragraph.

Peanut Butter Crackers

1. Get a jar of peanut butter, some crackers, a plate, and a knife.
2. Open the jar of peanut butter. Scoop out a small amount with the knife.
3. Spread the peanut butter on a cracker. Then put it on a plate.
4. Spread peanut butter on the other crackers.
5. Put the lid back on the peanut butter.
6. Wash and dry the knife.
7. Enjoy your snack.

And *Then* What Happened?

A good book provides the perfect opportunity for students to fine-tune their skills with predicting outcomes.

Skill: Predicting outcomes

Estimated Lesson Time: 45 minutes

Teacher Preparation:
1. Duplicate page 43 for each student.
2. Select a storybook to share with the class.

Materials:
1 copy of page 43 per student
1 story to read aloud to the class

Teacher Reference:
Suggested titles:

Arthur's Tooth
by Marc Brown
(Little, Brown and Company)

Chrysanthemum
by Kevin Henkes
(Greenwillow Books)

Emily At School
by Suzanne Williams
(Hyperion Books For Children)

In Trouble With Teacher
by Patricia Brennan Demuth
(Dutton Children's Books)

Lilly's Purple Plastic Purse
by Kevin Henkes
(Greenwillow Books)

Martha Speaks
by Susan Meddaugh
(Houghton Mifflin Company)

Mirandy And Brother Wind
by Patricia McKissack
(Alfred A. Knopf)

Ruby The Copycat
by Peggy Rathmann
(Scholastic Inc.)

The Talking Eggs
by Robert D. San Souci
(Dial Books For Young Readers)

READING

Introducing The Lesson:

Ask students if they have ever watched a movie or read a book and knew what was going to happen next. Have several volunteers give examples of situations when they were able to predict the outcome. Ask students to surmise why they were able to figure out the results. Point out that prior events sometimes give us clues as to what will happen next. Tell students that they are going to use the power of prediction as they hear a story and try to determine its outcome.

Steps:

1. Read the selected story to the class, pausing before the culminating event in the story.

2. Distribute page 43 to each student.

3. Have each student use the reproducible to complete information about what has happened in the story so far.

4. Have each student predict what will happen next in the story.

5. Finish reading the story to the class.

6. Have each student use the reproducible to evaluate his prediction and write what really happened next.

7. Challenge students to complete the Bonus Box activity.

The house was on fire and the family was inside sleeping.

But I knew their dog would wake them up and save them, because he was a really smart dog.

The bully at school was always pulling on the girl's braids.

I thought she would get her hair cut short, but she decided to be the bully's friend.

42   *Predicting outcomes*

And *Then* What Happened?

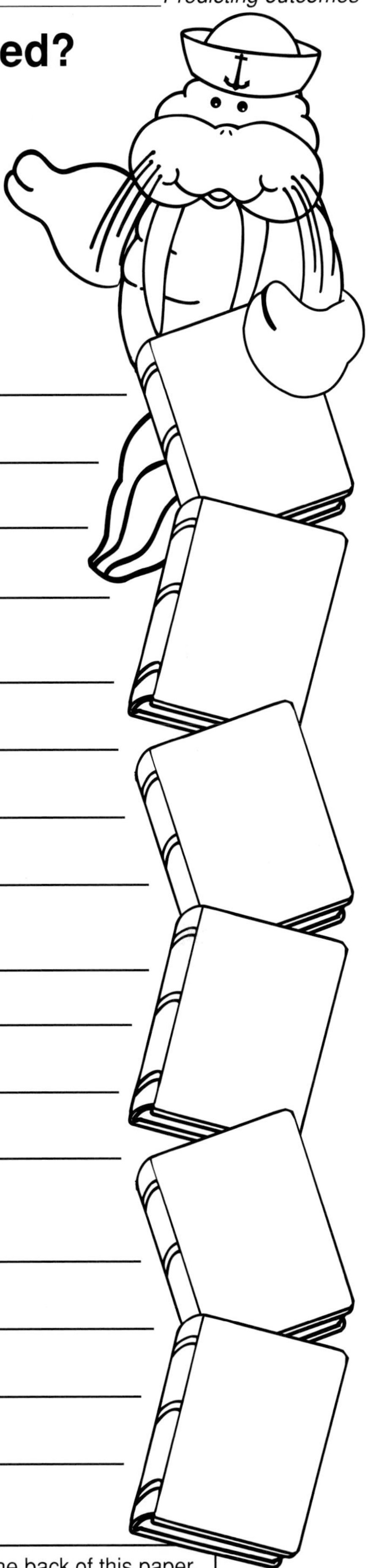

Title of book: _____

Author: _____

Illustrator: _____

This is what has happened so far:_____

_____

_____

_____

This is what I predict will happen next: _____

_____

_____

_____

I think it will happen because: _____

_____

_____

_____

This is what really happened next: _____

_____

_____

_____

Bonus Box: Did you like the outcome? Tell why or why not on the back of this paper.

How To Extend The Lesson:

- Read another story to the class. Stop reading at a critical part of the story. Place the students in small groups to discuss the events and predict the outcome. Have each group present its outcome before you read the rest of the story to the class.

- Ask each student to bring a mystery item for show-and-tell. Instruct the student to place her item in a paper bag before sharing with the class. When it's her turn to share, the student tells what the item is used for, where it came from, and other clues. Her classmates then predict what item is inside the bag. After a designated number of guesses, the student reveals the item.

- Turn a predicting activity into a lesson on graphing. Supply each student with a resealable plastic bag, a wet paper towel, and a lima bean. Instruct each student to place the bean and the paper towel in the bag before sealing it shut. Ask students to predict how long it will take before their beans sprout. Record the responses on a class graph. After all the beans have sprouted, discuss how the predictions compare to the actual results.

- Incorporate a lesson on math predictions by filling a clear container with marbles, jelly beans, or other small items. Have each student predict how many items are in the jar. If desired, have students record their predictions on copies of the form below. Then count the items together to see how close the predictions were to the actual count. Repeat the activity with items of assorted sizes, reminding students to use the information from the original count to help gauge their new predictions.

Name: _____

Name of item: _____

My prediction: _____

The highest prediction in the class is _____.

The lowest prediction in the class is _____.

The actual number of items is _____.

My prediction was (higher, lower) than the actual amount.

Main-Idea Matchup

Reinforce main-idea skills with this picture-perfect review activity.

Skill: Stating the main idea

Estimated Lesson Time: 45 minutes

Teacher Preparation:
1. Duplicate page 47 for each student.
2. Gather the materials listed below.

Materials:
1 copy of page 47 per student
scissors
crayons

The bee is buzzing by the flower.

The cow is jumping over the moon.

The mouse is hiding from the cat.

Introducing The Lesson:

Write the following words on the board: "chicken, pig, horse, cow, sheep." Ask students to read the words and raise their hands if they can name a title for the objects. Call on students to answer, and reinforce that *farm animals* is a good name because all the objects listed are animals that live on farms. Repeat the activity with words related to baseball, swimming, winter clothing, or other pertinent topics.

Steps:

1. Explain to your students that when they thought of names for the objects listed, they were thinking of the main, or most important, idea about the objects. Tell students that they will be identifying main ideas in a matching game.

2. Distribute a copy of page 47 to each student.

3. Instruct each student to draw a picture in the large square, then write a sentence in the rectangle telling the main idea of the picture.

4. Provide time for each student to draw and color a picture, write a sentence, and cut out the box.

5. Have each student show his picture to the class with the sentence folded behind the picture. His classmates volunteer main-idea sentences for the picture. After several responses have been given, the student unfolds his main-idea sentence and reads it to the class.

6. Challenge students to complete the Bonus Box activity.

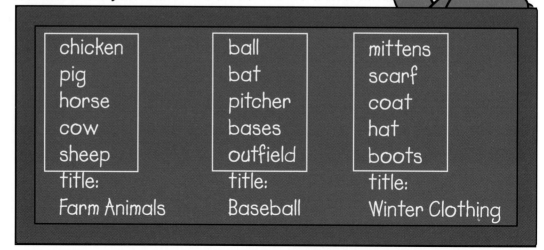

chicken	ball	mittens
pig	bat	scarf
horse	pitcher	coat
cow	bases	hat
sheep	outfield	boots
title:	title:	title:
Farm Animals	Baseball	Winter Clothing

Main-Idea Matchup

Draw a picture in the large box.
Write a main-idea sentence about the picture in the small box.
Cut out the shape.
Fold the sentence behind the picture.

Bonus Box: On another sheet of paper, draw a picture that shows the main idea of your favorite season or holiday.

How To Extend The Lesson:

- Write a main-idea sentence on the board for students to use as a story starter. Have each student copy the sentence and add three or four more sentences that support the main idea. Provide time for students to share their paragraphs with the class.

- Each morning write a short paragraph on the board. Include one sentence in the paragraph that does not support the main idea. Have students rewrite the paragraph, omitting the sentence that does not belong. For an added challenge, have students add one more supporting sentence to the paragraph.

- Select a book with short chapters to read to your students. Read one chapter at a time to the class, but do not disclose the name of the chapter. At the end of each reading, have students suggest an appropriate title for the chapter. Then reveal the title of the chapter to the class.

- Display a print of a famous painting on a bulletin board. Have each student create a title for the painting. After a few days, post the correct title of the artwork.

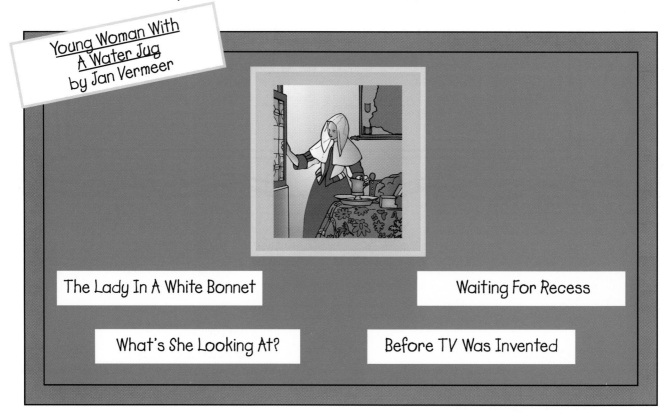

Young Woman With A Water Jug by Jan Vermeer

The Lady In A White Bonnet

Waiting For Recess

What's She Looking At?

Before TV Was Invented

What A Character!

Capitalize on best-loved literature to introduce some real characters into your classroom!

Skill: Analyzing characters in literature

Estimated Lesson Time: 45 minutes

Teacher Preparation:

1. Duplicate page 51 for each student.
2. Provide a library book for each student, or use a story from a basal reader.

Materials:

1 copy of page 51 per student
1 storybook per student
scissors
stapler

Teacher Reference:

Suggested Titles:

Abiyoyo
By Pete Seeger
(Simon & Schuster Children's Books)

Flossie And The Fox
By Patricia C. McKissack
(Dial Books For Young Readers)

The Mud Pony
By Caron L. Cohen
(Scholastic Inc.)

Mufaro's Beautiful Daughters
By John Steptoe
(Lothrop, Lee & Shepard Books)

The Rough-Face Girl
By Rafe Martin
(G. P. Putnam's Sons)

Yeh Shen
By Al-Ling Louie
(Philomel Books)

Introducing The Lesson:

Write the titles of several fairy tales on the board. Ask students to tell who these stories were about. Record the responses under each title. After the lists are complete, reinforce to the students that the names they have listed are *characters* in the stories.

Steps:

1. Instruct each student to identify one of the characters in his library book. Tell the student that he will create a minibook about that character.

2. Distribute page 51 to each student.

3. Challenge students to complete the Bonus Box activity.

Cinderella	Little Red Riding Hood	Jack And The Beanstalk
Cinderella	Red Riding Hood	Jack
stepmother	Grandmother	mother
stepsisters	Wolf	cow
fairy godmother	woodcutter	giant
prince		

Name _____   *Analyzing characters*

What A Character!

Tell about the character in your book.
Complete the sentences in each box.
Cut, sequence, and staple the boxes to make a minibook.

✂--------

A Minibook About _____ (character's name) by _____ (student's name)	This character was in a book called _____. The character looked like this: [ ] **1**	One thing that happened to the character was _____ _____ _____. This made the character feel _____. **2**
Another thing that happened to the character was _____ _____ _____. This made the character feel _____. **3**	The character likes _____ _____ _____. But the character does not like _____ _____. **4**	My favorite thing about the character is _____ _____ _____ _____. **5**

Bonus Box: Would you like to be friends with this character? On a piece of paper, tell why or why not.

How To Extend The Lesson:

- Use the reproducible to supplement stories from your basal or reading curriculum. Have each student complete the minibook by using the main character, or assign a different character from the story to each student.

- Pair your students and have them compare the characters in their stories. Have each pair list the similarities and differences in their characters.

- Encourage students to find a series of books that feature the same character in different stories. Look for the Curious George books by H. A. Rey, the Frances series by Russell Hoban, stories about Lilly by Kevin Henkes, and books featuring Arthur by Marc Brown. Have students determine how the character is alike and different in each story.

- Invite your students to become a favorite character for a day. Encourage students to come to school dressed as one of their favorite literary characters. Have students stay in character by asking them to write the character's name on their papers for the day, play games at recess that are typical of the character, and bring a snack that the character would enjoy. End the day with a discussion of what it felt like to be someone else for a while.

- Enlarge the suitcase pattern below and duplicate a copy for each student. Instruct the student to fill the suitcase with drawings of items that a certain character might take on a trip.

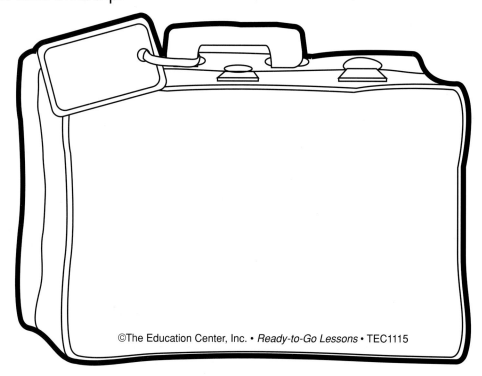

All Aboard!

*Put students on the right track for mapping a story
with this locomotive approach to literature!*

Skill: Mapping a story

Estimated Lesson Time: 45 minutes

Teacher Preparation:
1. Duplicate page 55 for each student.
2. Select a story to be mapped. You may use a story that the class has read together, or have students use library books that they have read individually.
3. Gather the materials listed below.

Materials:
one copy of page 55 per student
one 12" x 18" sheet of white construction paper per student
scissors
crayons
glue

Teacher Reference:

author: the person who wrote the book

character: a person appearing in the story

illustrator: the person who created the pictures in the book

plot: the structure of a story, including the problems or challenges that a character faces

setting: where the story takes place

title: the name of the book

Introducing The Lesson:

Ask students to think about the different parts of a story. Direct responses to include discussions on character, setting, and plot. Record the responses on the board. Tell students that they will each use all the parts of a story to construct a story train.

Steps:

1. Distribute crayons, scissors, glue, a sheet of construction paper, and a copy of page 55 to each student.

2. Instruct each student to complete the information on each section of the train.

3. Provide time for each student to color and cut out the pieces of the train, then glue them to the construction paper. If desired have her draw a track under the assembled train.

4. Challenge students to complete the Bonus Box activity.

Characters	Settings	Plots
• Curious George	• the woods	• pigs try to stay away from a wolf
• Big Bad Wolf	• Italy	• a boy climbs a giant beanstalk
• Alexander	• a castle	• a monkey gets into mischief at the circus
• Stega Nona	• Grandma's house	• a frog needs the kiss of a princess to help him break a spell
• Flossie	• a cave	
• Flat Stanley		

All Aboard!

Fill in the blanks with information about a story you have read.
Color and cut out the train.
Glue the train to a sheet
    of paper.

Author: _____
_____
_____

Title:
_____
_____

The characters
in the story
_____
_____
_____

The setting of the story is
_____

This book is about
_____

Bonus Box: Draw a scene from the story in the background of your picture.

How To Extend The Lesson:

• Challenge students to find stories about trains in the library. Have them work in pairs to create story maps about the books.

• Place students in cooperative groups to read a story together; then have each member complete a section of the train. If desired enlarge the train pattern so that each group makes a poster-size display about its story.

• Have each student write a story that features a train. Use the train pattern as a prewriting activity to help each student generate story ideas. The student can then use the assembled train as a paper topper for his completed story.

• Display the completed story maps in the hallway. Post a banner proclaiming "Our Class Is On The Reading Railroad."

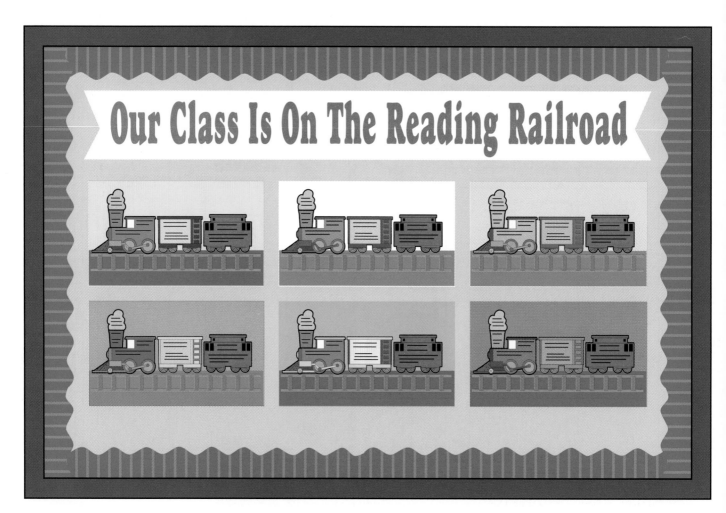

"Tic-Fact-Toe"

*Involve your students in a game of tic-tac-toe
where facts and opinions really make their marks!*

Skill: Determining fact and opinion

Estimated Lesson Time: 30 minutes

Teacher Preparation:
Duplicate page 59 for each student.

Materials:
1 copy of page 59 per student

Teacher Reference:
Suggested fact-filled, bird-related resources:

The Bird Atlas
By Barbara Taylor
(Dorling Kindersley, Inc.)

Everything You Never Learned About Birds
By Rebecca Rupp
(Storey Communications, Inc.)

Outside And Inside Birds
By Sandra Markle
(Aladdin Paperbacks)

What Is A Bird?
By Robert Snedden
(Sierra Club Books For Children)

Our Living World: Birds
By Edward R. Ricciuti
(Blackbirch Press, Inc.)

Introducing The Lesson:

Announce to students that they are going to play a game to review fact and opinion statements. Ask students to explain the difference between a fact and an opinion. Confirm that a fact is a statement that can be proven, and an opinion is a statement that tells someone's view or judgment about a topic. Tell students that to play the game, they will need several facts and opinions about a topic. (If desired, use a topic that the class is currently studying.) Ask students to state facts and opinions about the topic while you list their responses on the board.

Steps:

1. After recording 10 to 12 fact and opinion statements, draw a tic-tac-toe grid on the board. Divide the class into two teams; one team will be the X team, and the other will be the O team.

2. Read a statement on the board to a member of the X team. The student must determine if the statement is a fact or an opinion. If he is correct, he may place his mark on the tic-tac-toe grid.

3. Repeat the procedure with a member of the O team. Continue play until one team has three marks in a row. Play several games to ensure that every student has had a turn.

4. Distribute a copy of page 59 to each student.

5. Provide time for students to complete the reproducible.

6. Challenge students to complete the Bonus Box activity.

> Rain forests have many kinds of birds.
> The parrots are cute.
> Birds are fun to watch.
> Toucans have large, colorful bills.
> Rain forest birds are beautiful.
> Harpy eagles live in the rain forest.
> Butterflies are prettier than birds.
> Many rain forest birds eat fruit.
> Macaws make a horrible noise.
> Some rain forest birds are endangered.

"Tic-Fact-Toe"

Read the statement in each box.
If it is a fact, put an F in the box.
If it is an opinion, put an O in the box.
Determine if F or O won the game.

Birds make good pets.	Many birds build nests.	Humming-birds are cute.
Ostriches are funny looking.	Birds hatch from eggs.	Some birds can swim.
Eagles are birds.	Birds have feathers.	Birds are fun to watch.

Who won the game? _____

Birds are covered in feathers.	Nests keep baby birds safe.	Robins have the prettiest song.
A chicken is a bird.	Parrots are the best birds.	Some birds build nests in trees.
Baby birds are cute.	Peacocks are nice birds.	Some birds have colorful feathers.

Who won the game? _____

Bonus Box: Think of an animal. Write two facts and two opinions about the animal on the back of this paper.

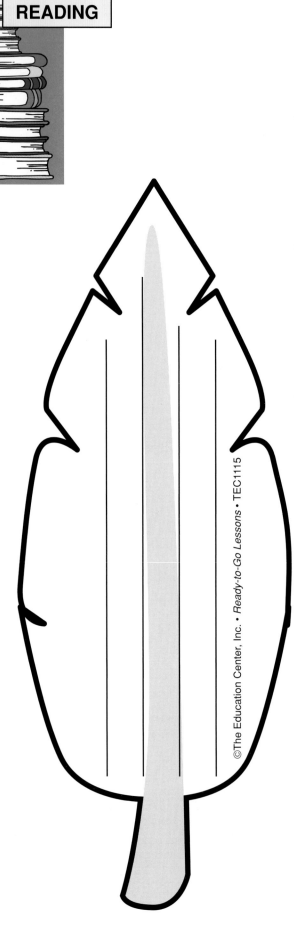

How To Extend The Lesson:

- Have each student research a type of bird. Instruct the student to list five facts and one opinion about the bird. Provide time for each student to share his information with the class, then ask for opinions about his bird.

- Have each student make a simple bird feeder. Instruct the student to tie a length of string to the top of a pine cone. Then have the child press a mixture of suet and birdseed into the pine cone. Hang the feeder where it can be observed from a window.

- Display several types of bird nests in your classroom. Discuss with your class where each nest was found. Have them observe how the nest is woven or held together. Then instruct each student to write one fact and one opinion about each nest.

- Make a batch of yummy bird-nest treats with your students. Melt two 12-ounce bags of butterscotch morsels in a large pan over low heat. Stir eight ounces of dry-roasted peanuts and five ounces of chow-mein noodles into the melted morsels. Drop the mixture by spoonfuls onto waxed paper. As it cools, have each child form a portion of the mixture into a small bird nest. If desired, small jelly beans can be added to each nest for eggs.

- Distribute a copy of the feather pattern on the left to each student. Instruct the student to locate a fact about bird feathers. Have him write the fact on the pattern. Mount the completed patterns on a bulletin board with the title "Fine-Feathered Facts."

Proud As A Peacock

Students will create fanciful feathers
as they demonstrate a flair for following directions.

Skill: Following written directions

Estimated Lesson Time: 30 minutes

Teacher Preparation:
1. Duplicate page 63 for each student.
2. Gather the materials listed below.

Materials:
1 copy of page 63 per student
crayons
a class supply of small treats such as crackers, stickers, or jelly beans

Always follow directions when:
• completing your schoolwork
• playing a game
• preparing a recipe
• practicing safety procedures

Introducing The Lesson:

Without speaking, walk to the chalkboard and write "Clear your desk-top." After students have had time to follow the direction, write "Place both hands on your desk." As a final direction, write "Sit quietly as I walk by each desk." Walk by each student's desk, and place a treat on the desk of each student who has followed the directions.

Steps:

1. Ask your students to guess why they received treats on their desks. Confirm that you rewarded students for following directions.

2. Ask students to think of other ways that it is rewarding to follow directions. Possible answers may include that following directions helps you make better grades, helps with classroom conduct, helps you follow a recipe, and helps you locate a destination.

3. Distribute crayons and a copy of page 63 to each student. Tell students that they will follow the written directions to complete the activity.

4. Provide time for students to complete the reproducible.

5. Challenge students to complete the Bonus Box activity.

1. Clear your desktop.
2. Place both hands on your desk.
3. Sit quietly as I walk by each desk.

Proud As A Peacock

Follow the directions to color the peacock's feathers.
Make the peacock proud of the way he looks!

1. Color the first and last feathers purple.
2. Color the second and eighth feathers green.
3. Color the fourth and sixth feathers blue.
4. Draw red-and-pink stripes on the third and seventh feathers.
5. Draw green and yellow dots on the fifth feather.
6. Color the rest of the peacock.

Bonus Box: Give your peacock a name. Write a sentence about the peacock on the back of this paper.

How To Extend The Lesson:

- White-out the list of directions on the reproducible. Reprogram with another set of directions for your students to follow as they color the peacock.

- Have each student write her own set of directions for coloring the peacock. Instruct students to trade directions with a classmate. Then each student colors her peacock according to her classmate's directions.

- Read the story *The Spooky Tail Of Prewitt Peacock* by Bill Peet (Houghton Mifflin Company, 1973) to your class. After reading the story, have each student draw a picture of Prewitt. Then have the student write a list of directions telling how Prewitt should be colored.

- Treat your students to a tasty exercise in following directions. Duplicate copies of the recipe below or write the directions on the board. Supply students with the necessary ingredients and have them follow directions to create a scrumptious snack.

PEACOCK COOKIE TREATS

1. Wash your hands.
2. Spread peanut butter on a sugar cookie.
3. Select one candy of each color of M&M's®.
4. Place the candies around the edge of the cookie.
5. Eat your colorful treat!

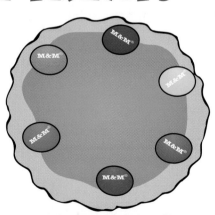

And That's What *Really* Happened!

*A touch of your students' imaginations will lend a spark
to this review of distinguishing reality and fantasy.*

Skill: Distinguishing reality and fantasy

Estimated Lesson Time: 30 minutes

Teacher Preparation:
Duplicate page 67 for each student.

Materials:
1 copy of page 67 per student

Teacher Reference:
Suggested topics for real and fantastic situations:

Reality:
- A student loses his lunch money on the way to school.
- A lost puppy shows up at a student's back door.
- A favorite TV show is interrupted for a special news report.
- Rainy weather delays a ball game.
- School is canceled because of bad weather.

Fantasy:
- An alligator sitting on the school steps eats a student's lunch money.
- A lost hippopotamus shows up at a student's back door.
- A TV show is canceled because of a news report that the sky is falling.
- Rainy weather causes baseball players to use umbrellas instead of bats during the game.
- School is canceled because the weather is so nice that the principal wants to go fishing instead of coming to school.

Introducing The Lesson:

Begin the lesson with a gigantic yawn and explain to students that you were up late last night. As you were getting ready for bed, there was a knock on the door. You went to answer the door and found a grumpy little penguin on your doorstep. He was on his way back to the South Pole and needed a place to stop for the night. He crawled inside your freezer and kept you awake with noises as he rearranged items in the freezer and played with the ice cubes.

Steps:

1. Pause in your story and ask if any students have had a similar experience. As students respond, reinforce the idea that such a situation could not really happen. Write the word *fantasy* on the board. Remind students that the term for a make-believe story is *fantasy*.

2. Ask students to name situations that might really cause someone to stay up late at night. After several responses, reinforce *reality* as the term for a situation that could really happen.

3. Distribute a copy of page 67 to each student. Explain to the class that they will compose realistic and fantasy situations for each topic on the reproducible.

4. Provide time for students to complete the activity.

5. Challenge students to complete the Bonus Box activity.

<u>Fantasy:</u> make-believe	<u>Reality:</u> could really happen
A penguin knocks at the door.	A thunderstorm keeps you awake.
A penguin plays in the freezer.	A barking dog keeps you awake.

And That's What *Really* Happened!

Read each topic.
Write a fantasy sentence about the topic sentence.
Then write a sentence telling what could really happen.

1. It's time for your birthday party!
   This could happen in a fantasy: _____
   _____.

   But this could really happen: _____
   _____.

2. You are going to spend the day at the zoo.
   This could happen in a fantasy: _____
   _____.

   But this could really happen: _____
   _____.

3. Grandmother is coming for a visit.
   This could happen in a fantasy: _____
   _____.

   But this could really happen: _____
   _____.

4. Mother says she has made a surprise for supper.
   This could happen in a fantasy: _____
   _____.

   But this could really happen: _____
   _____.

5. The teacher takes your class on a field trip.
   This could happen in a fantasy: _____
   _____.

   But this could really happen: _____
   _____.

Bonus Box: Write one of your sentences on a sheet of drawing paper. Draw a picture to go with the sentence.

How To Extend The Lesson:

- Use reality and fantasy themes in journal-writing activities. Once a week, have students use their imaginations to describe a fantasy day at school.

- Use an art project as a springboard for a lesson on fantasy. Ask each student to draw an imaginary creature, then paint the illustration with vivid colors. Challenge her to write a description of the creature telling about the fantastic things it can do.

- Have each student write a few sentences about a realistic topic. Instruct the student to include one sentence that is not realistic. Provide time for each student to read his sentences to the class. Have his classmates identify the sentence that is not realistic.

- Share a fairy tale with your students; then work as a class to write a realistic version of the story. For example, Jack's beanstalk might not grow high enough to reach a giant's house, but it might produce enough beans for him to make a pot of chili.

- Host a fantasy show-and-tell, where students tell fantastic stories about the objects they brought to show the class. Be sure to bring an item and tell a fantastic story of your own!

- Share these fantastic tales with your students:
  — *What Use Is A Moose?* by Martin Waddell (Candlewick Press, 1996)
  — *Tiny For A Day* by Dick Gackenbach (Clarion Books, 1993)
  — *Luck With Potatoes* by Helen Ketteman (Orchard Books, 1995)
  — *Martha Speaks* by Susan Meddaugh (Houghton Mifflin Company, 1992)
  — *No Moon, No Milk!* by Chris Babcock (Crown Publishers, Inc; 1993)
  — *Imogene's Antlers* by David Small (Crown Publishers, Inc.; 1985)

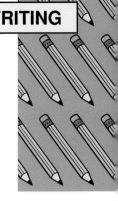

Punctuation Power!

Lead students through an assortment of activities that reinforce correct ending punctuation.

Skill: Using ending punctuation

Estimated Lesson Time: 30 minutes

Teacher Preparation:
Duplicate a copy of page 71 for each student.

Materials:
1 copy of page 71 per student

Teacher Reference:

Periods

- Use periods at the end of declarative sentences (statements) and imperative sentences (commands).
  Examples:
  I like ice cream.
  Bring me a spoon.

- Use a period after each part of an abbreviation or a person's initials.
  Examples:
  Mr. Pierson
  C. A. Weaver

Question marks

- Use a question mark at the end of an interrogative sentence (question).
  Example:
  Where is the office?

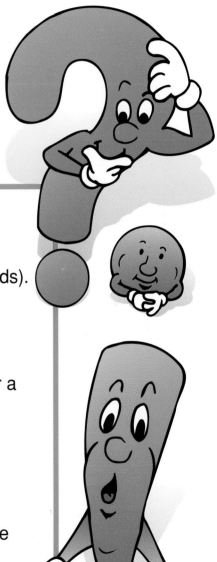

Introducing The Lesson:

As the lesson begins, address the class with the statement, "Put both feet flat on the floor." After the students have complied, follow with the question, "Would you place both hands on your desk?" After students have responded, ask them to think about the two directions you have given. If desired, write both sentences on the board. Discuss the differences between the two types of sentences. Review the concepts of statements and questions.

Steps:

1. Distribute a copy of page 71 to each student.

2. Allow time for students to follow the directions on the page and fill in the correct punctuation.

3. Challenge students to complete the Bonus Box activity.

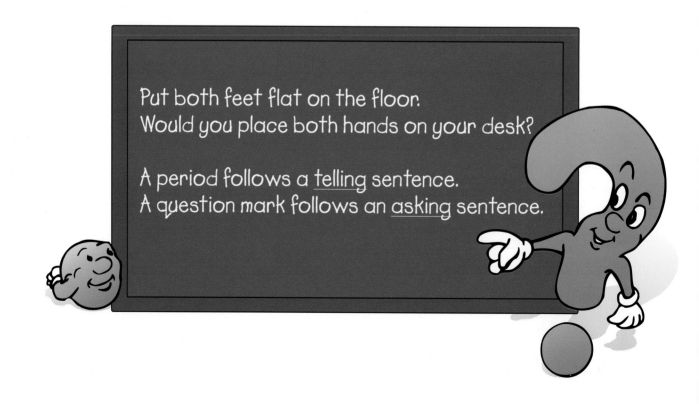

Put both feet flat on the floor.
Would you place both hands on your desk?

A period follows a <u>telling</u> sentence.
A question mark follows an <u>asking</u> sentence.

?\?/?!?\?\?/?! Punctuation Power! \?/?!?\

Write a question mark (?) or a period (.) in the blank after each sentence.
Then follow the directions given in each sentence.
Write your answers in the boxes.

1. Write today's date _____

2. Think of a word that rhymes with *bat* _____

3. How many letters are in the word *punctuation* _____

4. Draw a star shape _____

5. What is your first name _____

6. Who is sitting closest to you _____

7. Spell your name backwards _____

8. Can you name someone wearing green today _____

9. Count the students in your class _____

10. Which hand do you write with _____

11. Underline the answer in number ten _____

12. Name your favorite snack _____

1	
2	
3	
4	
5	
6	
7	
8	
9	
10	
11	
12	

Bonus Box: Write two questions and two statements on the back of this paper.

How To Extend The Lesson:

- Distribute a copy of the patterns below to each student. Read several sentences to the class. Have students hold up the correct punctuation pattern to tell whether each sentence is a statement or a question.

- Provide a supply of magazines and have each student cut out three pictures. Instruct each student to glue the pictures to a sheet of drawing paper. The student then writes a question and a statement relating to each picture.

- Share a short story with your class; then have each student write three questions about the story. Tell each student to switch papers with a classmate and answer the questions on the traded paper. After answering the questions, have the pair proofread each other's paper for punctuation errors.

- Invite the student helper or daily leader to write three unpunctuated sentences on the board. Have her call on student volunteers to add the missing punctuation. If desired, duplicate the patterns below for students to attach to the end of each sentence.

©The Education Center, Inc.   ©The Education Center, Inc.

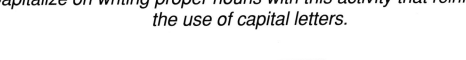

A Capital Idea

Capitalize on writing proper nouns with this activity that reinforces the use of capital letters.

Skill: Using capitalization

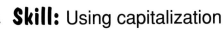

Estimated Lesson Time: 30 minutes

Teacher Preparation:
Duplicate page 75 for each student.

Materials:
1 copy of page 75 per student

Teacher Reference:

Tell students that to capitalize means to begin a word with a capital letter. The following items should always be capitalized:

- the first word in a sentence
  The girl went to the store.

- proper nouns
  Easter
  Beverly Cleary
  Tuesday
  December
  Florida

- the pronoun *I*
  Should I bring a sweater?

- titles and initials
  President Lincoln
  Mrs. Dunlap
  E. B. White

- the greeting and closing of a letter
  Dear John,
  Your friend,

- titles of written works
  The Borrowers
  Ranger Rick

- abbreviations of proper nouns or titles
  PTA
  M.D.

Introducing The Lesson:

Begin the lesson by calling student volunteers to the board to write the answers to such questions as "What is your first name?", "In what month were you born?", and "What state do you live in?" After several answers are on the board, ask the class to notice something that each answer has in common. Verify that each answer begins with a capital letter. Explain that these words are proper nouns and should always be capitalized.

Steps:

1. Review a list of words that should always be capitalized, such as days of the week; months of the year; names of streets, cities, states, and countries; names of holidays; people's names; and the first word of every sentence.

2. Distribute a copy of page 75 to each student. Allow time for students to complete the page.

3. Challenge students to complete the Bonus Box activity.

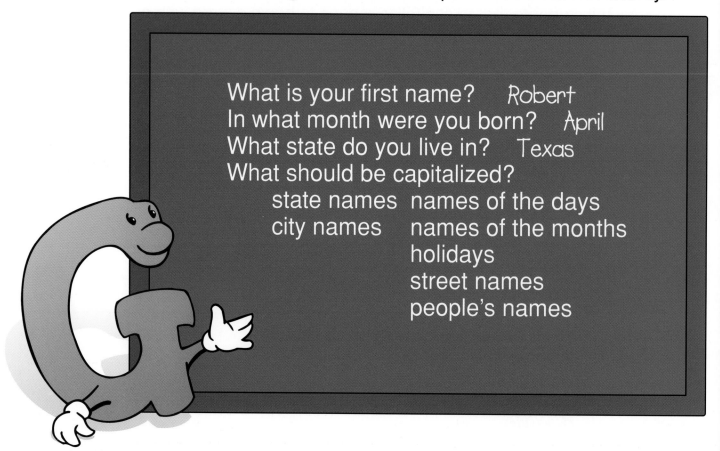

What is your first name?   Robert
In what month were you born?   April
What state do you live in?   Texas
What should be capitalized?
        state names   names of the days
        city names   names of the months
                      holidays
                      street names
                      people's names

A Capital Idea

Answer each question. Be sure to begin each word with a capital letter.

1. What is your first name? _____

2. What is your last name? _____

3. What is the name of your school? _____

4. What is your favorite holiday? _____

5. What day will tomorrow be? _____

6. What day was yesterday? _____

7. What month is it? _____

8. In what state were you born? _____

9. What is your friend's name? _____

10. On what street do you live? _____

Use your answers to write five sentences.

1. _____.

2. _____.

3. _____.

4. _____.

5. _____.

Bonus Box: On the back of the paper, write ten more words that each begin with a capital letter.

How To Extend The Lesson:

- Play a game of Capital Letter Trivia. Divide students into small groups and have them brainstorm words for categories, such as boys' names that start with the letter *M,* states that begin with *N,* and winter holidays. Each group earns a point for every reasonable answer that has been written with a capital letter.

- Use a roll of the die for a daily capitalization challenge. Instruct each student to write a sentence containing capitalized words. The amount of capitalized words the sentence should contain is determined by the number on the die.

- Give each student an old magazine, catalog, or newspaper. Instruct the students to find and cut out capitalized words. Have them glue the words on a chart that has been labeled with categories such as Days Of The Week, Months, Holidays, First Words In The Sentence, etc.

- Write a sentence on the board that contains several capitalization errors. Call on student volunteers to come to the board and correct the mistakes. If desired, use capitalization errors from student papers (anonymously) in the sentences on the board. Reward students for their efforts with copies of the award pattern below.

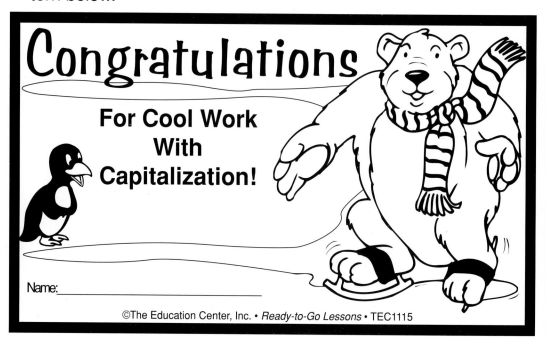

Congratulations

**For Cool Work
With
Capitalization!**

Name: _____

Beyond Description

This guessing game will inspire students to sharpen their writing skills as they describe a mystery object.

Skill: Writing with description

Estimated Lesson Time: 45 minutes

Teacher Preparation:
1. Duplicate page 79 for each student.
2. Prepare several Mystery Boxes. Each box consists of an object inside a shoebox or covered box.

Materials:
1 copy of page 79 per student
several Mystery Boxes

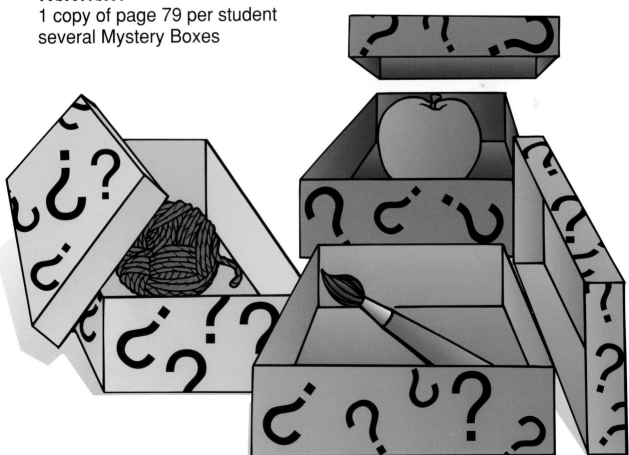

Introducing The Lesson:

Ask students if they have ever played a game called I Spy. Demonstrate the format by providing clues for an object in the room. (For example, "I spy with my little eye something red.") Continue giving clues until students guess the object.

Steps:

1. Tell students that they are going to use clues to describe a mystery object for their classmates to guess. Each student will peek into one of the Mystery Boxes and write a description of the object inside.

2. Distribute page 79 to each student.

3. Challenge students to complete the Bonus Box activity.

4. Have students read their descriptions to the class for a guessing game.

The Mystery Box

Answer the questions about the object in the Mystery Box.
Use the information to write a description of the object.

MYSTERY
BOX

What color is the object? _____

About how large is the object? _____

What shape does the object have? _____

What noise does the object make? _____

How does the object smell? _____

How would the object feel? _____

Where would the object usually be found? _____

How is the object used? _____

Now use the information to write a description of the object.

_____

_____

_____

_____

_____

_____

Bonus Box: Write a list of ten words to describe yourself.

How To Extend The Lesson:

- After students have read their descriptions to the class, make lists of words that were used to describe different attributes. Have students classify words that describe shapes, words that describe colors, and words that describe textures. Record the lists on chart paper so that they can be displayed for future writing assignments.

- Ask for student volunteers to each bring an object from home to be the focus of a descriptive writing assignment. Encourage students to look for items that have interesting detail or unusual features.

- Announce a description show-and-tell, where students must describe their objects before they show them to the class. Classmates might want to guess each object before it is actually shown.

- Duplicate a class supply of the pattern below. Instruct each student to write three sentences on her pattern describing an object in the room. Provide time for students to read their sentences aloud and have classmates try to identify the objects.

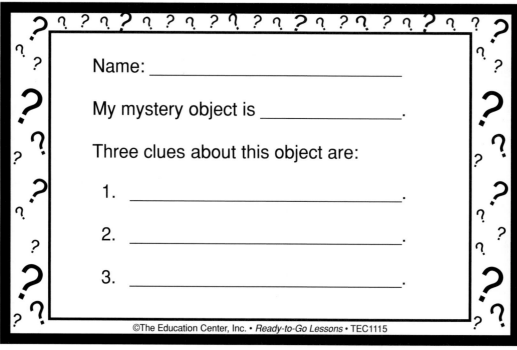

Name: _____

My mystery object is _____.

Three clues about this object are:

1. _____.

2. _____.

3. _____.

©The Education Center, Inc. • *Ready-to-Go Lessons* • TEC1115

Neat, Complete, And Hard To Beat!

Improve writing skills with this activity for making sentences neat, complete, and hard to beat!

Skill: Writing complete sentences

Estimated Lesson Time: 30 minutes

Teacher Preparation:
Duplicate page 83 for each student.

Materials:
1 copy of page 83 per student

Teacher Reference:
A sentence is a basic unit of language which must contain a *subject* and a *predicate*.

A *subject* is a word or phrase in a sentence that does the action, receives the action, or is described. The subject must agree with the predicate.
Examples: *Carol* went to the store.
Green is my favorite color.
The little rabbit hopped away.

A *predicate* is the portion of a sentence that tells something about the subject. It consists of a verb and possibly includes objects, modifiers, or verb complements.
Examples: John *is late.*
The lion *pounced.*
He *threw the ball.*

Introducing The Lesson:

Begin your lesson by giving students directions in incomplete sentences. Tell your students to "Get out your pencils and…" or "…the paper that you need to complete." Ask students if they understand the assignment. Discuss the importance of stating a complete thought to communicate ideas.

Steps:

1. Tell students that they will change some incomplete sentences into complete thoughts. If desired read aloud several of the fragments listed below. Ask student volunteers to restate each fragment as a complete sentence.

2. Distribute a copy of page 83 to each student.

3. Provide time for students to complete the activity.

4. Challenge students to complete the Bonus Box activity.

after we go to recess

under the desk

because it was raining

if you want to

maybe later

in a minute

before you begin

Name_____

Neat, Complete, And Hard To Beat!

Change each incomplete sentence into a complete thought.
Use your neatest handwriting.
Check your capitalization and punctuation.

1. under the table

   _____
   _____.

2. the big dog

   _____
   _____.

3. on Wednesday afternoon

   _____
   _____.

4. because the teacher

   _____
   _____.

5. running down the street

   _____
   _____.

6. at the zoo yesterday

   _____
   _____.

7. started the car

   _____
   _____.

8. drew a picture

   _____
   _____.

Bonus Box: Write two sentences about yourself. Make sure they tell complete thoughts.

How To Extend The Lesson:

• Write a sentence fragment on the board each morning. Have students copy it and make it a complete sentence. Provide time for students to share their sentences with the class.

• Assign each student a subject to write about. Instruct the student to write five complete sentences about the subject. Then have students trade papers with a classmate to check each other's work.

• Display a picture in your writing center. As students visit the center, they must write a complete sentence about the picture. At the end of the week, post the picture and sentences in the hallway for other classes to observe.

• Organize a classroom newsletter. Post a list of topics on the board. Encourage students to submit ideas to the paper by writing a complete sentence or two about a topic. Compile the ideas into a newsletter and duplicate a copy for each student to take home.

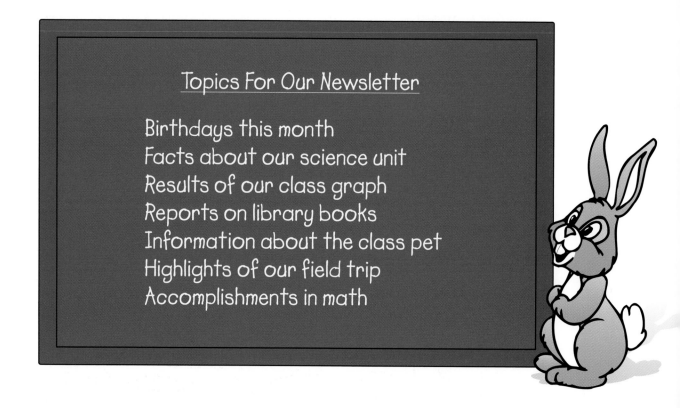

Topics For Our Newsletter

Birthdays this month
Facts about our science unit
Results of our class graph
Reports on library books
Information about the class pet
Highlights of our field trip
Accomplishments in math

Monkeying Around With Mail

Letter-writing practice is a barrel of laughs with this cast of characters on the mailing list!

Skill: Writing a friendly letter

Estimated Lesson Time: 30 minutes

Teacher Preparation:
Duplicate page 87 for each student.

Materials:
1 copy of page 87 per student

Background Information:
The parts of a friendly letter are:
- *date* (tells when the letter was written)
- *greeting* (tells to whom the letter was written)
- *body* (tells what the letter is about)
- *closing* (brings the letter to a close)
- *signature* (tells who wrote the letter)

Introducing The Lesson:

Ask students to recall letters they have received in the mail. Have them identify items such as thank-you notes, party invitations, and friendly letters. Write a sample letter on the board, such as the one shown below. Discuss the information included on the correspondence.

Steps:

1. Review the main parts of a letter: *date, greeting, body, closing,* and *signature.*

2. Distribute a copy of page 87 to each student.

3. Tell the students to read about the characters featured on page 87. Instruct each student to choose a character described on the page and write a letter to that character.

4. Provide time for students to choose a character and write a letter.

5. Challenge students to complete the Bonus Box activity.

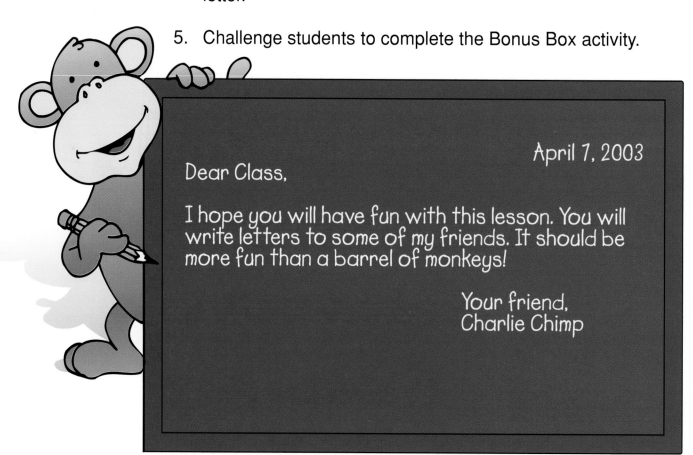

April 7, 2003

Dear Class,

I hope you will have fun with this lesson. You will write letters to some of my friends. It should be more fun than a barrel of monkeys!

Your friend,
Charlie Chimp

Monkeying Around With The Mail!

Read about each monkey.
Write a letter to one of the monkeys.

Marvin Monkey
Marvin is very sad because he lost his
  banana.
Now he doesn't have anything to eat for
  lunch.

Limber Larry
Larry wants to learn how to play basketball.
He needs someone to teach him the
  rules of the game.

Swingin' Sue
Sue wants you to come to her tree
  house.
She wants to teach you to swing from
  the trees.

Brenda Baboon
Brenda is having a dance recital.
She would like for you to come watch
  her dance.

_____
(date)

_____,
(greeting)

_____

_____

_____

_____

_____
(body)

_____
(closing)

_____
(signature)

Bonus Box: Pretend the monkey is writing a letter back to you. Write a letter showing what
the monkey would say.

How To Extend The Lesson:

• Have each student write a story about an encounter with one of the monkey characters. Provide time for students to share their stories with the class.

• Show students how to address an envelope. Have each student bring a stamped envelope from home. Instruct the student to address the envelope to herself. Collect the envelopes, and enclose in each one a monkey cutout made from the pattern below. If desired write a cheery note on each pattern before sealing it in the envelope. Mail the envelopes and tell students to watch for a special letter in the mail.

• Write each student's name on a piece of paper and place the names in a container. Have each student draw a name from the container, making sure that a student does not draw her own name. Instruct each student to write a letter to the person whose name she has selected. Collect the finished letters; then distribute them to the correct students.

• Call a local hospital or nursing home and ask if your students could write cheerful letters to the patients or clientele.

• Ask students to bring in envelopes they have received at home. Place the envelopes in a center so students can examine the postage stamps, postmarks, and states on the return addresses.

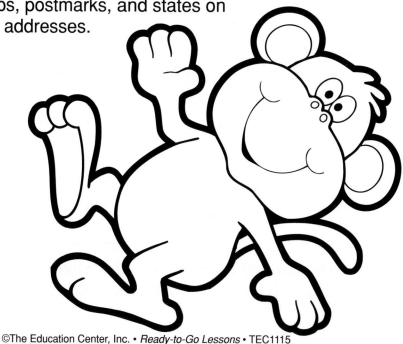

©The Education Center, Inc. • *Ready-to-Go Lessons* • TEC1115

"Eggs-actly" The Facts

*Reinforce basic facts with
this "egg-cellent" addition review.*

Skill: Reviewing addition facts to 12

Estimated Lesson Time: 30 minutes

Teacher Preparation:

1. Duplicate a copy of page 91 for each student.
2. Make an overhead transparency of the pattern on page 90.
3. Gather the materials listed below.

Materials:

1 copy of page 91 per student
1 overhead transparency
1 transparency marker
scissors
glue
crayons

Teacher Reference:

Have your students use manipulatives to solve the following problems about a dozen eggs:

• If three people shared a dozen eggs equally, how many eggs would each person get?

• How many eggs are in a half-dozen?

• If you ate four eggs each day, how long would a dozen eggs last?

• If your teacher had a dozen eggs and gave one egg to each student, how many students would not get eggs?

• If you started with a dozen eggs and scrambled one, boiled two, and made an omelette with three, how many eggs would be left over?

• Can you name a dozen ways to prepare eggs?

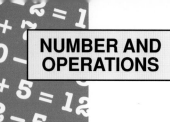

Introducing The Lesson:

Tell students that they are going to use a dozen eggs to review addition facts to 12. Display the transparency of the pattern below and have students count the eggs. Explain that a dozen is equal to 12 items; when we say a dozen eggs, we mean that there are 12 eggs.

Steps:

1. Use the transparency to review addition facts to 12. Color in three of the eggs with a transparency marker. Ask students to determine what number should be added to 3 to equal 12. Confirm that the correct answer is 9; then count the uncolored eggs to demonstrate the correct answer.

2. Repeat the procedure, coloring in a different amount of eggs each time, to review additional facts.

3. Distribute a copy of page 91 to each student. Instruct the students to cut out the eggs at the bottom of their pages to use in solving the math problems.

4. Provide time for students to complete the reproducible; then challenge them to complete the Bonus Box activity.

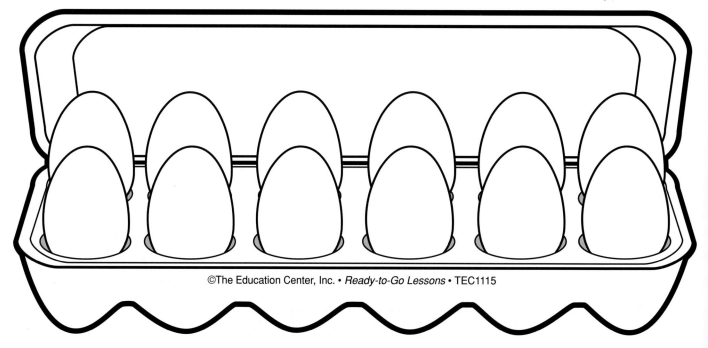

©The Education Center, Inc. • Ready-to-Go Lessons • TEC1115

"Eggs-actly" The Facts

Cut out the eggs.
Use the eggs to help solve each problem.

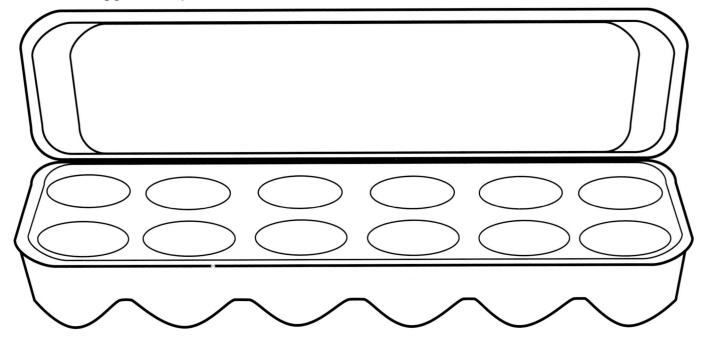

1. 8 + ___ = 12
2. ___ + 7 = 12
3. ___ + 6 = 12
4. 3 + ___ = 12

5. ___ + 10 = 12
6. 4 + ___ = 12
7. 9 + ___ = 12
8. ___ + 11 = 12

9. ___ + 0 = 12
10. 2 + ___ = 12
11. ___ + 1 = 12
12. ___ + 5 = 12

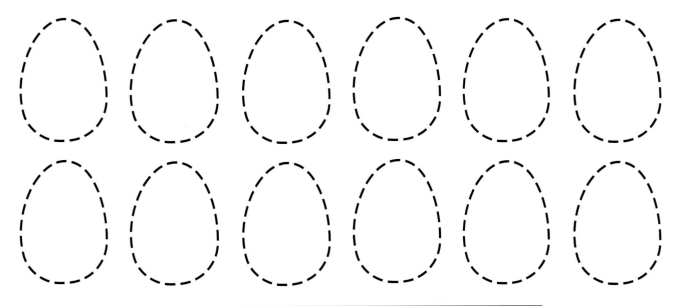

Bonus Box: Color each egg. Glue the colored eggs in the carton.

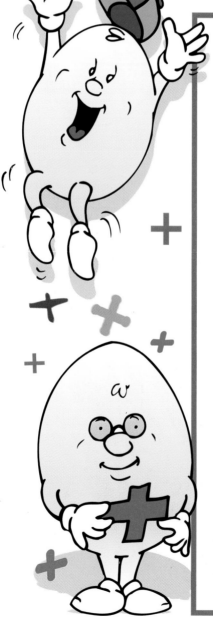

How To Extend The Lesson:

• Introduce students to fact families using the egg-carton transparency. After students identify two addends (such as 5 and 7) that equal 12, explain that the numbers 5, 7, and 12 form a *fact family*. Show your students how the numbers in the family can be arranged to create two addition facts and two subtraction facts.

• Reinforce the concept of a dozen with Dozen Day. Incorporate the following 12 activities into the celebration.

— Have each student bring a dozen crackers, cookies, or pieces of fruit to school. Arrange the treats on a table and let each student select 12 items to snack on during the day.

— Tell each student to write her name a dozen times in her best handwriting.

— Call out a dozen words for a spelling test.

— Write a dozen vocabulary words with definitions on the chalkboard. Challenge each student to use each word at least once during the day.

— Ask students to list a dozen things to do on a rainy day.

— Have students visit the library and select a dozen books for you to read to them during the next month.

— Have students write the names of the 12 months and their abbreviations.

— For math practice, have students solve a dozen addition and a dozen subtraction problems.

— Have students brainstorm a list of things that come in 12s. Be sure to include the numbers on a clock, the inches in a foot, the months of the year, a dozen roses, and a dozen doughnuts on the list.

— Ask students to list a dozen things they know about dinosaurs, plants, weather, or animals.

— List a dozen states and have students locate them on a map.

— Have each student select a dozen crayons from her supply box. Ask her to create a picture using those crayons.

Addition On The Wing

*Let a bright bunch of butterflies
reinforce addition practice.*

Skill: Solving addition with regrouping

Estimated Lesson Time: 30 minutes

Teacher Preparation:
1. Duplicate page 95 for each student.
2. Program a 9" x 12" sheet of construction paper with a numeral from 1 to 9 for each student.

Materials:
1 copy of page 95 per student
1 programmed sheet of construction paper per student
crayons

Quick Tip:
Help students keep numerals in line when working with column addition. Create a set of practice problems on a sheet of notebook paper turned sideways. Duplicate a class supply, making sure that the lines of the notebook paper show clearly on the copies. Then have students use the lines to help them keep numerals in the correct columns when solving the problems.

Introducing The Lesson:

Draw ten butterfly shapes across the top of the chalkboard. Tell students that they will use regrouping skills to solve some addition problems. Each time an addition problem is solved, you will color in a butterfly shape.

Steps:

1. Write "+ 9" on the chalkboard. Distribute a programmed sheet of construction paper to each student.

2. Tell the class that you will call one or two students to come to the front of the room with their numerals. The students will form a number that the class will add to the number on the board.

3. Call a student to the front of the room. Write his numeral on the board to form a column addition problem with nine as the other addend. Ask students to help you solve the problem while you model the steps for regrouping. Then color in one butterfly shape.

4. Repeat the process, using different student volunteers. Call individual students as well as student pairs to reinforce both single- and double-digit addition. Continue until all the butterfly shapes have been colored in.

5. Distribute a copy of page 95 to each student. Have each student complete the page independently.

6. Challenge students to complete the Bonus Box activity.

Name _____

Addition On The Wing

Add the numeral in the balloon to each numeral on the butterfly's wings.
Write the answers on the wings.
The first one is done for you.

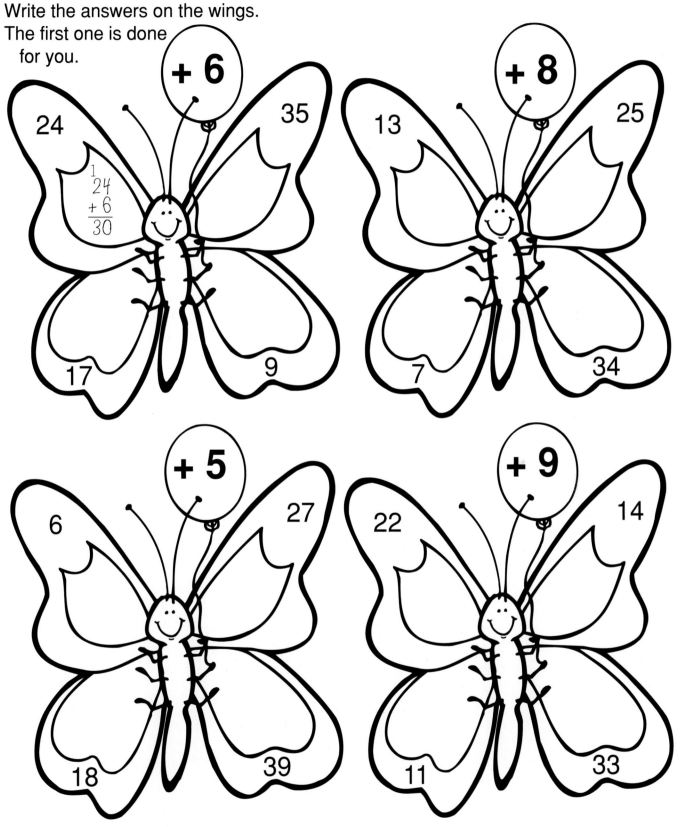

$$\begin{array}{r} \overset{1}{2}4 \\ + 6 \\ \hline 30 \end{array}$$

24   35
17   9

+ 6

13   25
7   34

+ 8

6   27
18   39

+ 5

22   14
11   33

+ 9

Bonus Box: Look at each answer. Then use the code to color the wings:
10–19 blue, 20–29 green, 30–39 red, 40–49 yellow.

©The Education Center, Inc. • *Ready-to-Go Lessons* • TEC1115 • Key p. 318

95

How To Extend The Lesson:

- Use the numeral cards from the activity on page 94 for a partner activity. Distribute a numeral card and a blank sheet of paper to each student; then group students in pairs. Instruct each pair to create a two-digit number with their numerals and to use this number throughout the activity. Have the partners meet with another pair of students, then write and solve an addition problem using their two numbers. Continue the activity until all student pairs have met together.

- Place students in pairs for some high-rolling addition practice. Each student pair will need a die, a sheet of paper for scoring, and a pencil. To play, each student takes turns rolling the die and adding the number from each roll to his score. To begin earning points, a student must roll a six on his turn. He is then awarded six points and may begin adding points from subsequent rolls to his score. The first player to earn exactly 50 points is the winner.

- Create an alphabet chart with an assigned numerical value for each letter. Begin with a value of ten for the *a,* and continue in sequence, ending with 35 for the *z.* Then have students find the values of the two-letter words shown below.

a	b	c	d	e	f	g	h	i	j	k	l	m
10	11	12	13	14	15	16	17	18	19	20	21	22

n	o	p	q	r	s	t	u	v	w	x	y	z
23	24	25	26	27	28	29	30	31	32	33	34	35

at

$a = 10 \quad t = 29$

$$\begin{array}{r} 10 \\ +29 \\ \hline 39 \end{array}$$

is if me to of my do he

up an so it we no us go

Subtraction Stars

Give students a chance to shine as they practice subtraction skills.

Skill: Solving subtraction facts to 12

Estimated Lesson Time: 30 minutes

Teacher Preparation:

1. Duplicate page 99 for each student.
2. Gather the materials listed below.

Materials:

1 copy of page 99 per student
12 index cards or construction-paper squares per student

Quick Tip:

Show students how to check their subtraction answers by using addition to work the problem in reverse. For example, $12 - 8 = 4$ can be checked by adding the difference (4) to the subtrahend (8). The answer should result in the minuend (12).

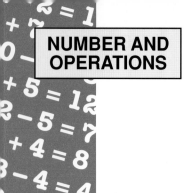

NUMBER AND OPERATIONS

Introducing The Lesson:

Tell students that they will work in pairs to play a subtraction game. In order to play the game, students need to know subtraction facts to 12. To prepare for the game, students will practice writing and solving some problems as a class.

Steps:

1. Call two student volunteers to come to the chalkboard. Ask each volunteer to write a numeral from 1 to 12 on the board.

2. Ask the class to name a subtraction problem that could be made using the two numerals. Remind students that in a subtraction problem, the larger number *(minuend)* must be above the smaller number *(subtrahend)*.

3. Write the subtraction problem on the board and ask the class to name the correct answer.

4. Repeat the activity until every student has had a chance to participate.

5. Distribute 12 index cards (or construction-paper squares) and a copy of page 99 to each student. Instruct each student to write a numeral from 1 to 12 on each card (or square).

6. Place students in pairs to complete the reproducible. Each student shuffles his cards and places them face-down in a stack. To complete the first problem, each student turns over the first card in his stack. The pair determines which number is the minuend and which is the subtrahend. The students write and solve the problem on their reproducibles. They continue this procedure until 12 problems have been written and solved.

7. Challenge students to complete the Bonus Box activity.

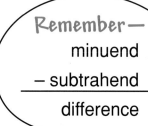

Remember—
$$\begin{array}{r} \text{minuend} \\ -\ \text{subtrahend} \\ \hline \text{difference} \end{array}$$

Name _____

Subtraction Stars

Follow your teacher's directions to become a subtraction star!

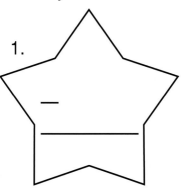

1.

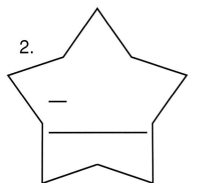

2.

3.

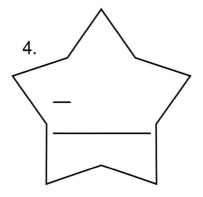

4.

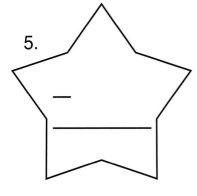

5.

6.

7.

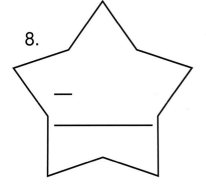

8.

9.

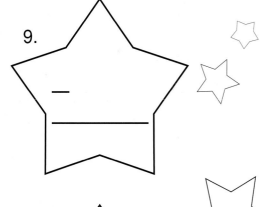

10.

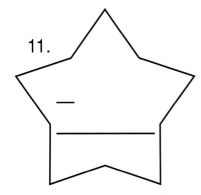

11.

12.

Bonus Box: How many letters are in your first name? Subtract the number from 12.

How To Extend The Lesson:

• Use an empty egg carton for a math center activity. Place an object in each section of the carton. Have each student work with a partner to complete the activity as follows: One student turns his back while his partner removes some of the objects from the carton and closes the lid. The student turns around and counts the objects his partner removed, then determines how many objects remain in the carton. After he gives his answer, his partner opens the lid and they count the remaining objects to check the answer. The partners switch roles and repeat the activity.

• Incorporate a measurement activity into subtraction practice. Place objects less than 12 inches long in a math center. Have each student measure the objects in inches, then subtract the length of each object from 12. Change the objects periodically to provide students with additional practice.

• Reward students for their efforts with copies of the award pattern below.

When it comes to subtraction, you really SHINE

To: _____

From: _____

©The Education Center, Inc. • *Ready-to-Go Lessons* • TEC1115

Bubble-Gum Subtraction

This subtraction activity shows that math facts can be fun, by gum!

Skill: Subtracting to 18

Estimated Lesson Time: 40 minutes

Teacher Preparation:

1. Draw a gumball machine on the chalkboard as shown.
2. Cut out a supply of construction-paper circles to use as gumballs for the machine. Each pair of students will need one cutout. (Or, if desired, use the variation described in the Quick Tip below.)
3. Duplicate page 103 for each student.

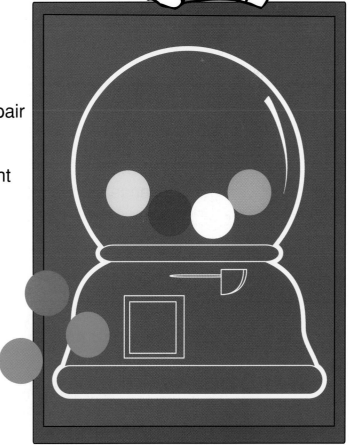

Materials:

1 gumball cutout per student pair
tape
1 paper clip per student
1 copy of page 103 per student

Quick Tip:

Instead of using gumball cutouts, supply each student pair with a piece of scrap paper to use in Step 1 on page 102. Then, for each correct response, draw a gumball in the machine instead of following the directions in Step 2.

Introducing The Lesson:

Draw a gumball machine similar to the one on page 101 on the chalkboard. Tell students that they are going to get the chance to fill the machine with gumballs. Divide students into pairs; then distribute a gumball cutout to each pair of students. (Or, if desired, follow the alternate directions described in the Quick Tip on page 101.)

Steps:

1. Ask each student pair to write a subtraction problem, with facts to 18, on one side of the gumball cutout. Then have them write the answer on the other side of the cutout.

2. Ask a student from one pair to read his subtraction problem to the class. Have the other student in the pair call on a volunteer to answer the problem; then have him check the answer on the back of the cutout. If the answer is correct, the volunteer tapes the gumball cutout inside the gumball machine.

3. Repeat the activity until all student pairs have shared their subtraction problems.

4. Distribute a copy of page 103 and a paper clip to each student.

5. Demonstrate to students how to use a paper clip and a pencil to create a spinner on the gumball machine as shown below.

6. Challenge students to complete the Bonus Box activity.

Bubble-Gum Subtraction

Use a pencil and a paper clip to make a spinner with
   the gumball machine.
Spin the paper clip.
Write the number in the box.
Subtract.
Write the answer in the gumball.

1. 18 – ☐ = ◯

2. 11 – ☐ = ◯

3. 9 – ☐ = ◯

4. 16 – ☐ = ◯

5. 6 – ☐ = ◯

6. 15 – ☐ = ◯

7. 8 – ☐ = ◯

8. 17 – ☐ = ◯

9. 7 – ☐ = ◯

10. 14 – ☐ = ◯

Bonus Box: Use the spinner to spin five more
subtraction problems. Write the problems and
the answers on the back of this sheet.

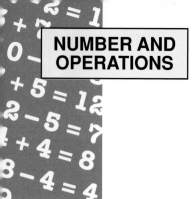
How To Extend The Lesson:

- Have students use calculators to check their answers on the previous activity (page 103).

- Use clear Con-Tact® paper to attach a copy of the gumball-machine pattern below to each student's desk. When a student hands in a math homework assignment, apply a sticker to the machine. Use this record-keeping method to keep track of students' assignments; then provide a reward when it's full.

- Have each student write a story problem about gumballs on an index card. Collect the cards; then have students solve the problems as you read them aloud to the class.

- Enlarge the pattern below on construction paper; then cut out the large gumball machine and display it on a classroom wall. Invite each student who does well on a math test or who shows tremendous improvement to write his name on a construction-paper gumball and tape it to the machine.

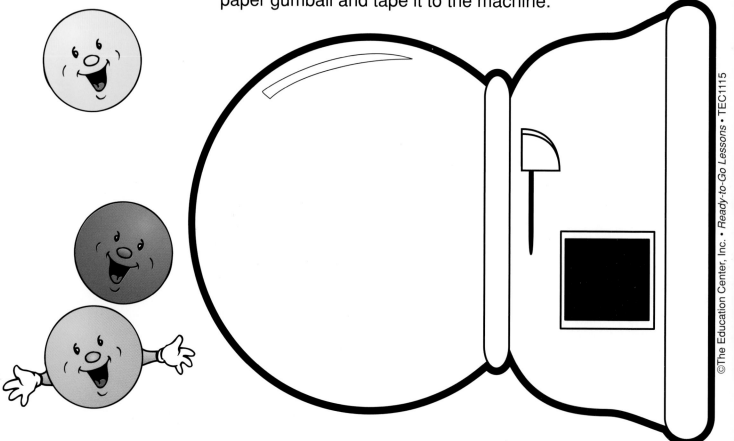

Trade Ten

*Put students on a roll to reinforce grouping objects
by tens in a race to reach 100.*

Skill: Determining place value to 100

Estimated Lesson Time: 30 minutes

Teacher Preparation:
1. Duplicate page 107 for each student.
2. Gather the materials listed below.

Materials:
1 copy of page 107 per student
1 set of place-value manipulatives for each student (See the
   patterns on page 313.)
1 die for each group of three students (If desired, use the number-
   cube pattern on page 108 to make a die.)

Teacher Reference:
Reinforce the concept of 100 items by asking
your students to consider the following:

Is 100 very many…

pennies to have?
cars to own?
hairs on your head?
blades of grass to mow?
houses in a neighborhood?
grains of sand?

dishes to wash?
scoops of ice cream?
pieces of rice to eat?
candles on a cake?
dogs to own?
leaves on a tree?

Introducing The Lesson:

Tell students they will use a die to roll and add to reach 100 points. Ask students to think about using a die: What could the largest number of a roll be, and what could the smallest number be? Then ask students how many groups of ten it would take to reach 100. Confirm the answer by having students count to 100 by tens. Tell students that they will be working in groups of three as they race each other to roll 100 points, and they must keep score on a chart that counts by ones and tens.

Steps:

1. Distribute a copy of page 107 and a set of manipulatives to each student.

2. Divide the class into groups of three. Give each group a die.

3. Explain the rules of the game as follows:

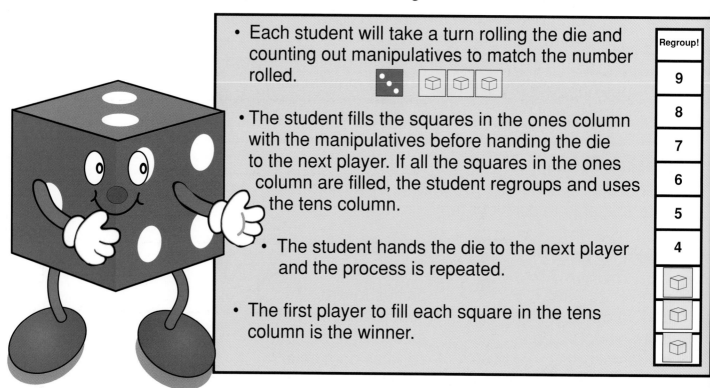

- Each student will take a turn rolling the die and counting out manipulatives to match the number rolled.

- The student fills the squares in the ones column with the manipulatives before handing the die to the next player. If all the squares in the ones column are filled, the student regroups and uses the tens column.

- The student hands the die to the next player and the process is repeated.

- The first player to fill each square in the tens column is the winner.

Regroup!
9
8
7
6
5
4

4. Challenge students to complete the Bonus Box activity.

Name _____

Place value

Trade Ten

Roll the die.

Fill the spaces in the ones column with counters.

Each time the ones column is filled, trade 10 ones for a place in the tens column.

The first player to reach 100 wins!

Trade 10 ones for 1 ten.

	100

Regroup! Trade 10 tens for 1 hundred.	Regroup!
90	9
80	8
70	7
60	6
50	5
40	4
30	3
20	2
10	1

★ **Start here.**

Bonus Box: Have everyone in the group roll the die. Write the numbers on the back of the paper. Add them up. Tell how many tens and ones are in the sum.

©The Education Center, Inc. • *Ready-to-Go Lessons* • TEC1115

107

How To Extend The Lesson:

• Have each student in the group roll the die two times. The first roll represents the number in the ones column and the second roll represents the number in the tens column. Instruct the student to fill in his chart with manipulatives to show the two-digit number. After each student has had a turn, the students compare numbers to see who rolled the largest numeral.

• Have each student in the group roll the die. Instruct the group to use the resulting numbers to create the largest numeral and smallest numeral possible.

• Write a two-digit numeral on the board. Have students use their reproducibles and the manipulatives to show the numeral in place-value form. Then try the reverse: Describe a number by telling its place values, and have students come to the board to write the numeral.

Number-Cube Pattern
If desired, use with the activity on page 107.

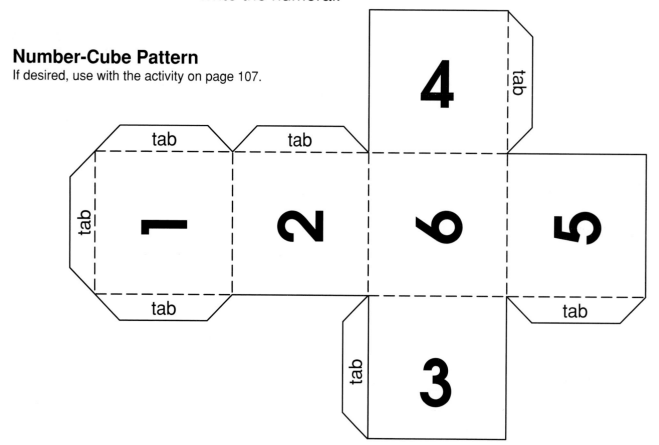

Place-Value Power!

*Reinforce place-value skills with a game
that puts numbers in their place!*

Skill: Determining place value through hundreds

Estimated Lesson Time: 30 minutes

Teacher Preparation:
1. Duplicate page 111 for each student.
2. Program ten index cards, each with a different numeral from 0 to 9.
3. Copy and assemble the spinner on page 112.
4. Gather the materials listed below.

Materials:
1 copy of page 111 per student
5 blank index cards per student
spinner (see page 112)
programmed index cards
an envelope or a container to hold the
   programmed index cards
scissors

Teacher Reference:
Reinforce place value with numbers students experience in everyday situations.
Ask students to determine the place value of these numerals:

- the page numbers in textbooks
- the date on the calendar
- grades on their papers
- the daily temperature
- the numbers in their street addresses
- prices in catalogs or sale advertisements

- menu prices
- coin combination values
- sporting event scores
- heights and weights

Introducing The Lesson:

Tell students that they are going to play a game in which place value will be very important. Review the concept of ones, tens, and hundreds places with your students. (If desired, use the suggestions in the Teacher Reference on page 109.) Tell students that they will have to identify numerals in each place to earn points in the game.

Steps:

1. Distribute a copy of page 111 and five index cards to each student.

2. Instruct students to cut each index card in half. Have them program each half with a different numeral from 0 to 9.

3. Explain to students the rules of the game as follows:

   • At the beginning of each turn, you will randomly select three number cards from a container. As you show the cards to the class, each student will find her corresponding cards.

   • Each student will place her cards in the place-value boxes on the reproducible to create a three-digit number.

   • After students have placed their cards, you will spin the spinner to determine which number wins a point for the turn. Every student with the winning number earns one point.

   • At the end of ten rounds, points are totaled to determine the winner(s).

4. Provide time for students to complete the questions on the reproducible.

5. Challenge students to complete the Bonus Box activity.

Place-Value Power!

Use your cards to play a game with your teacher.
Then answer the questions.

Hundreds	Tens	Ones

Use the numerals 3, 5, and 8 to answer these questions.

_____ 1. What is the largest number you can make?

_____ 2. What is the smallest number you can make?

_____ 3. Write a number with the largest numeral in the tens place.

_____ 4. Write a number with the smallest numeral in the tens place.

Use the numerals 2, 7, and 9 to answer these questions.

_____ 5. What is the largest number you can make?

_____ 6. What is the smallest number you can make?

_____ 7. Write a number with the largest numeral in the tens place.

_____ 8. Write a number with the smallest numeral in the tens place.

Use the numerals 1, 4, and 6 to answer these questions.

_____ 9. What is the largest number you can make?

_____ 10. What is the smallest number you can make?

_____ 11. Write a number with the largest numeral in the tens place.

_____ 12. Write a number with the smallest numeral in the tens place.

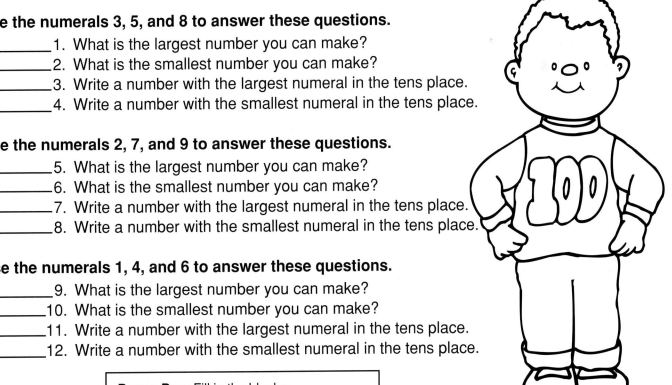

Bonus Box: Fill in the blanks:
I would like to have 100 _____.
I would *not* like to have 100 _____.

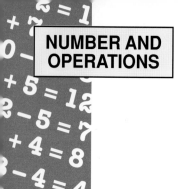
How To Extend The Lesson:

- Have students use their cards from the reproducible activity in a three-digit number challenge. Place your students in pairs. Instruct each student to shuffle his cards and stack them facedown. Have each student turn over the first three cards and arrange the numerals to create the highest possible number. The partner with the highest number earns a point. Have students play until one player reaches ten points to win the game.

- Place students in small groups to play a variation of the game described on page 110. Make tagboard copies of the pattern below. Provide a spinner for each group of students. Using his cards from the reproducible activity, each student in the group arranges three cards to form a three-digit number. A group member spins the spinner to determine which number wins a point for the round. Have students play ten rounds, then total their points to see which student earned the highest score.

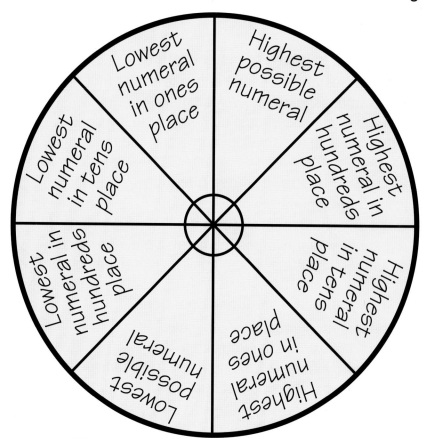

Classroom Count

Leapin' lizards! Have students use objects in the classroom for a greater-than and less-than review.

Skill: Determining greater than and less than

Estimated Lesson Time: 30 minutes

Teacher Preparation:
Duplicate page 115 for each student.

Materials:
1 copy of page 115 per student

Teacher Reference:
Poll your students to determine the greater-than or less-than status of:
- pencils and crayons in each student's desk
- red backpacks and blue backpacks in the classroom
- summer and winter student birthdays
- dog owners and cat owners in the classroom
- students' brothers and sisters
- blue-eyed and brown-eyed students
- bus riders and walkers
- students' preference of hamburgers to cheeseburgers

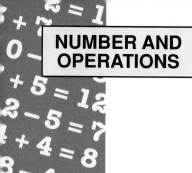

Introducing The Lesson:

Tell students that they will help design the math lesson by counting objects in the classroom; then use the information in a greater-than and less-than review. Call on several students to help confirm the count of each item on page 115.

Steps:

1. Distribute a copy of page 115 to each student.

2. For each object listed, assign several students to count the total number in the classroom.

3. Call on students to announce the count of their assigned objects. Instruct the class to fill in the totals in the appropriate places on page 115.

4. Provide time for students to complete the greater-than and less-than portion of page 115.

5. Challenge students to complete the Bonus Box activity.

girls	14	today's date	7
boys	11	lunch hour	11
lunchboxes	9	# on clock	12
lunch trays	16	teacher's buttons	8
plants	4	bookshelves	3
pets	2	windows	5

Name _____

Classroom Count

Find the total number of each object.
Then complete the greater-than and less-than sentences.

1. The number of boys in the room =
   _____
   The number of girls in the room =
   _____

   _____ > _____

   _____ < _____

2. The number of students who brought
   a lunch = _____
   The number of students buying
   lunch = _____

   _____ > _____

   _____ < _____

3. The number of plants in the room =
   _____
   The number of pets in the room =
   _____

   _____ > _____

   _____ < _____

4. The date on the calendar = _____
   The hour that lunch begins = _____

   _____ > _____

   _____ < _____

5. The highest numeral on the
   clock = _____
   The number of buttons on your
   teacher's clothing = _____

   _____ > _____

   _____ < _____

6. The number of bookshelves in the
   classroom = _____
   The number of windows in the
   classroom = _____

   _____ > _____

   _____ < _____

7. The number of chairs in the
   room = _____
   Your room number = _____

   _____ > _____

   _____ < _____

8. The number of people wearing
   red = _____
   The number of people wearing
   yellow = _____

   _____ > _____

   _____ < _____

9. The number of letters in your school's
   name = _____
   The number of letters in your
   teacher's last name = _____

   _____ > _____

   _____ < _____

10. The number of people wearing white
    shoes = _____
    The number of people wearing blue
    jeans = _____

    _____ > _____

    _____ < _____

Bonus Box: Find another pair of items to count. Then write a greater-than and
less-than sentence about them.

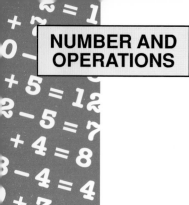

How To Extend The Lesson:

- Compile student-written ideas for another Classroom Count project. Collect ideas from the Bonus Box challenge on page 115, or have students develop ideas as a homework assignment.

- Take students into the cafeteria, gym, or library. Have them work quietly to count preassigned objects in each place. Take the information back to the classroom and use it for greater-than and less-than practice.

- Instruct students to color-code the totals of the objects on page 115. Have them circle each odd number with a blue crayon and each even number with a red crayon.

- Create a file-folder game using the patterns below. Duplicate, color, and cut out each pattern. Glue the patterns to a file folder; then laminate it for durability. Program a set of index cards with number pairs as shown. A student decides which symbol belongs between each number pair and places the card on the correct symbol. Program the back of each card for self-checking. Store the cards in a Press-On Pocket or a zippered plastic bag clipped to the folder.

Greater Than   **Less Than**

Pizza By The Slice

Add pizzazz to math with this tasty lesson on fractions!

Skill: Recognizing fractions (halves, thirds, and fourths)

Estimated Lesson Time: 45 minutes

Teacher Preparation:
1. Duplicate page 119 and the patterns below for each student pair.
2. Gather the materials listed below.

Materials:
1 copy of the patterns below per student pair
1 copy of page 119 per student pair
1 paper clip per student pair
1 piece of drawing paper per student
scissors
crayons
rulers (optional)

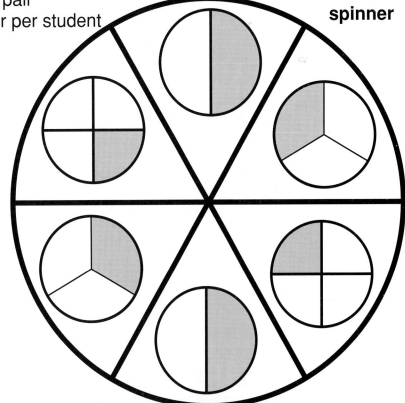

spinner

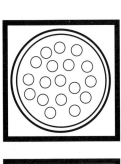

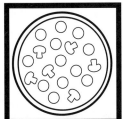

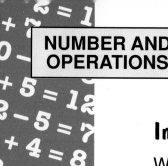

Introducing The Lesson:

Welcome your students to a pretend pizza parlor. Provide each child with a piece of drawing paper and ask him to draw his favorite kind of pizza. Be sure to tell students to draw the whole pizza and not just a slice.

Steps:

1. Draw a pizza on the chalkboard. Tell students that a friend is going to help you eat the pizza. Call on a volunteer to draw a line to divide the pizza in half so that you and your friend will have an equal amount of pizza. Review with students the concept of one half.

2. Draw two additional pizzas on the board. Repeat the activity, dividing one pizza into thirds and the other pizza into fourths.

3. Have each child choose a way to divide the pizza he drew (in half, in thirds, or in fourths). If desired, provide each child with a ruler and instruct him to use it to draw lines dividing his pizza. Then have him label each piece with a fraction. Check for understanding.

4. Pair students. Distribute a copy of the spinner and game-marker patterns to each pair. Ask them to cut out each piece. Then give each pair a paper clip. Show them how to use it as the spinner indicator by placing it around a pencil-point positioned at the center of the spinner.

5. Distribute page 119 to each student pair. Explain the directions for playing the game as follows:

- Place your game markers on START.
- In turn, spin the spinner and identify the fraction.
- Move your game marker to the next space on the gameboard that names the fraction determined by the spinner. Follow any additional directions on the space.
- Continue taking turns until one player reaches FINISH.

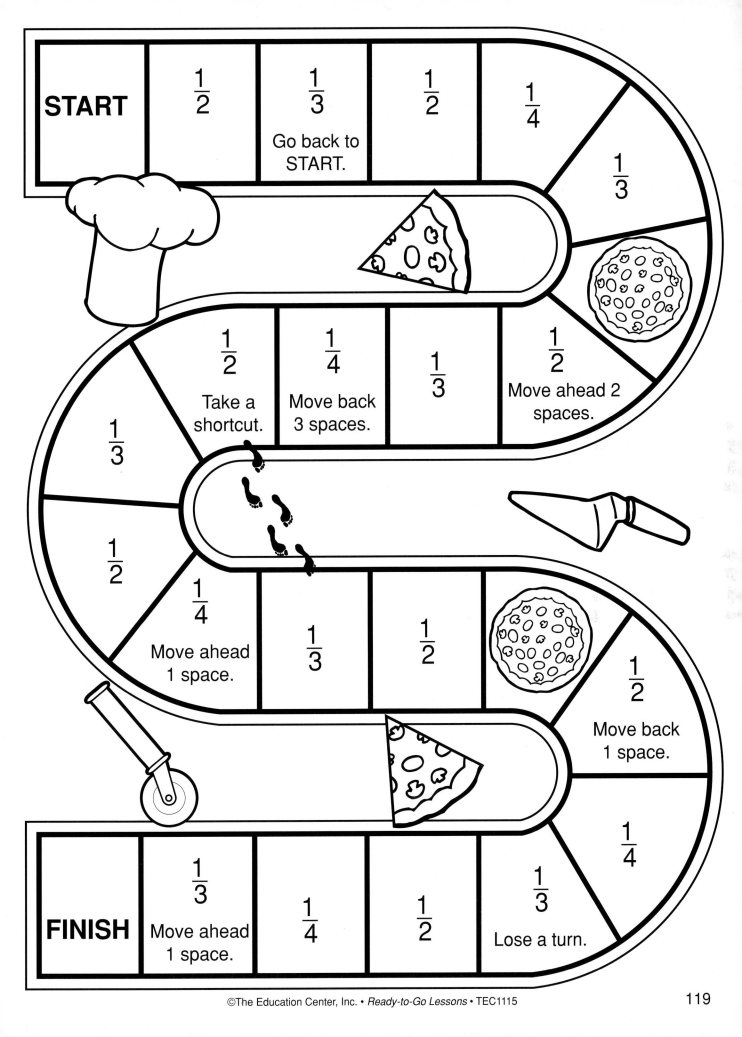

START

$\frac{1}{2}$

$\frac{1}{3}$ Go back to START.

$\frac{1}{2}$

$\frac{1}{4}$

$\frac{1}{3}$

$\frac{1}{2}$ Move ahead 2 spaces.

$\frac{1}{3}$

$\frac{1}{4}$ Move back 3 spaces.

$\frac{1}{2}$ Take a shortcut.

$\frac{1}{3}$

$\frac{1}{2}$

$\frac{1}{4}$ Move ahead 1 space.

$\frac{1}{3}$

$\frac{1}{2}$

$\frac{1}{2}$ Move back 1 space.

$\frac{1}{4}$

$\frac{1}{3}$ Lose a turn.

$\frac{1}{2}$

$\frac{1}{4}$

$\frac{1}{3}$ Move ahead 1 space.

FINISH

How To Extend The Lesson:

- Have students practice making halves, thirds, and fourths from play dough. Provide each child with a ball of play dough and a plastic knife. Have him flatten the dough into the shape of a pancake and then cut it in half. Ask each student to check to see if the halves are equal by placing one on top of the other. If they are not equal, have the student make another pancake and try again. Challenge students to also divide the dough into thirds and fourths.

- This center activity combines measurement and fractions. Gather a variety of containers marked 1/2, 1/3, or 1/4; a large plastic tub filled with sand; and several scoopers. Have students explore fractions by filling the jars with sand to their marked amounts.

- Enlist students' help in cooking up some practice with fractions. The following easy-to-make recipe requires ingredients to be measured in fractional amounts. Place students into groups and provide each group with the needed ingredients and supplies. Have students work together to measure the ingredients to make the treat, then enjoy the tasty results!

Perky Popcorn
3 cups popped corn
1/2 cup peanuts
1/3 cup chocolate candies
1/4 cup butterscotch chips

Measure each ingredient and pour into a large bowl.
Mix together.
Use a measuring cup to divide the mixture into equal portions.
Enjoy!

Words For Sale

Entice students to count money by putting the alphabet up for sale!

Skill: Adding pennies, nickels, dimes, and quarters

Estimated Lesson Time: 45 minutes

Teacher Preparation:
Duplicate page 123 and the letter-value chart on page 124 for each student.

Materials:
1 letter-value chart per student
1 copy of page 123 per student
scrap paper for each student

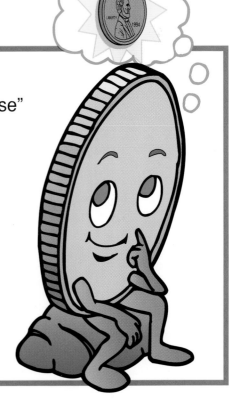

Teacher Reference:
Show students that they can "coin a phrase" with these expressions:
- Penny-pincher
- Putting in your two cents' worth
- A penny for your thoughts.
- A penny saved is a penny earned.
- Money doesn't grow on trees.
- You look like a million bucks!

Introducing The Lesson:

Tell students to imagine that they have to buy letters to make words. Write your name on the chalkboard and tell students that you need their help in determining how much your name would cost. Distribute a letter-value chart to each student. Demonstrate to students how to look at the chart to determine the value of each letter and then add the value of each letter to determine your name's total price.

Steps:

1. Enlist students' help in determining the prices of other school helpers' names, such as the principal and the school secretary.

2. Next ask each child to use the chart and a piece of scrap paper to determine how much her name costs. Then have her exchange papers with a partner, check her partner's work, and then get her own paper back.

3. Ask students questions about the prices of their names, such as "Who has a name that costs more than 50¢?" or "Who has a name that costs less than 90¢?"

4. Distribute page 123 to each student. Have each child choose six spelling words, seasonal words, or theme-related words and write one word on the top line of each problem. (If desired, have students copy a predetermined list of six words from the chalkboard.) Next instruct each student to determine the value for each letter, write the value under each letter, and then add the numbers together to determine the price of each word. Ask students to write the price of each word in its price tag.

5. Challenge each child to complete the Bonus Box activity.

Ms.   Murphy

1¢ + 5¢   1¢ + 1¢ + 10¢ + 1¢ + 1¢ + 1¢ = 21¢

Name _____

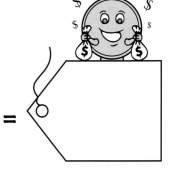

Words For Sale

Follow your teacher's directions to complete this page.

1. _____

_____

=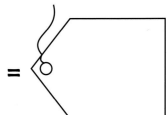

2. _____

_____

=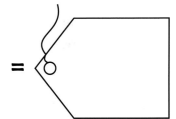

3. _____

_____

=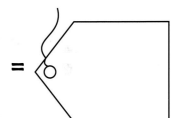

4. _____

_____

=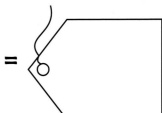

5. _____

_____

=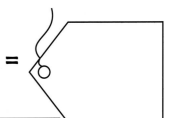

6. _____

_____

=

Bonus Box: Choose three friends' names. How much does each name cost?

How To Extend The Lesson:

- Encourage students to choose other favorite words and determine how much they cost.

- This cooperative-group activity is sure to be a class favorite. Divide students into small groups. Label a sheet of construction paper with an amount of money (less than $1) for each student group. Provide each group with one programmed sheet of construction paper and a supply of dime, nickel, and penny cutouts. Have each group of students work together to glue as many different coin combinations as possible for the amount shown on the construction paper.

Letter-Value Chart
Use with the activity on page 122.

A	B	C	D	E	F	G	H	I

J	K	L	M	N	O	P	Q	R

S	T	U	V	W	X	Y	Z

©The Education Center, Inc. • *Ready-to-Go Lessons* • TEC1115

Piggy-Bank Parade

*Help students cash in on coin comparisons
as they try to collect a dollar's worth.*

Skill: Comparing coins

Estimated Lesson Time: 30 minutes

Teacher Preparation:
1. Duplicate page 127 for each student.
2. Gather the materials listed below.

Materials:
1 copy of page 127 per student
5 pennies and 1 nickel to place in your pocket
scissors for each student
1 die per group of four students
1 resealable bag per student (optional)

Teacher Reference:

Why is some money made from paper and some made from metal? Share this fact with your students:

Because of its large population, China didn't have the resources to make metal coins for all its people. The Chinese came up with the idea of making paper money, since paper was much easier to come by. The first paper money was created, and other countries started using it as well.

Introducing The Lesson:

Tell students that you found ten cents on the sidewalk and you put it in your pocket. With that information, ask students to describe the contents of your pocket. After a few responses, show students that you have five pennies and one nickel in your pocket, which adds up to ten cents.

Steps:

1. Draw a diagram on the chalkboard as shown below. In the ten-cent category, write "5 pennies + 1 nickel." Ask students to name other coins that equal ten cents.

2. Have students help you complete the chart by describing ways to create one cent, five cents, and twenty-five cents.

3. Tell students they can refer to this chart as they play a game. To prepare for the game, distribute a copy of page 127 and a pair of scissors to each student. Instruct each student to cut out the coin patterns at the bottom of the reproducible. If desired, give each student a resealable bag in which to store the coins.

4. Place students in groups of four and give each group a die. Explain the rules of the game as follows:
   - Each player rolls the die. If a number lower than five is rolled, the player takes that number of pennies from his supply and places them on his chart. If a five is rolled, the player uses a nickel. If a six is rolled, the player uses one penny and one nickel.
   - The next player rolls the die and repeats the procedure.
   - At the beginning of each turn, the player exchanges coins on his chart for higher denominations whenever possible.
   - The first player to earn four quarters wins the game.

1 cent	5 cents	10 cents	25 cents	
1 penny	5 pennies	10 pennies	25 pennies	1 dime + 15 pennies
	1 nickel	2 nickels	5 nickels	4 nickels + 5 pennies
		5 pennies + 1 nickel	2 dimes + 1 nickel	3 nickels + 10 pennies
		1 dime	2 dimes + 5 pennies	2 nickels + 15 pennies
			1 dime + 3 nickels	1 nickel + 20 pennies
			1 dime + 2 nickels + 5 pennies	1 quarter
			1 dime + 1 nickel + 10 pennies	

Piggy-Bank Parade

Cut out the coins at the bottom of the page.
Then follow your teacher's directions to play a game.

25¢ Quarters	10¢ Dimes	5¢ Nickels	1¢ Pennies

Coin Patterns

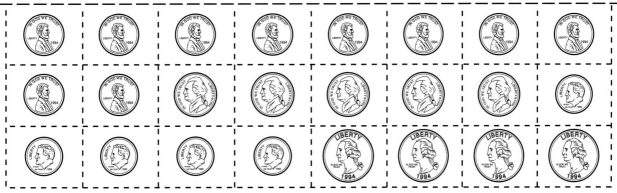

How To Extend The Lesson:

- Have students use their charts and coin cutouts to show different ways of making specified denominations. Record on the chalkboard all the different possible coin combinations for each denomination.

- Read to your class the story *Alexander, Who Used To Be Rich Last Sunday* by Judith Viorst (Atheneum, 1978). After hearing the story, have the students reenact parts of the story with their coin cutouts as you read it a second time. Begin by asking students to create $1.00 with their coins to show how much money Alexander received from his grandparents. As the story unfolds, have students subtract the amounts Alexander spends and figure out how much money he has left. By the end of the story, everyone will know why Alexander is no longer rich!

- Play Money Mystery with your students. Write a clue about a certain amount of money on the chalkboard. Challenge students to solve the mystery by showing which coins were used to create the amount. Here are some clues to get you started:

  - Show 22 cents using five coins. *(1 dime, 2 nickels, 2 pennies)*
  - Show 13 cents using four coins. *(1 dime, 3 pennies)*
  - Show 30 cents using nine coins. *(1 dime, 3 nickels, 5 pennies)*
  - Show 12 cents using four coins. *(2 nickels, 2 pennies)*
  - Show 18 cents using six coins. *(3 nickels, 3 pennies)*
  - Show 26 cents using five coins. *(1 dime, 3 nickels, 1 penny)*
  - Show 30 cents using two coins. *(1 quarter, 1 nickel)*
  - Show 40 cents using three coins. *(1 quarter, 1 dime, 1 nickel)*
  - Show 50 cents using seven coins. *(3 dimes, 4 nickels)*
  - Show 50 cents using four coins. *(1 quarter, 2 dimes, 1 nickel)*

Stepping Out

Students will put their best foot forward to keep their graphing skills sharp.

Skill: Creating a bar graph

Estimated Lesson Time: 30 minutes

Teacher Preparation:
1. Duplicate page 131 and the shoe pattern on page 132 for each student.
2. Gather the materials listed below.

Materials:
1 copy of page 131 per student
1 copy of the shoe pattern (see page 132) per student
crayons
tape
scissors

Teacher Reference:
Have students refer to the completed graph to answer the following questions:
• Which category has the most items?
• Which category has the least items?
• How many items are in the first category?
• How many items are in the second and third categories combined?
• How many more items are in the highest category than in the lowest category?
• How many items are in the highest and lowest categories combined?
• Rank the categories in order from highest to lowest.
• How many items are represented on the graph all together?

Introducing The Lesson:

Tell students that you saw a pair of shoes in a store window and you were amazed by the color. The shoes were bright green with purple stripes and yellow glow-in-the-dark laces. It made you wonder about the most popular shoe color worn by second-grade students in your classroom.

Steps:

1. Ask the class for suggestions on how you could organize information to find the answer. Allow for responses; then explain that a bar graph is a good way to organize information. Tell students they will use a bar graph to find the answer to your question.

2. Distribute a shoe pattern (page 132) to each student. Instruct the student to color the pattern to resemble her shoes and cut it out.

3. Draw a simple bar graph on the board and label it as shown. Have each student in turn tape her colored shoe pattern in the correct column. (For multicolored shoes, choose "other" or use the most prominent color on the shoe.)

4. Distribute a copy of page 131 to each student. Instruct the student to label the graph with the categories shown on the board.

5. Instruct each student to transfer the information from the board onto her graph, create a title for her graph, and then write a statement about the results.

6. Challenge students to complete the Bonus Box activity.

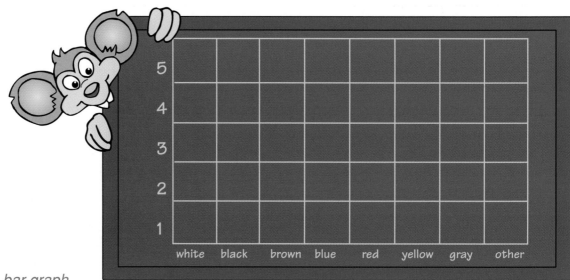

Stepping Out

Follow your teacher's directions to make a graph.
Color the squares to show the different colors of shoes.

10							
9							
8							
7							
6							
5							
4							
3							
2							
1							

Write a sentence about the information you collected on the graph.

_____

_____

Bonus Box: Trace your shoe pattern on the back of this paper. Design it with your favorite colors.

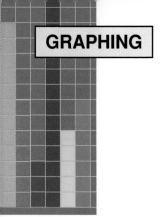

How To Extend The Lesson:

- Repeat the activity every Friday and compare the results on a monthly basis.

- Have the class work in groups to make graphs that show what color shoes teachers are wearing. Instruct groups to quietly survey the teachers so as not to interrupt another class.

- Give each of the students a blank graph to take home. Have them make graphs of their families' shoes.

- Program the graph for a different type of information, such as favorite flavors of ice cream, favorite school subjects, or colors of shirts worn by the class that day.

Pattern
Use with Step 2 on page 130.

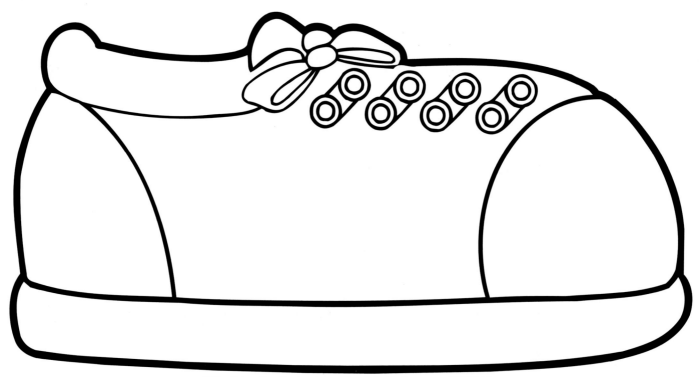

Presenting...Pictographs!

Students will wing their way to success with high-interest pictographs!

Skill: Creating pictographs

Estimated Lesson Time: 45 minutes

Teacher Preparation:
1. Duplicate a copy of page 135 for each student.
2. Gather the materials listed below.

Materials:
1 copy of page 135 per student
crayons
scissors
tape

Teacher Reference:
You can choose from a variety of topics for your students to graph, including:
- How many students prefer pepperoni, hamburger, or cheese pizza?
- How many students prefer the color blue, red, or green?
- How many students were born in the summer, fall, winter, or spring?
- How many students prefer football, soccer, baseball, or another sport?
- How many students have blond, brown, or black hair?
- How many students prefer math, science, or social studies?
- How many students have less than five, exactly five, or more than five letters in their names?
- How many students have younger siblings, older siblings, or both older and younger siblings?

Introducing The Lesson:

Ask students if they have ever heard the expression, "A picture is worth a thousand words." Have students explain what they think the statement means. After several responses, tell students that sometimes a picture can show us information that would normally take many words to express. Cite examples of helpful pictures, such as those found on instruction sheets, road maps, and advertisements.

Steps:

1. Tell students that they are going to use pictures to record and study information. They will do this on a special kind of graph—called a *pictograph*—which uses pictures to show the information that was collected.

2. Draw the pictograph below on the chalkboard. Have students interpret the graph to answer the questions.

3. Distribute crayons, scissors, and a copy of page 135 to each student. Instruct each student to color the pattern to represent his likeness, then cut out the shape.

4. Ask students a survey question (see the suggestions on page 133). Write the answer choices on the board. To answer the question, each student tapes his cutout to the appropriate place on the chalkboard.

5. Have students interpret the pictograph as you ask them questions about the results.

6. Continue asking survey questions to provide additional practice with graphing skills, or use the extension activities on page 136.

1. Who read the most books?
2. Which students read the same number of books?
3. Who read the least books?
4. What is the total number of books that John and Jane read?
5. Who read one more book than Lynn?

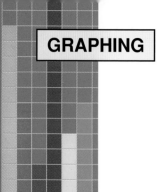
How To Extend The Lesson:

- After students have created a graph, provide each student with a sentence strip to write a statement about the results of the graph. Post the strips around the graph for the class to observe.

- Have students brainstorm a list of survey questions that can be represented on a pictograph. Record each question on a slip of paper and store the questions in a container. When you need a five-minute filler or want to review graphing skills, randomly select a question for students to answer by placing their cutouts on a graph.

- Use the student-made pattern cutouts for graphing activities throughout the year. After students color and cut out their patterns, laminate them or glue them onto tagboard for durability. Store the cutouts in an envelope for future graphing activities.

- Create a durable and inexpensive pictograph grid that can be used over and over again. Use a permanent marker to draw the grid on a shower-curtain liner or laminated sheet of bulletin-board paper. To prepare the graph for a specific activity, tape index cards programmed with the appropriate information to the graph. The student cutouts can be easily taped to the graph, and just as easily removed without damaging the cutout or the grid.

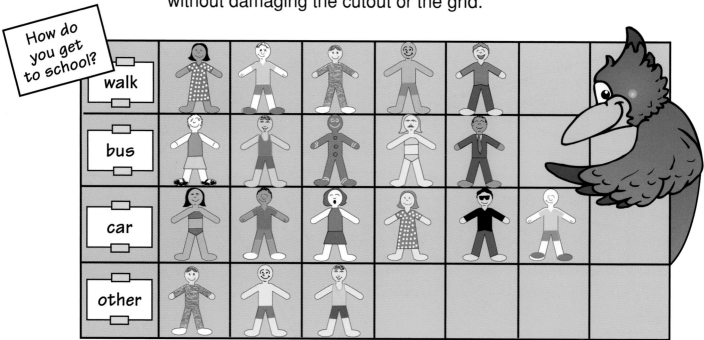

How do you get to school?

walk | bus | car | other

Measurement Mania

Create a frenzy of excitement with activities that build estimation and measurement skills.

Skill: Estimating and measuring

Estimated Lesson Time: 30 minutes

Teacher Preparation:
1. Duplicate page 139 for each student.
2. Gather the materials listed below.

Materials:
1 copy of page 139 per student
one 12-inch ruler per student
12 small paper clips per student

Teacher Reference:

Reinforce the concept of an *inch* by having students classify these objects as being shorter than, longer than, or about the same as an inch in length:

- a crayon
- a penny
- a quarter
- a macaroni noodle
- a jelly bean
- a toothpick
- a candy corn
- a cotton ball
- a lima bean
- a walnut

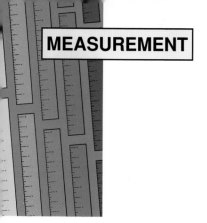
Introducing The Lesson:

Distribute a ruler and a small paper clip to each student. Ask the student to compare the size of the paper clip to an inch on the ruler. Solicit comments about the comparisons.

Steps:

1. Tell students that they will be using inches and paper clips to measure several items. Distribute the paper clips so that each student has a total of 12 clips. Show students how to link the clips together so that they each have a chain of clips. Point out to students that each of their measuring tools now has 12 sections.

2. Distribute a copy of page 139 to each student.

3. Allow time for students to complete the estimation and measurement activities.

4. Challenge students to complete the Bonus Box activity.

When *you* make an *estimate*, you make a guess about a number. If you tell someone that your pencil is about seven inches long, you have made an estimate.

Measurement Mania

Estimate the length of each object.
Then measure to find the actual lengths.

Object	Estimate	Actual
Your math book this way ➔ **Math**	Guess how many… inches _____ paper clips _____	Measure how many… inches _____ paper clips _____
Your math book this way ↑ **Math**	How many… inches _____ paper clips _____	How many… inches _____ paper clips _____
This paper this way ➔ Name____	How many… inches _____ paper clips _____	How many… inches _____ paper clips _____
This paper this way ↑ Name____	How many… inches _____ paper clips _____	How many… inches _____ paper clips _____

Bonus Box: Which tool was easier to measure with? Tell why.

How To Extend The Lesson:

• Reprogram the reproducible to include new objects to measure, or to add different units of nonstandard measurement. If desired, ask students to select these nonstandard units.

• Ask students how many inches are found in one foot. Then ask students to surmise how a foot got its name. Explain that the foot measurement began in ancient times and was based on the length of a human foot. Different countries had their own definitions of how long a foot was, ranging from lengths of 10 to 20 inches. In 1305, the English set the foot at a consistent length of 12 inches. Have each student measure his own foot and record the length; then compare the results. Then ask students to list problems that could occur if there were not a standard definition for the length of a foot.

• Send students on a classroom scavenger hunt by challenging them to find objects of specific lengths. If desired, place students in small groups and assign each group a different length to find. Have students create posters illustrating the objects they found. Display the posters on a bulletin board with the title "We Really Measure Up!"

• Read the story *Inch By Inch* by Leo Lionni (Mulberry Books, 1994) with your students. Discuss the size of the worm and the different birds he measured. Then have each student create a bird drawing. Give each student a copy of the ruler below to use to find measurements in his drawing. Instruct the student to record the attributes measured and their lengths under the illustration.

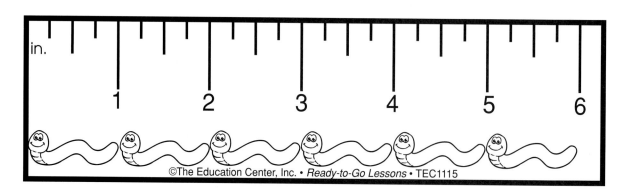

©The Education Center, Inc. • *Ready-to-Go Lessons* • TEC1115

Measuring With Moop

*Provide nonstandard-measurement practice
with the help of an unusual creature named Moop.*

Skill: Using nonstandard measurement

Estimated Lesson Time: 30 minutes

Teacher Preparation:

1. Duplicate page 143 for each student.
2. Make an overhead transparency or enlarged copy of the character on page 142.
3. Gather the materials listed below.

Materials:

1 copy of page 143 per student
1 copy of the character on page 142
1 pencil with an unused eraser per student
ink pads or small containers of tempera paint for students to access

The elephant's trunk
is __11__ Moop marks long.

The frog's leg
is __7__ Moop marks long.

Introducing The Lesson:

Begin the lesson by introducing your students to Moop, an unusual creature from a faraway planet. Show students a picture of Moop and explain that he is about as big as a man's thumb, and has only one little round toe the size of a pencil eraser on each foot. To measure an object, Moop dips his toes in a bucket of paint and walks the length of the object. He counts the number of toe prints to determine how long the object is.

Steps:

1. Tell students that they are going to practice measuring as Moop does. They will use pencil erasers to create prints similar to Moop's toes.

2. Distribute a copy of page 143 and a pencil with an unused eraser to each student.

3. Provide stamp pads or containers of tempera paint for students to access.

4. Use the example at the top of the reproducible to lead students in a guided practice. Have each student stamp the eraser over the "Moop marks" in the first example, then practice the technique with the second example.

5. Provide time for students to complete the reproducible.

6. Challenge students to complete the Bonus Box activity.

©The Education Center, Inc. • *Ready-to-Go Lessons* • TEC1115

Name _____ *Using nonstandard measurement*

Measuring With Moop

Practice measuring.
Use your eraser to stamp over these Moop marks:

Now practice making Moop marks on this line:

_____

Measure to find the length of each object in Moop marks.

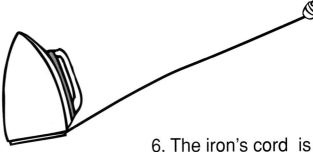

2. The worm is ___ Moop marks long.

1. The leaf is ___ Moop marks long.

4. The paintbrush is ___ Moop marks long.

3. The bunny's ear is ___ Moop marks long.

5. The broom handle is ___ Moop marks long.

6. The iron's cord is ___ Moop marks long.

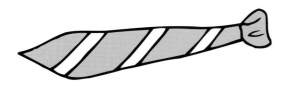

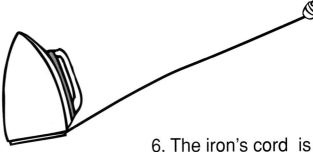

7. The tie is ___ Moop marks long.

8. The spoon is ___ Moop marks long.

Bonus Box: Where do you think Moop came from? Write your answer on the back of this paper.

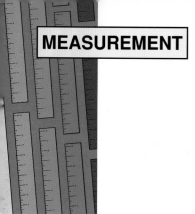

How To Extend The Lesson:

- Have each student choose five nonstandard units of measurement from objects available in the classroom. Instruct him to predict the width of his desk for each unit of measurement. Have him measure his desk with each object, then compare the results with his predictions.

- Have each student measure the length of the classroom using her footsteps as the unit of measurement. Compare the results; then discuss the need for standard units of measurement.

- Discuss the need for different units of measurement. Moop's marks work well when measuring a paintbrush, but how practical would it be to measure a house with them? Show students an example of an inch, a foot, and a yard. Discuss the types of objects you could measure with each unit.

- Program copies of the pattern below with activities for both standard and nonstandard units of measurement. Place the task cards in a learning center along with rulers, objects to use as nonstandard units, items to be measured, and answer keys.

Measure With Moop

©The Education Center, Inc. • *Ready-to-Go Lessons* • TEC1115

Time Flies

*Time will fly by as students review time-telling skills
with this enjoyable math activity!*

Skill: Telling time to the hour and half hour

Estimated Lesson Time: 40 minutes

Teacher Preparation:
Duplicate page 147 for each student.

Materials:
1 clock model with movable hands (A pattern is provided on page 314.)
1 copy of page 147 per student
1 piece of white construction paper per student
glue
scissors
crayons

Teacher Reference:
Share the following "time-ly"
expressions with your students:
- In the nick of time
- Time marches on
- Time-out
- Wasting time
- Once upon a time
- Time's up
- The time of your life
- Time on your hands

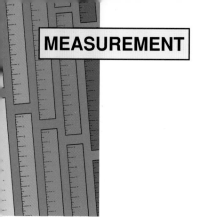

Introducing The Lesson:

Ask each child to decide on his favorite daily activity. Call on several student volunteers to describe the chosen activities, then name the approximate times these activities take place. Show the times using the clock model and reinforcing the concept of A.M. and P.M. Then invite student volunteers to think of activities that take place at designated times.

Steps:

1. Use the clock model to display various times throughout the day, specifying A.M. or P.M. Call on student volunteers to name activities that occur at those times.

2. Distribute page 147 and one piece of white construction paper to each student.

3. Instruct each child to write the time shown on each clock on page 147 on the lines. Then have him cut out the clock cards and glue each clock on the construction paper, keeping the clocks in numerical order. Next have the student write a sentence and draw a picture by each clock showing what he might be doing at that time of day.

4. Provide time for students to share their work with the class.

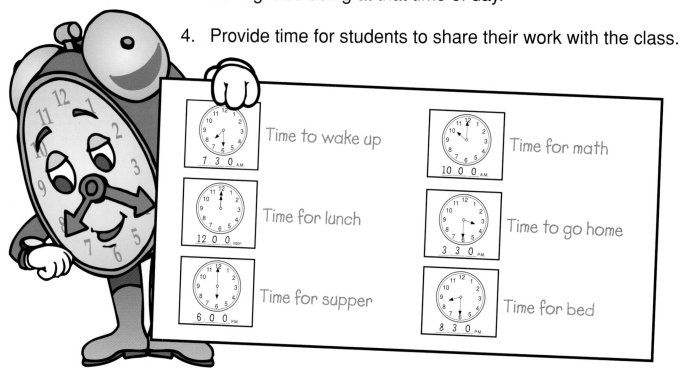

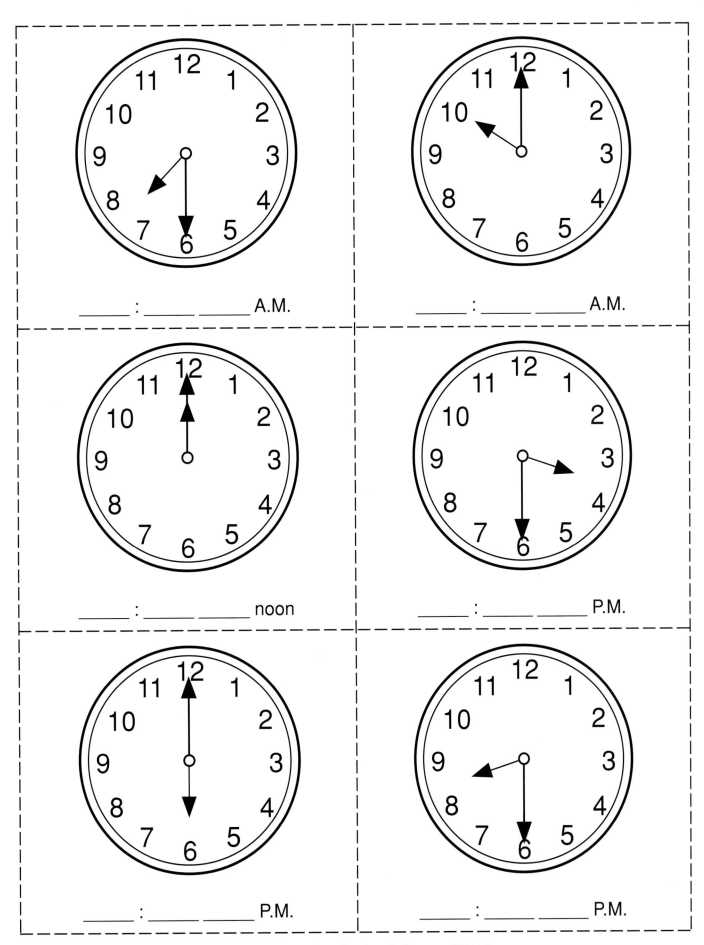

_____ : _____ _____ A.M.

_____ : _____ _____ A.M.

_____ : _____ _____ noon

_____ : _____ _____ P.M.

_____ : _____ _____ P.M.

_____ : _____ _____ P.M.

Note To The Teacher: See page 146 for directions for using this page.

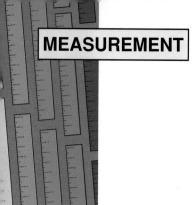
How To Extend The Lesson:

- Have students practice telling time throughout the day with this activity. At the beginning of the day, have each student number a piece of paper from one to ten. At ten various hour and half-hour times throughout the day, announce, "What's the time?" Instruct students to stop what they are doing, read the clock, and write the time on their papers. Be sure to record the times too. After the tenth time check, collect students' papers for assessment.

- Read *The Grouchy Ladybug* by Eric Carle (HarperCollins Children's Books, 1986) to your students. After sharing the story, have each student create his own version of this crabby critter's tale. Remind students to include their own clocks and times, as well as their own happenings, on each page.

- Create a set of flash cards with copies of the patterns below. Draw the clock hands to show the desired times; then program the back of each card for self-checking. Place the cards in a learning center for individual or partner practice.

©The Education Center, Inc.   ©The Education Center, Inc.

Calendar Calculations

*Students travel through the months of the year
in this calendar-based problem-solving activity.*

Skill: Using a calendar

Estimated Lesson Time: 30 minutes

Teacher Preparation:
Duplicate page 151 for each student.

Materials:
1 copy of page 151 per student
1 red and 1 blue crayon per student

Teacher Reference:
Listed below are two holidays or celebrations for each month of the year.

January
New Year's Day (1st)
Martin Luther King, Jr.'s Birthday (15th)

February
Groundhog Day (2nd)
Valentine's Day (14th)

March
St. Patrick's Day (17th)
First Day Of Spring (20th or 21st)

April
April Fools' Day (1st)
National Arbor Day (last Friday)

May
Mother's Day (2nd Sunday)
Memorial Day (last Monday)

June
Flag Day (14th)
Father's Day (third Sunday)

July
Independence Day (4th)
National Ice Cream Day (third Sunday)

August
Friendship Day (first Sunday)
National Relaxation Day (15th)

September
Labor Day (1st)
Grandparents Day (first Sunday after Labor Day)

October
Columbus Day (12th)
Halloween (31st)

November
Veterans Day (11th)
Thanksgiving (fourth Thursday)

December
St. Nicholas Day (6th)
Christmas (25th)

Introducing The Lesson:

Write the names of three months of the year on the board. Ask students to help you organize the months in chronological order. After arranging the months, ask one student at a time to name his birthday month and tell where it would fit in the list. Write each month as it is named, placing it in the correct order. After each student has had a turn, fill in the list with the names of any months that are missing. Tell students they will use this information to complete a partner activity.

Steps:

1. Distribute a red and a blue crayon and page 151 to each student.

2. Pair each student with a partner.

3. Have student pairs answer the questions, then trade papers to check the responses.

4. Challenge students to complete the Bonus Box activity.

Calendar Calculations

Use the calendar pages to answer the questions.
Then trade papers with your partner and check each other's work.

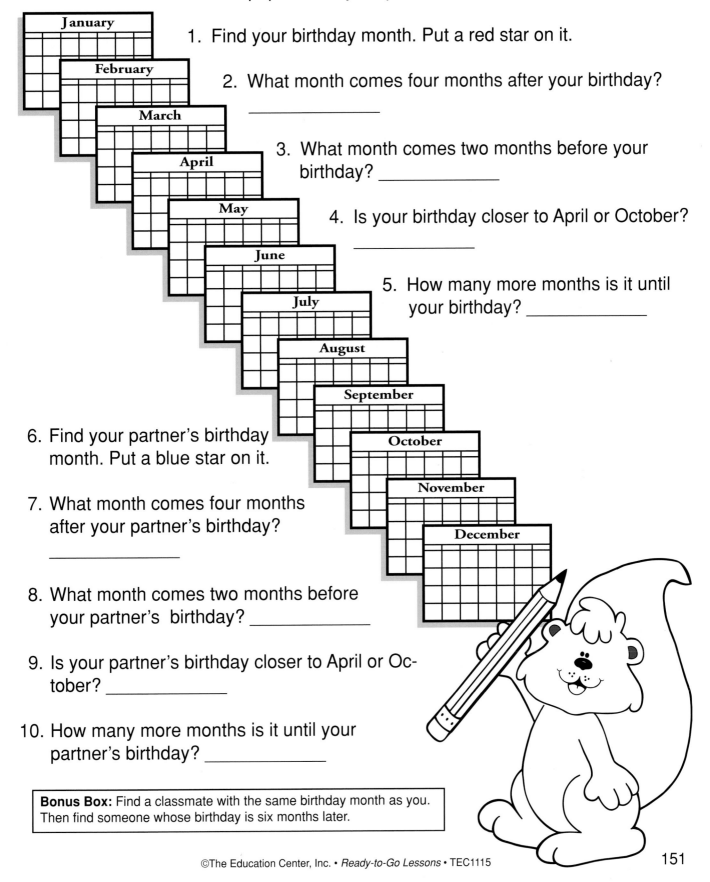

1. Find your birthday month. Put a red star on it.

2. What month comes four months after your birthday?
   _____

3. What month comes two months before your birthday? _____

4. Is your birthday closer to April or October?
   _____

5. How many more months is it until your birthday? _____

6. Find your partner's birthday month. Put a blue star on it.

7. What month comes four months after your partner's birthday?

   _____

8. What month comes two months before your partner's birthday? _____

9. Is your partner's birthday closer to April or October? _____

10. How many more months is it until your partner's birthday? _____

Bonus Box: Find a classmate with the same birthday month as you. Then find someone whose birthday is six months later.

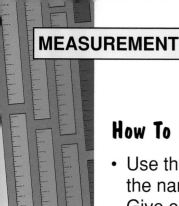

How To Extend The Lesson:

- Use the pattern below to make a class graph of student birthdays. Write the name of each month of the year on a piece of bulletin-board paper. Give each student a copy of the pattern to color and personalize. Instruct each student to tape the pattern above her birthday month on the graph. Have students discuss the resulting information, or have students write questions pertaining to the outcome of the graph for their classmates to answer.

- Challenge students to learn the abbreviations for each month of the year. If desired, use the abbreviations as bonus words on a spelling test or in a spelling-bee contest.

- Divide the class into 12 small groups and assign each group a month of the year. Instruct the groups to find holidays, celebrations, and important happenings in their assigned month. Provide each group with appropriate research material and a sheet of poster board on which to illustrate its findings. Display the completed posters under the title "Marvelous Months."

- Provide each student with a copy of the blank calendar on page 315 to program for the current month. Instruct students to keep the calendars with their journals. At the end of each day, have students jot down a few words telling about their feelings, something they learned, or a special event. Refer to the calendars for writing topics during the month.

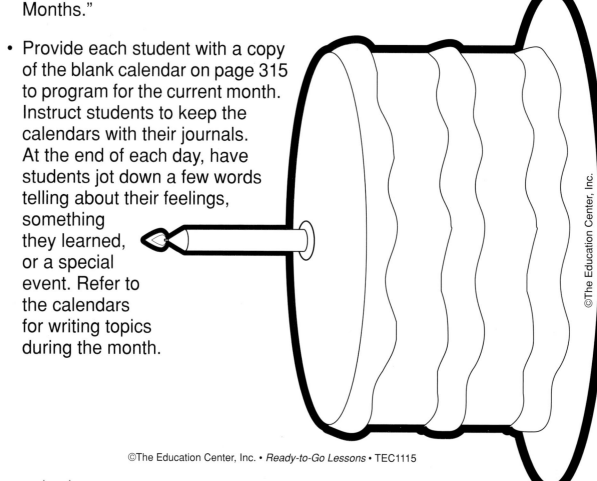

©The Education Center, Inc.

Patterns On Parade

Students will enjoy creating patterns with a variety of shapes and colors.

 Skill: Creating patterns

Estimated Lesson Time: 45 minutes

Teacher Preparation:
1. Duplicate page 155 for each student.
2. Make an overhead transparency of page 155. Cut apart several of each shape.
3. Gather the materials listed below.

Materials:
1 copy of page 155 per student
1 sheet of construction paper per student
overhead-transparency shapes
crayons
scissors
glue

Teacher Reference:
Pattern-Block Terminology

 trapezoid   **triangle**

 **parallelogram**   **hexagon**

 square   **rhombus**

Introducing The Lesson:

Tell students that they will be working with pattern-block shapes to create a variety of patterns. After learning the name of each type of block, students will learn the arrangement of several types of patterns. Students will then each make a set of pattern pieces and use them to demonstrate different designs.

Steps:

1. Display the shape transparencies to introduce each shape and identify it by name.

2. Use the transparencies to demonstrate the following patterns: ABAB, ABCABC, ABBC, and ABCB. After showing each type of pattern, have the children practice recognition by having student volunteers arrange the pieces in different patterns for their classmates to identify.

3. Distribute a copy of page 155 to each student. Provide time for students to color each pattern block in the appropriate color (see page 153) before cutting out the pieces.

4. Provide a sheet of construction paper for each student. Instruct each student to glue shapes to the paper to demonstrate each type of pattern listed in Step 2.

5. Challenge students to use the remaining pieces to create patterns of their choice. If desired, have students glue these patterns to the back of their construction-paper sheets.

ABAB

ABCABC

ABBC  ABCB

PROBLEM SOLVING

How To Extend The Lesson:

- Have students look for patterns in the classroom or on the school grounds. To get them started, point out patterns on students' clothing, bulletin-board borders, floor and ceiling tiles, carpet designs, and the flag.

- Have students identify and extend patterns using Unifix® cubes, buttons, dry pasta shapes, colored cereal pieces, or an assortment of dried beans.

- Incorporate movement into your study of patterns by having students create a sequence of activities in pattern form. Demonstrate a movement pattern by having students touch their toes, clap their hands, and snap their fingers on their right, then left hands. Repeat the pattern several times; then ask student volunteers to suggest new movements to add to the sequence.

- Challenge students to find patterns in a sequence of letters, a list of spelling words, or in skip-counting.

AaBbCcDd   pdqtglyf
1, 3, 5, 7, 9, 11, 13
3, 6, 9, 12, 15, 18
lake
take
shake
snake
bake
cake

Ready, Set, Go!

Help students look for special signals when solving addition word problems.

Skill: Identifying unnecessary information

Estimated Lesson Time: 30 minutes

Teacher Preparation:
1. Duplicate page 159 for each student.
2. Gather the materials listed below.

Materials:
1 copy of page 159 per student
1 red, 1 green, and 1 yellow crayon or colored pencil per student
red, green, and yellow colored chalks

Teacher Reference:
Share these problem-solving signals with your students:

Stop! . . . This information is not needed.

Caution! . . . Take your time to read the question.

Go! . . . Use this information to solve the problem.

Introducing The Lesson:

Tell your students that they are going to use some familiar signals to help them solve word problems. Draw a traffic signal similar to the one on page 157 on the chalkboard. Review with students what each color of the signal symbolizes. Then use the Teacher Reference information to explain how each color can help when solving word problems.

Steps:

1. Write one of the word problems shown below on the board. Tell students that you are going to carefully read the question stated in the problem. Have students help you locate the question; then underline it with yellow chalk.

2. Explain to students that you are going to read the problem again, but you are going to stop if you find information that will not help solve the problem. Have students help identify the unnecessary information; then underline it in red.

3. Tell students that you are ready to look for information to use in solving the problem. Have students locate the important information; then underline it in green.

4. Tell students that green means go—they can go ahead and solve the problem!

5. Write another problem for additional guided practice as needed.

6. Distribute red, green, and yellow crayons and a copy of page 159 to each student.

7. Provide time for students to finish the reproducible independently; then challenge them to complete the Bonus Box activity.

Lisa has 2 cats and 3 dogs.

Bruce has 4 cats.

How many cats are there?

Robert has 4 red marbles.

Chad has 3 red marbles and 2 blue marbles.

How many red marbles are there?

Ashley has 1 pencil and 2 pens.

Kristen has 3 pencils.

How many pencils are there?

Name _____

Ready, Set, Go!

Read each problem.
Underline the question in yellow.
Underline extra information in red.
Underline important information in green.
Go! Solve the problem!

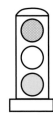
1. I see 2 cars and 5 trucks.
   Sam sees 4 cars.
   How many cars are there?

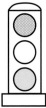
2. Jan's garden has 6 flowers.
   Mike's garden has 2 flowers and 3
     trees.
   How many flowers are there?

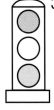
3. Bill has 5 frogs and 2 turtles.
   Jim has 3 frogs.
   How many frogs are there?

4. Tom has 2 pennies and 4 dimes.
   John has 3 pennies.
   How many pennies are there?

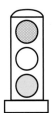
5. Sara found 6 shells and 5 rocks.
   Kim found 3 shells.
   How many shells are there?

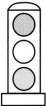
6. Bo has 2 cookies and 1 apple.
   Pete has 5 cookies.
   How many cookies are there?

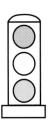
7. Dave has 7 hats and 3 ties.
   Eva has 2 hats.
   How many hats are there?

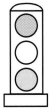
8. Jose has 4 sisters and 2 brothers.
   Alice has 3 sisters.
   How many sisters are there?

Bonus Box: Write a word problem that has extra information. Ask a friend to solve the problem.

How To Extend The Lesson:

- Place students in pairs to create word problems that contain unnecessary information. Provide time for each pair to present its problem to the class. Then have the class work through the problem together.

- Distribute one red, one green, and one yellow construction-paper circle to each student. Write a word problem on the board. Underline a section of the problem. Ask each student to hold up a colored circle to show whether the underlined section is the question, extra information, or information needed to solve the problem.

- Challenge students with word problems that contain two pieces of extra information. Caution students that they will need to use more red when solving these problems!

- Enlarge the pattern below and program it to match the example shown on page 157. Display the signal when students are solving word problems to remind them of the procedure.

Tasty Toppings

Students will enjoy this tasty approach to problem solving!

Skill: Solving problems with manipulatives

Estimated Lesson Time: 30 minutes

Teacher Preparation:
1. Duplicate a copy of page 163 for each student.
2. Gather the materials listed below.

Materials:
1 copy of page 163 per student
20 small candies per student
1 sheet of blank paper per student

Teacher Reference:

A dozen items to use as math manipulatives:

- beans
- bingo chips
- bottle caps
- buttons
- dry cereal
- dry pasta
- interlocking cubes
- milk-jug caps
- paper clips
- pattern blocks
- pennies
- shells

Introducing The Lesson:

Ask students if they have ever been to an ice-cream parlor. Have students name the different choices there are to make when ordering ice cream. Confirm responses such as flavors, sizes of cones, the number of scoops, and topping choices. Ask students if deciding on these choices can be a problem. Tell students that they will use problem-solving strategies to decide how many toppings belong on different ice-cream treats.

Steps:

1. Draw a figure as shown below on the board. Tell students that each circle is a scoop of ice cream. The numbers in between the scoops tell how many topping pieces are shared between the scoops. The students must determine how many topping pieces belong on each scoop to arrive at the specified numbers.

2. Tell students to look at the number 7 in between two of the scoops. Ask students to determine ways to share seven pieces between two scoops. (Responses should include 6 and 1, 5 and 2, 3 and 4, and 7 and 0.)

3. Remind students that one scoop already has four pieces. How many pieces belong on the other scoop? Confirm that 3 pieces should go on the other scoop to make a total of 7. Draw 3 pieces on the corresponding scoop.

4. Continue modeling the problem-solving strategy to complete the rest of the problem.

5. Distribute page 163 and 20 candy pieces to each student.

6. Instruct the students to use the candies as manipulatives in solving the problems on their reproducibles.

7. Challenge students to complete the Bonus Box activity.

Tasty Toppings

Use candy pieces to decide how many topping pieces belong on each treat.
Then draw topping pieces to show your answer.
When you are finished, you may eat your candies!

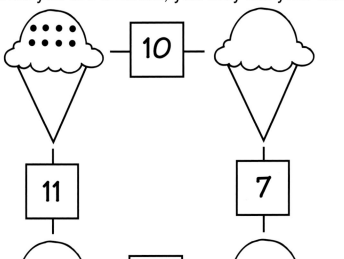

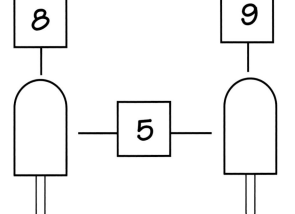

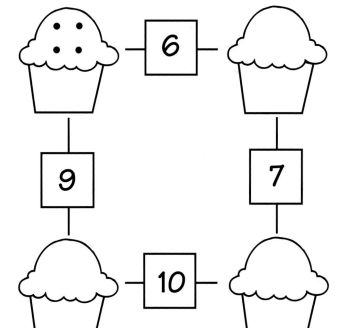

PROBLEM SOLVING

How To Extend The Lesson:

- Introduce multiplication and division concepts by having students divide manipulatives into equal sets. Instruct each student to draw four scoops of ice cream. Challenge students to place 12 manipulatives on the scoops so that there is an equal number on each. Discuss the results; then challenge students with another problem.

- Duplicate copies of the patterns below. Program each scoop with a different addend. Program each cone with a corresponding sum. Place the pieces in a learning center and instruct students to match each pair of scoops with the correct cone. Have students use manipulatives to check their answers.

- Duplicate the patterns below in several different colors. Challenge students to create as many combinations of ice-cream cones as possible using the different-colored pieces. For an added challenge, provide an assortment of toppings for students to use in creating combinations.

Patterns

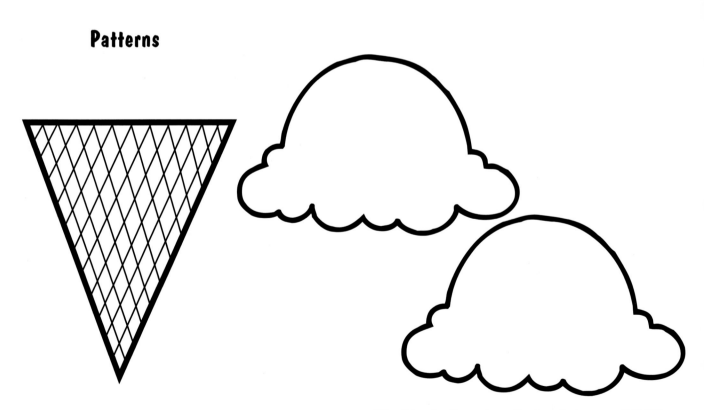

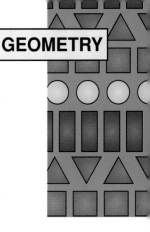

Caught On Camera!

Students will see the big picture as they identify congruent shapes.

Skill: Identifying congruent figures

Estimated Lesson Time: 30 minutes

Teacher Preparation:
1. Duplicate page 167 for each student.
2. Cut out a class supply of construction-paper shapes. Make several sizes and colors of each shape. (Patterns are provided on page 316.)

Materials:
1 copy of page 167 per student
class supply of construction-paper shapes

Teacher Reference:
Have students look for congruent shapes:

- in floor-tile patterns
- in their school-supply boxes
- on the cafeteria trays
- on the exterior of the school building
- on plants
- on insects
- on clothing
- on the computer keyboard
- on the playground
- in the school parking lot

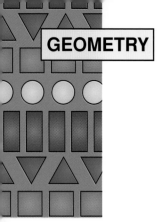

Introducing The Lesson:

Tell students that they are going to be on the lookout for congruent figures. To discover what *congruent* means, each student will be given a shape. Students will compare their shapes to determine similarities and differences.

Steps:

1. Distribute a shape to each student. Provide time for students to compare and discuss their shapes; then have students return to their seats.

2. Ask students to name some of the characteristics of the shapes. Record responses such as color similarities, shape similarities, and size similarities.

3. Inform students that congruent figures have both the same size and the same shape. Reinforce that congruent figures do *not* have to be the same color. Provide time for students to identify classmates with congruent figures.

4. Distribute a copy of page 167 to each student. Tell students to look carefully at each picture to find a pair of congruent figures.

5. Provide time for students to identify the congruent figures in each picture; then challenge students to complete the Bonus Box activity.

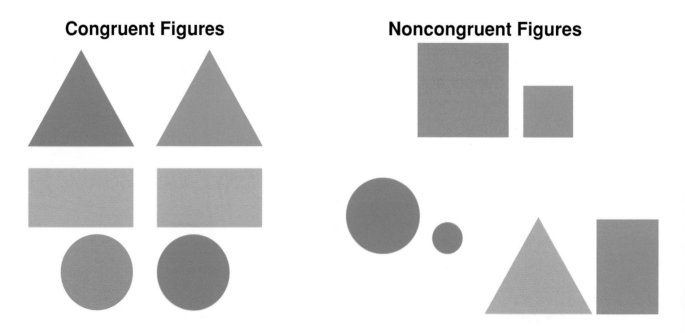

Congruent Figures   **Noncongruent Figures**

Caught On Camera!

Look at each picture.
Color the congruent figures in each picture.

Bonus Box: Draw a picture that has two congruent circles, two congruent squares, and two congruent triangles.

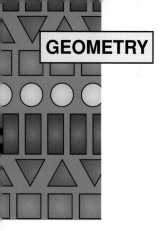

How To Extend The Lesson:

- Create a partner game to reinforce congruent figures. Program 20 index cards so that 10 pairs of congruent figures are made. Instruct the partners to arrange the cards facedown on a desk. Each student takes a turn selecting two cards and turning them faceup. If the figures are congruent, the student will pick up the cards and take another turn. If the figures are not congruent, the student replaces the cards and his partner takes a turn. The game continues until all pairs have been matched. The winner is the student with the most pairs at the end of the game.

- Use congruent figures as a means of dividing students into small groups. Create a set of construction-paper congruent figures for the number of students you want in each group. Place the figures in a bag, and then randomly distribute a figure to each student. Have all students holding congruent figures work together for the group activity.

- Have students use tempera paint to experiment with congruent figures. Provide each student with a sheet of construction paper. Instruct each student to fold the paper in half; then assist students in pouring a small amount of tempera in between the folded papers. Tell each student to gently press down on the top half of the paper, spreading the paint between the two sheets. Have students unfold their papers and examine the resulting figures.

- Create a set of templates by duplicating the patterns on page 316 onto tagboard. Place the templates in a learning center for students to use in creating designs with congruent figures. Display the completed works on a bulletin board titled "Congruent Collages."

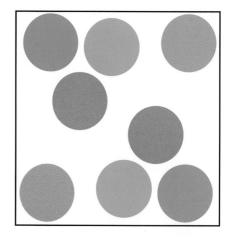

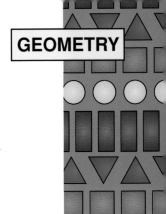

The ABCs Of Symmetry

Use the letters of the alphabet for a look at symmetrical figures.

Skill: Recognizing lines of symmetry

Estimated Lesson Time: 30 minutes

Teacher Preparation:

1. Duplicate a copy of page 171 for each student.
2. Prepare an overhead transparency of the shapes on page 170.
3. Gather the materials listed below.

Materials:

1 copy of page 171 per student
1 ruler per student
1 overhead transparency and projector

Teacher Reference:

Show your students examples of symmetrical objects…

in the classroom…   and in nature.

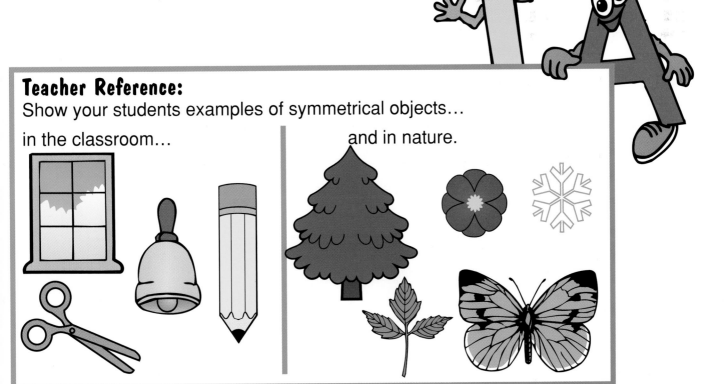

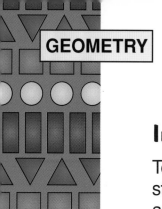

Introducing The Lesson:

Tell students that they are going to look at shapes in a special way. Ask students to name some common shapes, such as a circle, triangle, square, and rectangle. As each shape is mentioned, draw it on the board. (For this example, draw an equilateral triangle.) Then tell students that they will look at each shape to determine if it has a line of *symmetry,* or a line that divides the shape into two parts that are mirror images of each other.

Steps:

1. Draw a vertical line through the middle of the circle. Ask students to observe that each half is identical. Show students that a horizontal line will also create a line of symmetry on the circle.

2. Repeat the demonstration with the other shapes, showing both the vertical and horizontal lines of symmetry. Students should observe that the triangle does not have two lines of symmetry; the horizontal line does not create two identical images.

3. Show students a transparency of the shapes below. Have students determine if a line of symmetry can be drawn for each shape.

4. Distribute a ruler and a copy of page 171 to each student. Provide time for students to complete the reproducible.

5. Challenge students to complete the Bonus Box activity.

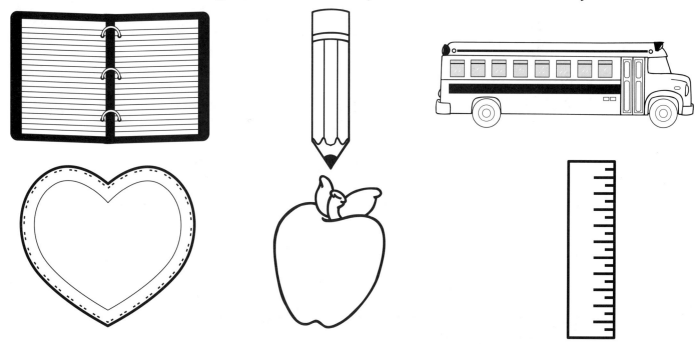

Name _____

The ABCs Of Symmetry

Draw a vertical (↑) line through the center of each letter.
If it makes a line of symmetry, color the box.

A	B	C	D	E	F	G

Draw a horizontal (→) line through the center of each letter.
If it makes a line of symmetry, color the box.

A	B	C	D	E	F	G

Draw a capital letter in each box.
Then draw a line through the center of each letter.
If it makes a line of symmetry, color the box.

Bonus Box: Write your name in capital letters. Circle the letters that have symmetry.

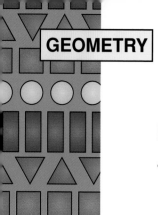

How To Extend The Lesson:

- Have students create symmetrical designs of their own. Distribute a sheet of construction paper to each student. Instruct her to fold her paper in half, then cut an abstract shape from the folded paper. Have each student unfold the shape and observe the symmetrical halves.

- Have students use the shapes described above for an art activity. Provide each student with a sheet of construction paper and instruct her to glue her shape in the center. Then provide a supply of markers for each student to use to create a picture incorporating the shape as part of the design. Display the finished artwork on a bulletin board.

- Gather a supply of old magazines for students to use in a symmetrical drawing activity. Instruct each student to look through the magazines to find a picture of a symmetrical object. Tell him to draw a line of symmetry on the object and cut it on the line. Have each student glue one-half of the picture to a sheet of drawing paper; then challenge him to draw the missing half of the picture.

- Take students on a Symmetry Scavenger Hunt. Lead your class on a walk around the school grounds in search of examples of symmetry. Make a list of the different symmetrical objects your students observe. After you return to the classroom, have students create categories for the objects on the list.

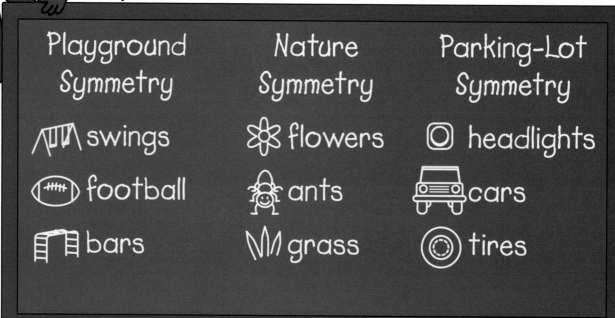

LIFE SCIENCE

Everything's Coming Up Pumpkins!

Plant a seed of knowledge with this life-cycle lesson and harvest a bumper crop of learning fun!

Skill: Sequencing the life-cycle stages of a pumpkin

Estimated Lesson Time: 30 minutes

Teacher Preparation:
Duplicate page 175 for each student.

Materials:
1 copy of page 175 per student
one 12" x 18" sheet of construction paper per student
crayons
scissors
glue

Background Information:
Pumpkins begin as small white seeds that are planted approximately one inch deep in soil. After several days, roots begin to grow downward and stems grow upward. After the stems break through the soil, two *seed leaves* appear where each seed was planted. Next, jagged-edged leaves called *pumpkin vine leaves* quickly grow and stems twist along the ground as they become vines. On the vines, curly tendrils appear and yellow flowers bloom. Below some of the flowers, tiny green bulbs grow. They slowly turn from green to orange and become ripened pumpkins. This process from seed to mature pumpkin takes about four months. If the seeds from a mature pumpkin are planted, the cycle will begin again.

Life cycle of a pumpkin   173

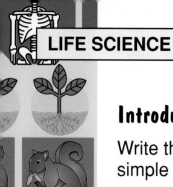

Introducing The Lesson:

Write the word *pumpkin* on the right side of the chalkboard and draw a simple picture of a pumpkin beside it. Invite youngsters to describe a fully grown pumpkin while you record their responses below the word *pumpkin*. Next ask youngsters to tell where pumpkins come from. Verify that pumpkins come from seeds; then write and illustrate the word *seed* on the left side of the chalkboard. Have students tell what a pumpkin seed looks like while you write their descriptions below the word *seed*. Invite youngsters to predict some of the changes that occur as a small pumpkin seed develops into a large orange pumpkin. Accept all responses and write them between the words *seed* and *pumpkin*. Tell students that they will learn about a pumpkin's life cycle with this lesson.

Steps:

1. Use the Background Information on page 173 to describe to youngsters the life-cycle stages of a pumpkin. Then have students orally compare and contrast this information with their ideas recorded on the chalkboard. Erase the chalkboard after this discussion.

2. Give each student a copy of page 175, a 12" x 18" sheet of construction paper, crayons, scissors, and glue. Tell youngsters that each of them will use these materials to create a poster of a pumpkin's life cycle.

3. Read with students the sentences on page 175. Then list the following words on the chalkboard: *orange*, *flower*, *stem*, *vine*, *bulb*, and *root*.

4. Have each student use the listed words to complete the sentences on his sheet. Then direct him to color and cut out each box and to personalize the cover.

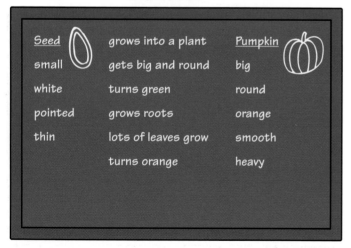

5. Next instruct each youngster to fold and cut his sheet of construction paper in half lengthwise. Have him glue the two resulting pieces together to make one long strip and then sequence and glue the boxes onto the strip.

6. Have youngsters orally summarize a pumpkin's life-cycle stages and then display their completed posters in the classroom or hall.

Everything's Coming Up
PUMPKINS!

Name _____

Next the stem grows into a

_____. Leaves grow, too.

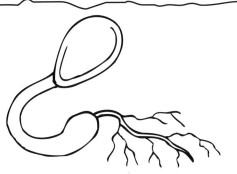

A pumpkin seed is planted. Its

_____ grows downward, and

its _____ grows upward.

The pumpkin slowly turns

_____ and is ready to pick.

A small green _____ grows
from the flower.

A yellow _____ blooms on
the vine.

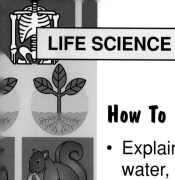

How To Extend The Lesson:

- Explain to students that most plants, including pumpkins, need sunlight, water, soil, and air. Then have each youngster conduct an experiment with a partner to determine how the amount of one of these needs—sunlight—affects plants. To do this, each student pair plants fast-germinating seeds, such as radish seeds, in two different containers. (The containers should have the same amount and same kind of soil.) Then each twosome places one container in a sunny location and the other in a dark location, waters them the same way, and predicts what will happen. At the end of a designated period of time, invite youngsters to share their results and compare them with their predictions. If desired, conduct similar experiments varying the amount of water, soil, and air that plants receive.

- Reinforce students' understanding of a pumpkin's life cycle with this creative-writing activity! Begin by reading aloud a book about pumpkins, such as *The Pumpkin Patch* by Elizabeth King (Viking Penguin, 1996) or *Too Many Pumpkins* by Linda White (Holiday House, Inc.; 1996). Then have youngsters write a story with the following story starter: "Peter LaPlante wanted to grow a perfect pumpkin to enter in the state fair. So one day…." Encourage them to use the information they've learned from the lesson on page 175 and from the book just shared in their stories. Direct students to illustrate their completed stories; then display your young authors' work on a bulletin board titled "Presenting The Perfect Pumpkin."

Group Number	Circumference of Pumpkin	Number of Seeds	
		Prediction	Actual
1	20"	100	
2	24"	150	
3	30"	110	
4	18"	60	
5	22"	50	
6	24"	75	
7	17"	40	

- Remind youngsters that a pumpkin's life cycle begins with a seed. Divide youngsters into small groups, assign each group a number, and give it a pumpkin. Then have each group measure the circumference of its pumpkin. Divide a sheet of chart paper into four columns, and record each pumpkin's circumference as shown. Next have each group predict how many seeds its pumpkin has and record its prediction. Cut off the top of each group's pumpkin; then have the group members take turns using a large spoon to scoop out the seeds. Record the actual number of seeds for each pumpkin; then discuss the results. How does the pumpkin's size correspond with the number of seeds? Does the pumpkin with the largest circumference have the most seeds? If desired, use these seeds for additional science explorations. Or clean and bake them for a nutritious snack!

Focus On Flowers!

Student learning will blossom with this "plant-astic" lesson!

Skill: Identifying the parts of a flower

Estimated Lesson Time: 25 minutes

Teacher Preparation:
1. On the chalkboard, draw a simple diagram of a flower. Use the illustration on page 178 as a reference, but do not include the labels.
2. Duplicate page 179 for each student.

Materials:
colored chalk
1 copy of page 179 per student

Background Information:
   Many plants have flowers. Flowers are important because they hold seeds—the beginnings of new plants. Several other parts of flowers that are important to the reproductive cycle of plants are described below.

- **Petals:** Petals shelter the reproductive parts of a flower. Some petals are brightly colored or have markings to attract insects for pollination.

- **Pistil:** The pistil is a tube in the middle of the flower.

- **Stigma:** The stigma is the sticky part at the top of a pistil.

- **Stamens:** The stamens are the stalks surrounding the pistil.

- **Anther:** The anther is the tip of a stamen. Anthers produce a yellow powder called *pollen*.

   In order for a flower to reproduce, pollen from its stamen needs to be transferred to the stigma of a flower of the same type. This process—*pollination*—occurs in different ways. For example, wind may blow pollen from flower to flower, or insects may carry pollen on their bodies from one flower to another. After pollination, a long tube grows through the pistil into an *ovule*. This is the beginning of a seed. Fruit grows around the seed. When the fruit ripens, the seeds are ready to develop into new plants, and the reproductive cycle continues.

Introducing The Lesson:

Ask students to think about why many flower petals are brightly colored or have markings. Give youngsters an opportunity to share their ideas; then explain that the appearance of petals attracts certain insects that are important to the process of pollination. Explain to students that pollination is necessary for new plants to be created. Then tell students that this lesson will teach them about some of the flower parts that play a role in this process.

Steps:

1. Direct students' attention to the diagram on the chalkboard. Use the relevant part of the Background Information on page 177 to explain each of the following flower parts: petals, pistil, stamens, anthers, and stigma. As you introduce each part, outline it on the diagram with colored chalk and label it (refer to the illustration below).

2. Describe pollen and indicate on the diagram where it is located on a flower. Then use the last paragraph of the Background Information to review the process of pollination.

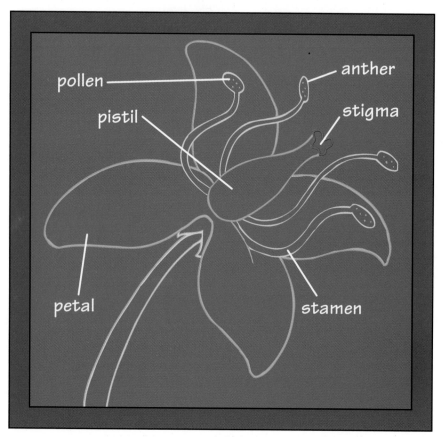

3. Give each student a copy of page 179. Have her refer to the chalkboard diagram and use the information you have presented to mark the illustration as indicated and complete the sentences on her sheet.

4. Challenge students to complete the Bonus Box activity.

Name _____

Focus On Flowers!

Read each sentence.
Follow the directions.

Trace the **petals** with a red crayon.

Make a check mark on each **stamen**.

Trace the **pistil** with a black crayon.

Circle the **stigma**.

Mark one **anther** with an X.

Color yellow **pollen** on one anther.

Complete each sentence.
Use the Word Bank.

1. The _____ is a tube in the middle of a flower.
2. Some _____ attract insects with bright colors.
3. The stalks around a pistil are called _____.
4. The sticky part at the top of a pistil is a _____.
5. The _____ is the tip of a stamen.
6. Anthers make a yellow powder called _____.

Word Bank					
pistil	stamens	pollen	stigma	petals	anther

Bonus Box: On the back of this sheet, write two ways that pollen can be transferred from one flower to another.

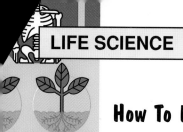

How To Extend The Lesson:

• Obtain one flower for every two or three students in your class. For best results, acquire a few different types. Give each student group an opportunity to examine its flower and share observations. Then review each of the basic flower parts with youngsters while they find them on their flowers. Tell students that during this lesson they will examine petals more closely. Assign each group a number. Then on a large sheet of paper, make a chart with the following column headings: Group, Color, Markings, Shape, and Number (the last four columns refer to petal characteristics). Add other columns and headings as desired. Have each group examine its flower for the listed characteristics and share them with the class. Then record each group's information on the chart. Lead youngsters in a discussion about the completed chart. What do they notice? How does the number of petals compare for flowers that are the same type? Different types? How about the shape of each petal? No doubt youngsters' observation skills will bloom with this hands-on activity!

• Your young botanists' love of literature will grow with these terrific titles!
— *The Tiny Seed* by Eric Carle (Simon & Schuster Children's Division, 1991)
— *Miss Rumphius* by Barbara Cooney (Puffin Books, 1985)
— *The Rose In My Garden* by Arnold Lobel (William Morrow & Co., Inc.; 1993)

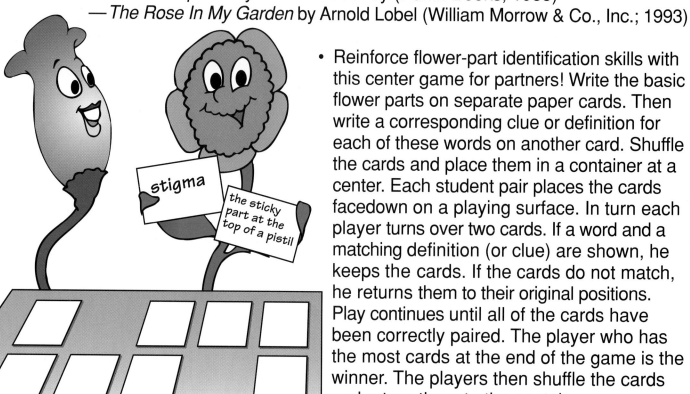

stigma

the sticky part at the top of a pistil

• Reinforce flower-part identification skills with this center game for partners! Write the basic flower parts on separate paper cards. Then write a corresponding clue or definition for each of these words on another card. Shuffle the cards and place them in a container at a center. Each student pair places the cards facedown on a playing surface. In turn each player turns over two cards. If a word and a matching definition (or clue) are shown, he keeps the cards. If the cards do not match, he returns them to their original positions. Play continues until all of the cards have been correctly paired. The player who has the most cards at the end of the game is the winner. The players then shuffle the cards and return them to the container to prepare the center for other students.

Absolutely "Tree-rific!"

Students' appreciation of trees will take root with this valuable learning activity!

Skill: Recognizing the value of trees

Estimated Lesson Time: 25 minutes

Teacher Preparation:

1. Write the following words on the chalkboard: "furniture," "chocolate," "soap," and "bulletin boards."
2. Divide a sheet of bulletin-board paper into two columns. Label one column "Products" and the other column "Benefits."
3. Duplicate page 183 for each student.

Materials:

1 labeled sheet of bulletin-board paper
1 copy of page 183 per student
crayons

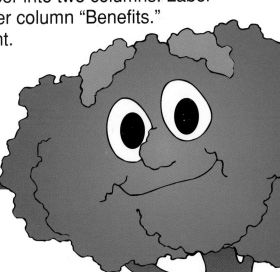

Background Information:

Trees are among the most useful plants. Some of the many products and benefits of trees are listed below.

- **Products**
  - **Food:** Trees are a source of food for people as well as animals. They provide many different types of food, such as fruits, chocolate, and nuts.
  - **Wood:** Wood products made from trees include furniture, houses, paper, and cardboard.
  - **Sap:** Sap from some trees is used to make maple syrup, chewing gum, and soap.
  - **Bark:** Some tree bark is used to make bottle stoppers or bulletin boards.
- **Benefits**
  - **Soil And Water Conservation:** Trees act as windbreaks in some areas, and their roots hold soil in place, keeping it from washing away in heavy rains or floods. Tree roots also store water in the ground.
  - **Air:** Trees help keep the balance of gases in the air by absorbing carbon dioxide and producing oxygen.
  - **Shelter/Recreation:** Forests provide shelter for many animals and recreational areas for people. They also offer shade and beautify our landscapes.

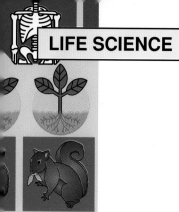

Introducing The Lesson:

Direct students' attention to the words on the chalkboard. Challenge youngsters to determine what the listed items have in common. Lead them to the conclusion that furniture, chocolate, soap, and bulletin boards are products from wood, seeds, sap, and bark, respectively. Tell students that trees are very useful to people and animals, and that this lesson will explore additional products and benefits of these plants.

Steps:

1. Share the Background Information on page 181.

2. Show students the prepared chart. Ask students to brainstorm products and benefits of trees and identify the listed category in which each of these belong. Record youngsters' ideas in the appropriate columns on the chart.

3. Give each student a copy of page 183. Have her use the Word Bank to complete the sentences and label the pictures on her sheet.

4. Challenge youngsters to complete the Bonus Box activity. If desired provide an opportunity for students to share this work with classmates.

Products	Benefits
fruit	produce oxygen
maple syrup	give shade
bottle stoppers	homes for animals
furniture	hold soil in place
cardboard	make yards pretty
paper	fun to climb
chewing gum	windbreaks

Name _____

Absolutely "Tree-rific!"

Use the Word Bank to complete each sentence.
Label each picture on the tree with the matching word.
Color the pictures.

1. Trees give us _____ on a hot day.

2. Some trees grow _____ for us to eat.

3. Tree _____ hold soil in place.

4. Some animals make their _____ in trees.

5. Sap from some trees is used to make _____.

6. Trees make our _____ look pretty.

Word Bank

soap   fruits

shade   yards

homes   roots

Bonus Box: On the back of this sheet, list ten products that come from trees.

183

©The Education Center, Inc. • *Ready-to-Go Lessons* • TEC1115 • Key p. 319

How To Extend The Lesson:

- Trees and other types of plants provide many valuable products. For example, trees provide lumber for building homes, and the bark from some trees is used for medicinal purposes. Food is obtained from several different parts of plants, such as seeds, roots, leaves, flower buds, and fruits. And cotton is one plant product that is used to make clothing. Discuss these and other plant products with youngsters; then divide students into small groups. Have each group compile a list titled "We thank plants for…." If desired challenge youngsters to categorize the items on their lists. Give each group an opportunity to share its work; then mount students' completed lists on a classroom wall.

Trees give us shade.

- What better way to teach youngsters about caring for our natural resources than with engaging literature? Read aloud *The Lorax* by Dr. Seuss (Random House Books For Young Readers, 1971). Then discuss how the Once-ler's factory affected plant life and other aspects of the environment. Ask each child to write a letter to the Once-ler expressing how he feels about the impact of the Thneed factory. Encourage students to give the Once-ler suggestions for taking better care of natural resources. To conclude this activity, have each student imagine that he is in charge of the last Truffula seed and discuss what he would do with it.

- Highlight the importance of trees with this "tree-mendous" bulletin-board activity! Take students outside to a wooded area. Direct each youngster to use a brown crayon and a sheet of drawing paper to make a rubbing of tree bark. Then have each student find one or two leaves that have fallen to the ground and take them back to the classroom with his crayon rubbing. Next each student makes several leaf rubbings with a green crayon and drawing paper. Direct each student to create a likeness of a tree by cutting out his rubbings and gluing them onto a sheet of paper. Have each youngster write on his paper one reason that trees are important. Mount students' completed work on a brightly colored bulletin board titled "Trees Are Tops!" With this creative display, it's easy to see that trees are tops!

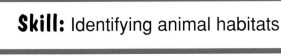

Home, Sweet Home

Whether it's a nest, log, or cave, there's no place like home!

Skill: Identifying animal habitats

Estimated Lesson Time: 25 minutes

Teacher Preparation:
Duplicate page 187 for each student.

Materials:
1 copy of page 187 per student
1 sheet of chart paper per student group
several real estate ads (optional)
scissors
glue
crayons

Background Information:

Every animal is suited to live in a particular environment or habitat. Information about the seven major types of habitats is provided below.

- **Mountains:** Mountain habitats range from dense forests to bare, rocky ground. Bears and tigers are among the animals that live at the forested bases of some mountains. Birds of prey and mountain goats are found on mountains at higher altitudes.
- **Grasslands:** Few trees grow in the grasslands because of insufficient rainfall or ground that is too sandy. Giraffes, elephants, and lions live in the grasslands of Africa, also known as the African savannah.
- **Temperate Forests:** Temperate forests have many deciduous and evergreen trees. Animals that live in this habitat include chipmunks, owls, and salamanders.
- **Tropical Forests:** In these forests near the equator, it is very hot and it rains frequently. Anteaters, chimpanzees, and a large number of insects make their homes in this habitat.
- **Deserts:** Deserts are extremely dry. Some deserts are vast areas of sand, but others are rocky regions. Camels, geckos, and scorpions live in deserts.
- **Polar Regions:** These areas in the Arctic and Antarctica are bitterly cold. Winters in the polar regions are stormy and dark. The summers are short and there is daylight nearly 24 hours a day. Polar bears, walruses, and puffins make their homes in the polar regions.
- **Oceans:** The oceans and seas are the largest natural habitat and are heavily populated by creatures such as blue whales, dolphins, and starfish.

Introducing The Lesson:

Ask youngsters to brainstorm words, such as *hilly* or *flat,* that describe the areas in which they live; record them on the chalkboard. Explain that animals are similar to people in that each of them lives in a particular type of environment. Unlike people, though, some animals can live only in one type of environment because they are uniquely suited to its special features and cannot survive in a different location. Tell students that they will learn about several different animal habitats, or environments, in this lesson.

Steps:

1. Use the Background Information on page 185 to describe to students the seven major habitats and some of the animals that live in them.

2. Divide students into seven groups and assign each group a different habitat. On a large sheet of chart paper, have each group write the name of its assigned habitat and a list of animals that live in it.

3. Have each group share its completed list; then display the lists in the classroom for reference.

4. Read aloud some real estate ads or the ads shown on this page. Discuss with students how special features of homes are highlighted in this type of ad.

5. Give each student a copy of page 187. Explain that on this sheet each habitat is described in a brief real estate ad. Have each student color and cut out his animal pictures. Next read each ad with students as they glue the pictures beside the appropriate ads. Remind students to use the Background Information and the group lists as references.

6. For added learning fun, challenge students to complete the Bonus Box activity.

Excellent Location
Furnished two-bedroom house with a screened-in porch. Air conditioning and new appliances. Close to shopping center.

Lake Area
Three bedrooms, two baths. Brick home in rural area. Seven rooms, new carpet, fenced yard, and patio. Walking distance to lake.

Name _____

Home, Sweet Home

Color and cut out each animal card.
Read each habitat ad.
Glue each animal card beside the matching ad.

For Sale

1. A high-rise home atop a rocky mountain. Perfect for surefooted animals that love to graze.

Available For Immediate Occupancy!

2. Large home in dry, sandy location. If you like hot weather and you store your own water, this is the place for you!

Cool Home!

3. Icy waterfront home for sale. Great for strong swimmers that love to eat fish.

Spacious Home

4. Looking for a home in a wide-open area? If so, this grassy home is for you!

Well-Landscaped Area

5. This lush forest is the perfect home for tree-loving animals that enjoy hot weather.

For Rent

6. One-room tree apartment. Great place for animals who like to sleep in during the day.

Swimmers' Delight

7. Very large watery home with well-populated neighborhood. Many schools in the area.

Bonus Box: Choose one of the seven habitats. On the back of this sheet, draw and label a picture of it with at least three animals that live there.

©The Education Center, Inc. • *Ready-to-Go Lessons* • TEC1115 • Key p. 319

polar bear · owl · elephant · mountain goat · dolphin · camel · chimpanzee

187

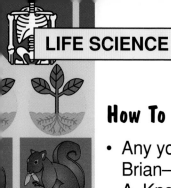

How To Extend The Lesson:

- Any youngster who has ever asked his parent for a pet will readily identify with Brian—the main character of *The Salamander Room* by Anne Mazer (Alfred A. Knopf Books For Young Readers, 1994). Brian wants to keep a salamander for a pet, but his mother doesn't seem to like this idea. In response to her questions about how he will care for it, Brian envisions transforming his bedroom into the perfect salamander habitat—complete with trees, frogs, and birds. Share this imaginative story with youngsters; then ask each student to name the animal she would most like to have. Next direct each youngster to write and illustrate a story about how she would provide an appropriate environment and good care for her pet. Bind students' completed work with a cover, and title the resulting book *Our Perfect Pet-Care Guide.*

- Youngsters will love being habitat detectives with this clue-filled activity! Cut a class supply of paper strips and program each strip with the name of a different animal. Then place the programmed strips in a large container. To play, each student in turn takes a strip from the container and silently reads the corresponding animal name. He orally gives clues about this animal's home and habitat, and challenges his classmates to identify the described animal. After they name the correct animal, the activity continues in a similar manner until every youngster has taken a turn.

- Students will be right at home with this creative class-book project! Read aloud *A House Is A House For Me* by Mary Ann Hoberman (Puffin Books, 1993), an inviting book that presents a variety of houses from a unique perspective. After sharing this delightful story, have students brainstorm animals and their homes as you record their responses on a chart (similar to the one shown). Next instruct students to use the list to create a class book. To do this, each student selects one animal and, on a sheet of paper, writes and illustrates a sentence about its home, using Hoberman's book as a model. Then, on another sheet of paper, a student volunteer draws a picture of the class and writes "And a school is a house for us." Using this sheet as the last page, bind all of the completed pages with a cover. No doubt your classroom library will be the perfect house for this student-made book!

Animals	Homes
beaver	lodge
grizzly bear	cave
chicken	coop
sheep	fold
cow and horse	barn
rabbit	hutch
centipede and beetle	rotting log
chipmunk and mole	underground tunnels
ant	hill
bee	hive
mountain lion	den
badger	burrow
raccoon	hollow tree
spider	web
bird	nest
sow	sty

Critter Cover-Ups

Uncover the facts about fur, feathers, and scales
with this animal classification activity!

Skill: Classifying animals

Estimated Lesson Time: 25 minutes

Teacher Preparation:
1. Divide a sheet of chart paper into three columns and label each column with one of the following headings: "fur," "feathers," and "scales."
2. Duplicate page 191 for each student.

Materials:
1 sheet of prepared chart paper
1 copy of page 191 per student
crayons

Background Information:
Animals are often classified by common characteristics. For example, animals can be classified by the number of legs they have, their habitats, or how they move. This activity focuses on classifying animals by three types of skin coverings—fur, feathers, and scales.

- **Fur:** Mammals are the only animals that have fur. The fur of mammals, such as cats, dogs, mice, and giraffes, helps retain body heat. Mammal fur varies from the curly wool of sheep, to the stiff short-haired covering of horses.
- **Feathers:** This skin covering is unique to birds. This group of animals includes chickens, parrots, and ducks. Feathers are birds' primary protective coverings. Some male birds have brightly colored or decorative feathers to attract mates. Other birds have feathers that camouflage them in their surroundings.
- **Scales:** The skin of reptiles is covered with scales. Some reptiles, such as lizards and snakes, have one sheet of overlapping scales. Other reptiles, including turtles and crocodiles, have scales that grow in individual areas called *plates*.

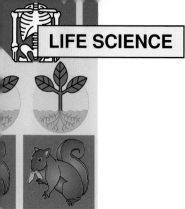

Introducing The Lesson:

Write the words "turtle," "owl," and "chicken" on the chalk-board. Challenge students to determine which animal does not belong in this group and to explain their reasoning. Be sure to encourage a variety of responses. For example, youngsters might state that the turtle doesn't belong because it doesn't have feathers, or students might explain that the turtle is different because it has four feet and the other animals do not. Continue in a similar manner with several other groups of three animals—two that have the same type of skin covering and one that does not. (See the list below for examples of animal groups.) Then tell youngsters that with this lesson, they will learn more about one of the ways to group or classify animals—by skin coverings.

Steps:

1. Have youngsters name the skin coverings of the animals discussed in the previous activity—fur, feathers, and scales. Then share with students the Background Information on page 189.

2. Ask students to brainstorm animals that have fur, feathers, or scales. Write each of their responses below the appropriate heading on the prepared chart.

3. Give each student a copy of page 191. With students, review each of the pictured animals and read the directions and questions.

4. Have each youngster color the animals and color the squares to graph her results according to the directions. Then instruct her to answer the questions.

5. Challenge students to complete the Bonus Box activity.

turtle	owl	chicken
fox	mouse	snake
duck	dog	bear
crocodile	snake	cat
giraffe	parrot	fox
snake	bear	turtle

Name _____

Critter Cover-Ups

Look at each animal.
Color it brown if it has **fur**.
Color it blue if it has **feathers**.
Color it green if it has **scales**.
Graph your results below.

Look at your graph.

1. What type of skin covering do most of the animals have? _____

2. How many of the animals have fur *or* scales? _____

3. How many of the animals have scales *or* feathers? _____

4. What group of animals has fur? _____

5. What group of animals has feathers? _____

6. What group of animals has scales? _____

Bonus Box: Choose three animals. On the back of this sheet, write a riddle about each of them. Ask a friend or family member to guess the answers.

Fur	Feathers	Scales

191

How To Extend The Lesson:

- Boost students' creativity with this one-of-a-kind animal project! Have each student fold a sheet of drawing paper in half and then unfold it. On one side of the paper, have him create and draw an animal that has fur, feathers, *and* scales. On the other side, instruct each youngster to write the name of his animal and a description of it. Encourage each student to include information about how each of the different types of skin coverings protects his animal. Give each youngster an opportunity to share his completed work, then display these unique projects on a bulletin board titled "Critter Creations."

- Reinforce critical-thinking skills with this open-ended classification activity. Give each student a copy of the pictures below and have her cut them apart. Next ask each youngster to sort her animal pictures by a rule of her choice, such as the number of legs or the type of skin covering. Instruct each student to write her rule and the corresponding animal names on a sheet of paper. Then, in a like manner, ask her to sort her cards by two other rules and record her work. For added learning fun, have each student show a classmate her favorite set of animals and challenge him to determine her sorting rule.

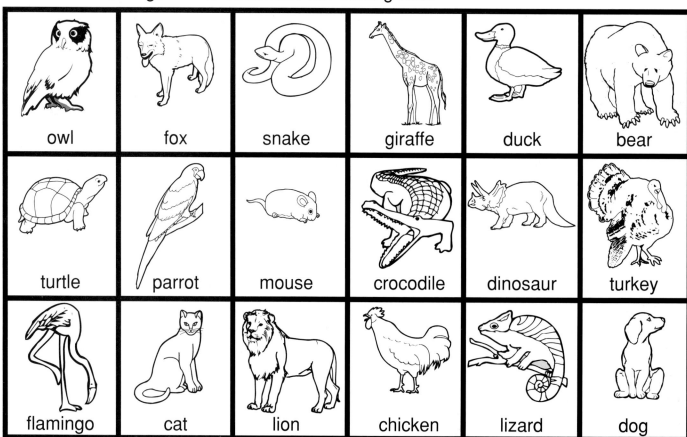

owl	fox	snake	giraffe	duck	bear
turtle	parrot	mouse	crocodile	dinosaur	turkey
flamingo	cat	lion	chicken	lizard	dog

Creepy, Crawly Lotto

Youngsters will go buggy over this insect-identification game!

Skill: Identifying insects

Estimated Lesson Time: 30 minutes

Teacher Preparation:

1. Enlarge the Background Information below. Cut the information about each insect into a strip. Fold each strip in half and place all of the strips in a container.
2. Duplicate page 195 for each student.

Materials:

1 copy of page 195 per student
12 game markers, such as kidney
   beans or buttons, per student
1 enlarged copy of the Background
   Information for the teacher

1 container to hold paper strips
scissors
glue

Background Information:

All insects have six legs and three main body parts. Each insect has a *head*, where eyes, antennae, and jaws are found; a *thorax*, where legs and wings are attached; and an *abdomen*, where food is digested and eggs are produced. Scientists have discovered and named about 1 million insects. Here is information about 12 of them:

- A **dragonfly** can fly backward or hover in one place. As it flies, it holds its legs together, forming a basket for capturing mosquitoes—its prey.
- A **honeybee** is important for pollination. People have collected honey from bees' nests for hundreds of years.
- An **ant** lives in a colony. Most ants make underground nests with many tunnels and rooms.
- A **praying mantis** has a long narrow body and thin legs. Its grasping front legs give it the appearance of praying.
- A **grasshopper** has strong hind legs that are used for jumping and singing.
- A **fly** has only one pair of wings, unlike other insects. Some flies have sticky, hairy pads on their feet to help them walk on smooth, slippery surfaces.
- A **stag beetle** has hardened front wings that cover its hind wings. Its powerful jaws are probably used for fighting.
- A **butterfly** is usually brightly colored and flies during the day. When it rests, it folds its wings upright over its back.
- A **moth** is dull in color and flies at night. When a moth is at rest, it holds its wings flat and rooflike over its body.
- A **walkingstick** is the longest insect. It resembles a twig and blends in with its background.
- A **ladybug** is helpful to gardeners because it eats insects that attack plants.
- A **firefly** makes a bright greenish light that can be seen at night.

Introducing The Lesson:

Ask students to imagine that they are outside and they see an ant, a honeybee, and a butterfly. Ask them to brainstorm the common characteristics of these creatures. Record their responses on the chalkboard. Lead youngsters to the conclusion that these creatures are insects. Use the Background Information on page 193 to explain that all insects have six legs and three main body parts. Tell students that they will learn about 12 different types of insects with this activity.

Steps:

1. Give each student a copy of page 195. Have him cut apart the insect pictures at the bottom of the page and then set aside the lotto board (at the top of the page) for later use.

2. Use the Background Information on page 193 to share with students some of the distinguishing characteristics of one of the pictured insects. Have each student hold up his corresponding picture card. Verify students' responses; then continue in a like manner with the remaining insects.

3. Tell youngsters that they will play a game with their picture cards. Instruct each student to randomly glue his insect pictures onto his lotto board. Then give each youngster game markers.

4. To play the game, take a paper strip from the container and read aloud the information on it without revealing the insect's name. Have each student place a game marker on the corresponding picture on his lotto board.

5. Continue the game in a similar fashion until one student has placed a game marker on each picture in one row. After verifying his marked pictures, declare him the winner of this round.

6. Prepare to play additional rounds in a similar manner by returning all of the strips to the container and having students clear their boards. Each winner becomes the caller for the following round.

Creepy, Crawly Lotto

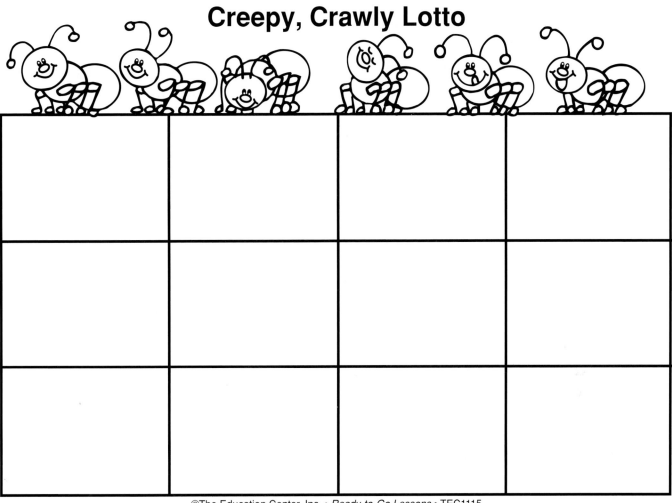

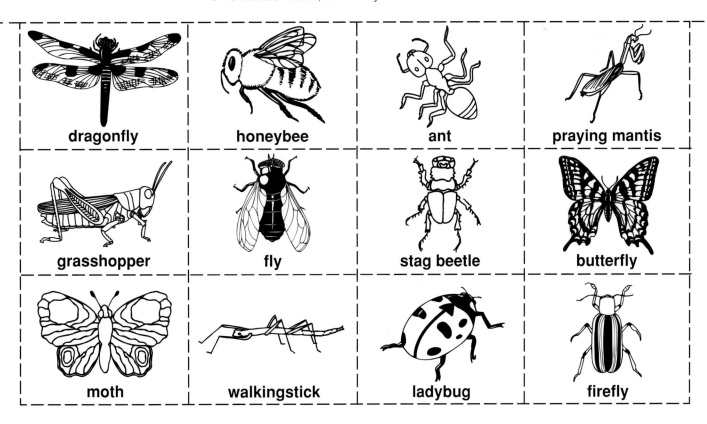

195

How To Extend The Lesson:

• Your young entomologists will be all abuzz over this fabulous selection of literature!
   — *Bugs!* by David T. Greenberg (Little, Brown And Company; 1997)
   — *Night Letters* by Palmyra LoMonaco (Dutton Children's Books, 1996)
   — *Insects Are My Life* by Megan McDonald (Orchard Books, 1997)
   — *Two Bad Ants* by Chris Van Allsburg (Houghton Mifflin Company, 1988)

• Give students an opportunity to be insect inventors! First remind students that every insect has six legs and three body parts: a head, an abdomen, and a thorax. Also discuss with youngsters the wide variety of insects. For example, a fairy fly is about one-hundredth inch long and can crawl through the eye of a needle. In contrast, the Goliath beetle grows to more than four inches. Not only do insects vary in size, but they also differ in color, markings, and shape. After this discussion, provide students with a selection of colored paper and craft materials, such as glitter, sequins, and buttons. Have each youngster use these supplies to create a poster of a new insect. Instruct her to include her insect's name and a summary of its distinguishing features on her poster. After your inventive students share their completed work, display the posters in the hall for everyone to enjoy. No doubt youngsters will buzz with enthusiasm over this project!

• Integrate math and science with this problem-solving activity. On an index card, write an insect word problem, such as "Jenny sees 18 insect legs. How many insects are there?" Write the answer on the back of the card. Program several other cards in a similar manner. Place them in a large decorated envelope titled "Going Buggy Over Math!" and place the envelope in a center with a supply of blank paper. To use the center, a student takes a card from the envelope, writes and illustrates his solution on a sheet of paper, and checks his work.

Going Buggy Over Math!

Jenny sees 18 insect legs. How many insects are there?

6   6   6

There are 3 insects.

Prehistoric Puzzlers

Your young paleontologists will travel back in time as they solve these remarkable reptile puzzles!

Skill: Identifying different kinds of dinosaurs

Estimated Lesson Time: 30 minutes

Teacher Preparation:
1. Duplicate page 199 for each student.
2. Enlarge and duplicate page 200. Cut apart the dinosaur pictures.

Materials:
1 enlarged copy of page 200 for the teacher
1 copy of page 199 per student
tape

Background Information:
Dinosaurs were reptiles that lived long ago. Most were four-footed plant eaters, but some were meat eaters that walked on their hind legs. There were many types of dinosaurs, and their sizes, shapes, and other distinguishing features varied greatly. Several different kinds of dinosaurs are described below.

- **Herbivores (plant eaters):** Most plant eaters had long necks that helped them reach treetops. Some herbivores had as many as 960 teeth!
  — A **Brachiosaurus** was so tall that it could have looked over a four-story building.
  — A **Stegosaurus** had bony plates on its back. It was as long as two cars, but its brain was only the size of a walnut!
  — An **Ankylosaurus** used its tail as a club to fight enemies. Bony plates covered its back, and sharp spines grew on its sides.
  — A **Triceratops** had a bony frill around the back of its head. It used its three horns to protect itself.
  — An **Apatosaurus** often stood in water to keep safe from its enemies. It used to be known as *Brontosaurus*.
  — An **Ammosaurus** was eight feet long. Its front legs were shorter than its hind legs.
- **Carnivores (meat eaters):** The majority of carnivores walked on their hind legs. Their front limbs were free for catching and holding prey. They had short necks.
  — An **Allosaurus** was twice as tall as a man. It had a ridge along the front of its skull, unlike other meat-eating dinosaurs.
  — A **Tyrannosaurus** had six-inch-long teeth and was a great hunter. It was the largest meat-eating dinosaur.

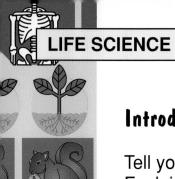

Introducing The Lesson:

Tell youngsters that they will learn about several types of dinosaurs. Explain that each of these dinosaurs was either a *herbivore* (plant eater) or a *carnivore* (meat eater). Invite youngsters to guess some of the physical characteristics that would have helped each of these types of dinosaurs survive. Then discuss the features of herbivores and carnivores summarized in the Background Information on page 197. For example, herbivorous dinosaurs often had long necks that helped them reach leafy treetops. Most carnivorous dinosaurs walked on their back legs, leaving their front limbs free for catching and holding prey.

Steps:

1. Write the word "herbivores" at the top of one side of the chalkboard and "carnivores" at the top of the other side.

2. Show youngsters a dinosaur picture card from page 200. Have them use what they learned about herbivores and carnivores to guess if the pictured dinosaur ate plants or meat. Then tape the picture card onto the chalkboard under the correct heading.

3. Using the Background Information on page 197, name and describe this dinosaur.

4. Continue classifying and discussing the remaining dinosaurs with youngsters in a like manner.

5. Give each student a copy of page 199. Read the directions, sentences, and each of the dinosaur names with students. Then instruct youngsters to fill in the blanks at the end of each sentence.

6. Challenge students to complete the Bonus Box activity.

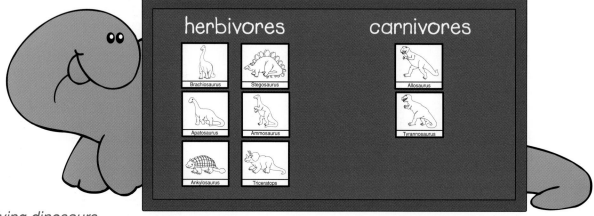

Name _____

Prehistoric Puzzlers

Write the name of each dinosaur in the boxes beside the matching clue.
Use the Dinosaur Word Bank.
Cross out each word as you use it.

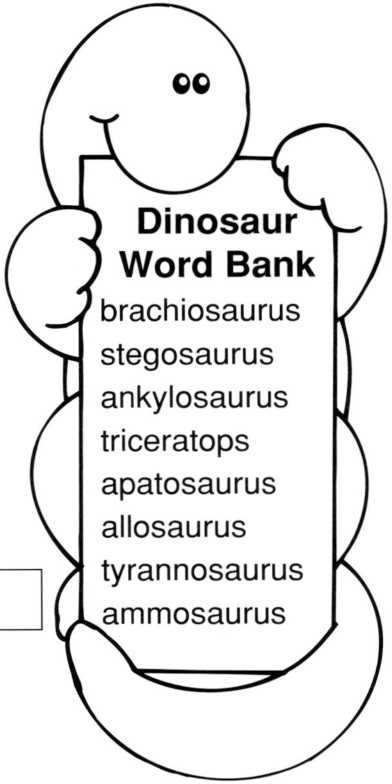

Dinosaur Word Bank

brachiosaurus
stegosaurus
ankylosaurus
triceratops
apatosaurus
allosaurus
tyrannosaurus
ammosaurus

1. This dinosaur often stood in water to keep safe.

2. This plant-eating dinosaur was eight feet long.

3. This meat eater was twice as tall as a man.

4. With six-inch-long teeth, this dinosaur was a great hunter.

5. Bony plates covered the back of this plant-eating dinosaur.

6. This dinosaur used its tail to fight enemies.

7. This plant eater used its three horns to protect itself.

8. This dinosaur could have looked over a four-story building.

Bonus Box: On the back of this sheet, write about your favorite type of dinosaur. Illustrate your work.

©The Education Center, Inc. • *Ready-to-Go Lessons* • TEC1115 • Key p. 319

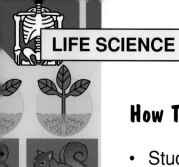

LIFE SCIENCE

How To Extend The Lesson:

- Students will discover what's in a name with this word-building activity! Explain that many dinosaurs are often given names made of root words that describe their shapes, sizes, or other characteristics. For example, stegosaurus means roofed *(stego)* reptile *(saurus)*. On chart paper, display the root words shown below and ask each youngster to use them to invent a new dinosaur name. Then, on a sheet of paper, have him draw and label a dinosaur to correspond with this name. Invite each student to share his completed work. Challenge his classmates to use the root-word list to determine the meaning of this unique reptile's name. No doubt your young "name-asaurs" will have a colossal good time!

alti: tall, high	**mega:** huge	**saurus:** reptile, lizard
bi: two	**mono:** single	**stego:** roofed
bronto: thunder	**ptero:** winged	**stereo:** twin
don, den: tooth	**rex:** king	**top:** head, face
luro: tail	**rhino:** nose	**tri:** three

- A love of literature will never be extinct with "dino-mite" titles like these!
  — *An Alphabet Of Dinosaurs* by Peter Dodson (Scholastic Inc., 1995)
  — *Can I Have A Stegosaurus, Mom? Can I? Please!?* by Lois Grambling (BridgeWater Books, 1997)
  — *How Big Were The Dinosaurs?* by Bernard Most (Harcourt Brace & Company, 1995)

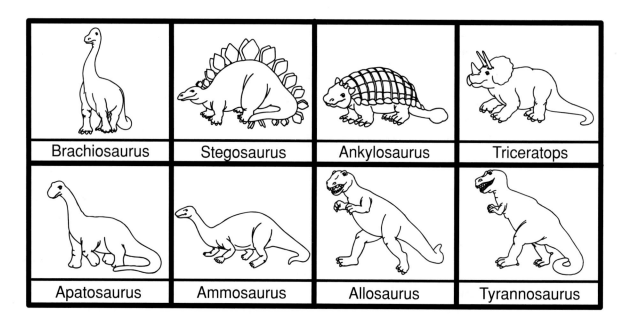

Brachiosaurus	Stegosaurus	Ankylosaurus	Triceratops
Apatosaurus	Ammosaurus	Allosaurus	Tyrannosaurus

Nutrition News

Extra! Extra! Read all about it! Second graders make headlines with nutrition know-how!

Skill: Interpreting and using the Food Guide Pyramid

Estimated Lesson Time: 45 minutes

Teacher Preparation:
1. Draw the Food Guide Pyramid shown below on a sheet of chart paper.
2. Duplicate page 203 for each student.

Materials:
1 copy of the day's school-lunch menu
1 prepared sheet of chart paper
1 copy of page 203 per student

Background Information:
The U.S. Department of Agriculture used its research about good nutrition to develop the Food Guide Pyramid. This dietary guide outlines a range of daily recommended servings for each major food group. The actual number of servings that a person needs varies depending on how many calories his body requires. Here are examples of foods in each Pyramid category:

- **Fats:** butter, chocolate, mayonnaise
- **Dairy:** yogurt, cheese, milk
- **Protein:** eggs, turkey, chicken
- **Vegetables:** carrots, celery, lettuce
- **Fruits:** oranges, strawberries, apples
- **Grains:** cereal, pasta, bread

Fats
very few
servings

Dairy
2–3

Protein
2–3

Vegetables
3–5

Fruits
2–4

Grains
6–11

Introducing The Lesson:

Tell youngsters that during this lesson, each of them will be an investigative reporter and write about the nutritional value of a school lunch. To begin, have students recall and name the items on the previous day's school menu as you write them on the chalkboard. Explain to students that they will prepare for their investigations by learning about the food groups in which these foods belong.

Steps:

1. Direct students' attention to the Food Guide Pyramid on the prepared chart. Use the Background Information on page 201 to tell students about the different food groups and serving suggestions shown.

2. Have students use the Pyramid to identify the group(s) in which each menu item belongs. Then ask youngsters to determine if the menu includes something from each of the food groups. If it does not, have students suggest additions to the menu. Also ask students how the menu could be changed in order to be more healthful. For example, a baked potato or mashed potatoes could be substituted for potato chips.

3. Erase the chalkboard. Have a student volunteer read today's lunch menu; write it on the chalkboard.

4. Give each student a copy of page 203. On his sheet, have him list each menu item and the food group(s) to which it belongs.

5. Explain to students that newspaper writers share their opinions about the news in editorials. Instruct each youngster to complete the editorial section on his sheet by listing the healthful menu items, then suggesting menu changes to make the lunch even more nutritious. Encourage students to be creative. For instance, a slice of tomato or cheese could be added to a hamburger, or a fresh apple could be substituted for cake.

6. Ask each youngster to draw an illustration of the school lunch in the box provided. Then have him write a short comment or description below it.

7. Challenge students to complete the Bonus Box activity.

8. On a bulletin board titled "Nutrition News," display students' completed work "hot off the press"!

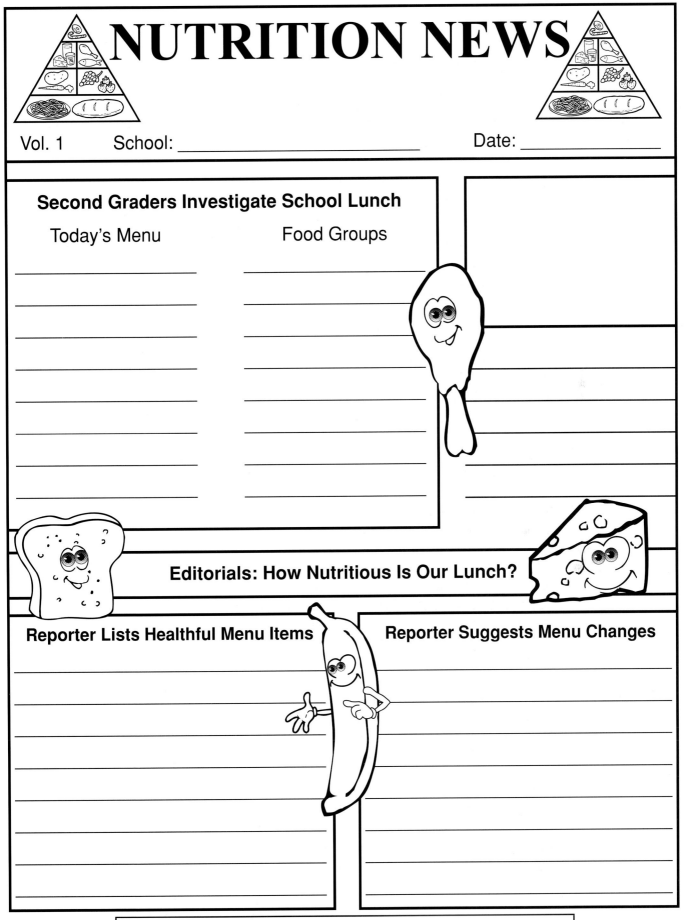

NUTRITION NEWS

Vol. 1   School: _____   Date: _____

Second Graders Investigate School Lunch

Today's Menu   Food Groups

_____   _____
_____   _____
_____   _____
_____   _____
_____   _____
_____   _____
_____   _____
_____   _____

Editorials: How Nutritious Is Our Lunch?

Reporter Lists Healthful Menu Items   Reporter Suggests Menu Changes

Bonus Box: On the back of this sheet, write a menu for a nutritious breakfast.

How To Extend The Lesson:

- Make a yummy display of healthful food choices! First, from discarded magazines, have each youngster cut out pictures of healthful foods that together would make a well-balanced, nutritious meal. Then have her glue them onto a paper plate. Cover a bulletin board with a red and white checkered vinyl tablecloth. Mount the completed projects on the bulletin board and add the title "Sink Your Teeth Into Good Nutrition." Now that's a surefire recipe for learning fun!

- Satisfy youngsters' appetites for food-related literature with these tasty titles!
  - *Milo's Great Invention* by Andrew Clements (Steck-Vaughn Company, 1998)
  - *The Seven Silly Eaters* by Mary Ann Hoberman (Harcourt Brace & Company, 1997)
  - *Chocolatina* by Erik Kraft (BridgeWater Books, 1998)
  - *The Edible Pyramid* by Loreen Leedy (Holiday House, Inc.; 1996)

- Give this lunch-ratings activity two thumbs-up! Ask each student to write an original lunch menu on a sheet of paper. Explain to him that for this activity, he may write a healthful menu or one that has little nutritional value. Next direct each youngster to trade his completed menu with a classmate. Then write the menu-rating scale shown below on the chalkboard. Have each student review his classmate's menu and then use the scale to rate it. Ask him to write the rating at the top of the menu. Instruct each student to return the rated menu to its owner and explain to him how he determined the rating. Also have him give the owner suggestions for making the menu more nutritious. No doubt this activity will give students food for thought!

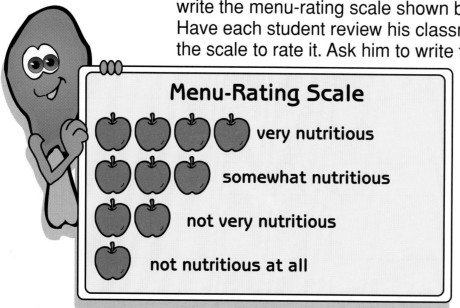

Menu-Rating Scale

🍎🍎🍎🍎 very nutritious

🍎🍎🍎 somewhat nutritious

🍎🍎 not very nutritious

🍎 not nutritious at all

Busy Bones

Standing up or sitting down, our bones help us get around!

Skill: Identifying parts of the human skeletal system

Estimated Lesson Time: 30 minutes

Teacher Preparation:
Duplicate page 207 for each student.

Materials:
1 copy of page 207 per student
scissors
glue

Background Information:
A skeleton is a very important part of a human body. It provides a strong framework for the body; protects its organs, such as the brain and heart; and helps it move. Without a skeleton, a body would be floppy and shapeless. An adult skeleton has 206 bones that vary in size and shape. Each bone has a special function.

- The **backbone**, or *spine*, links together the top and bottom parts of a skeleton and provides its primary support. It also balances the top part of a body over its hips and legs.
- The **skull** has 22 bones and protects the brain.
- The **upper arm** bone is also known as the *humerus*. Arms are the most mobile parts of a body.
- The **hand** has 27 bones. It is the most flexible part of the human skeleton.
- The **rib** bones curve around the body, forming a strong cage that guards the heart and lungs.
- The **pelvis**, a bowl-shaped bone, has two sockets into which the thighbones fit.
- The **thighbone**, or *femur,* is a person's longest bone. The length of one thighbone is equal to one-quarter of a person's total height.
- The **foot** bones grow faster than any other bones in the human body. They are flatter than hand bones, which helps people balance.

Introducing The Lesson:

Ask each student to sit up as straight as possible in her chair. Next tell her to place her hand on the center of her back and then to relax her position. Repeat these steps several times and have youngsters share their observations. Explain to each student that the bumps she felt are actually small bones that are part of her backbone, or spine—the primary support for a skeleton. Tell students that the human body has 206 bones and that this lesson will teach them about several of them.

Steps:

1. Use the Background Information on page 205 to tell students about the importance of the human skeletal system.

2. Have each student find and feel his skull; then share the related facts on page 205. Continue in a like manner with the following skeletal parts: *upper arm, hand, ribs, pelvis, thighbone,* and *foot.*

3. Give each student a copy of page 207, scissors, and glue. Review the directions with students; then have each of them complete the reproducible activity.

4. Challenge youngsters to complete the Bonus Box activity.

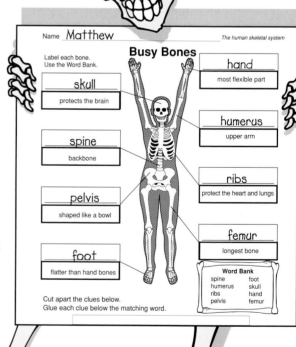

Name Matthew   The human skeletal system

Busy Bones

Label each bone.
Use the Word Bank.

skull — protects the brain

hand — most flexible part

humerus — upper arm

spine — backbone

ribs — protect the heart and lungs

pelvis — shaped like a bowl

femur — longest bone

foot — flatter than hand bones

Word Bank
spine   foot
humerus   skull
ribs   hand
pelvis   femur

Cut apart the clues below.
Glue each clue below the matching word.

Name _____

The human skeletal system

Busy Bones

Label each bone.
Use the Word Bank.

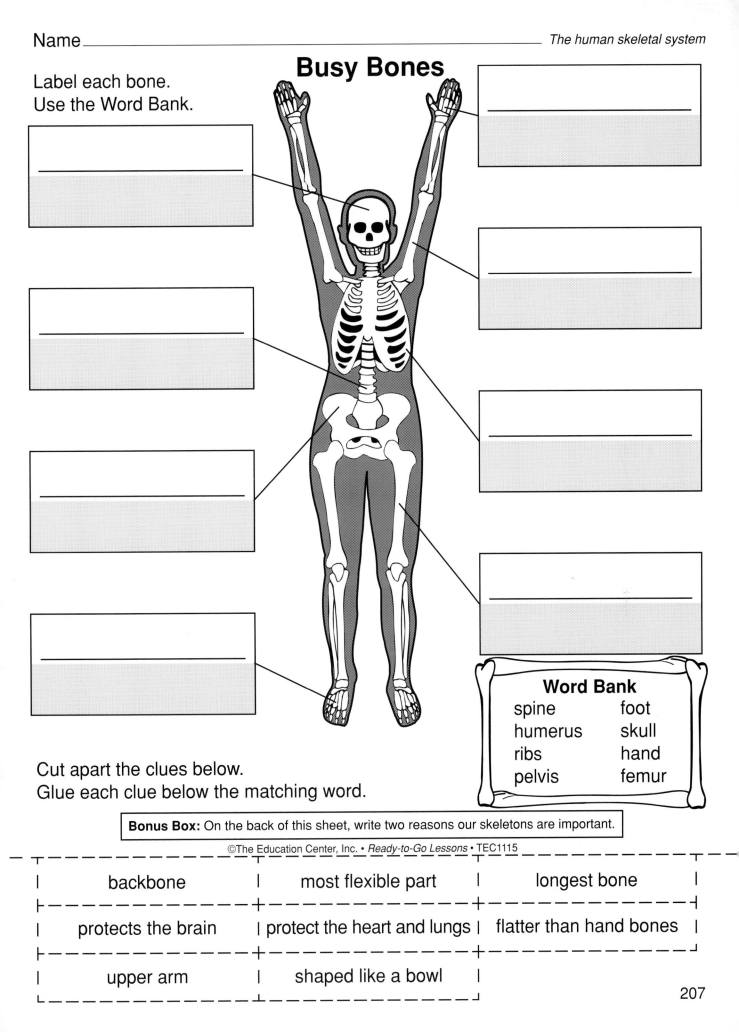

Cut apart the clues below.
Glue each clue below the matching word.

Word Bank

spine	foot
humerus	skull
ribs	hand
pelvis	femur

Bonus Box: On the back of this sheet, write two reasons our skeletons are important.

©The Education Center, Inc. • *Ready-to-Go Lessons* • TEC1115

backbone	most flexible part	longest bone
protects the brain	protect the heart and lungs	flatter than hand bones
upper arm	shaped like a bowl	

207

How To Extend The Lesson:

- Keep students on the move with this lesson about joints. Explain that the place where two bones meet is called a *joint. Ball-and-socket joints* are found in a person's shoulders and hips, and they swivel in almost any direction. *Hinge joints* are found in a person's fingers, elbows, and knees. Each of them allows movement in only one direction, like a door hinge. Have students demonstrate the movements of these two types of joints. Then show youngsters what it would be like if they didn't have joints. To begin, help a student volunteer tape a crayon to each of his fingers on one hand so that his knuckles will not bend. Next have him try to pick up a pencil or book as his classmates observe. Ask the volunteer and other students to share their observations. Repeat this exercise with other students, or complete similar experiments by taping a ruler to a student volunteer's elbow or wrist joint. If desired, provide time later in the day for the remaining students to try this exercise. Make no bones about it—this activity is a winner!

- Bone up on the skeletal system with these terrific titles!
  — *The Skeleton Inside You* by Philip Balestrino (HarperCollins Publishers, Inc.; 1989)
  — *Dem Bones* by Bob Barner (Chronicle Books, 1996)
  — *Body Books: Bones* by Anna Sandeman (The Millbrook Press, Inc.; 1995)

- Host a "bone-a fide" bone-building snack time! Tell students that calcium-rich foods—such as milk, cheese, and spinach—help to grow strong bones. Ask each student to bring a calcium-rich snack to school on a predetermined day. As youngsters munch away on their healthful treats, share the facts below.
  — Both the human neck and the giraffe neck have seven bones.
  — Skeletons in laboratories are white because their bones have been lightened. The bones of a living skeleton vary from beige to pink.
  — A very young person has approximately 300 bones. As he grows, some of them fuse together, so an adult skeleton has 206 bones.
  — A person's muscles weigh more than his bones.
  — The smallest human bone is in the ear. It is smaller than a grain of rice.

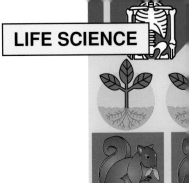

Tooth Wisdom

Smile! It's time to brush up on dental health!

Skill: Identifying good dental-health habits

Estimated Lesson Time: 45 minutes

Teacher Preparation:

1. Visually divide a sheet of bulletin-board paper into two columns. Label one column "Foods That Make My Smile Bright." Label the other column "Foods That Make My Smile A Fright."
2. Draw a tooth character with a bright smile in the left column of the labeled paper and a tooth character with a gap-toothed grin in the right column, as shown on page 210.
3. Duplicate page 211 for each student.

Materials:

1 large sheet of prepared bulletin-board paper (see page 210)
1 discarded magazine per every two students
1 copy of page 211 per student
scissors
glue

Background Information:

Good dental habits prevent most cases of tooth decay. Three major components of dental care recommended by dentists follow.

- **A healthful diet:** Eat well-balanced meals and few sugary foods to avoid cavities. Foods that are high in calcium—such as cheese, yogurt, and milk—are especially important for keeping teeth strong and healthy. Fluorides are also helpful; they help teeth resist cavity-forming acid. You can get fluorides in a variety of ways (drinking water, tablets prescribed by your dentist, toothpaste, etc.).
- **Clean teeth:** Brush your teeth after every meal and floss once a day. These practices remove food particles and plaque from teeth. Food particles attract germs, which gather on the surface of teeth and form a thin layer called plaque. If the plaque is not brushed away, it will cause tooth decay.
- **Dental checkups:** Visit your dentist at least once a year. With regular appointments, dentists can recognize and treat dental diseases before they cause serious damage.

Introducing The Lesson:

Display the prepared chart (similar to the one shown below). Read the first column heading with youngsters and ask them to brainstorm nutritious foods that help keep teeth healthy. Then read the second heading with youngsters. Tell them that foods with a lot of sugar can make teeth unhealthy. Ask students to name some foods that belong in this category.

Steps:

1. Tell students that they will complete this chart as a class by adding magazine pictures to it. Divide students into pairs and give each pair a magazine and scissors.

2. Ask each youngster to cut out one picture of food from the magazine.

3. Have each student in turn show the class his picture, classify it as either a food that is good for teeth or one that is harmful, and glue it onto the chart in the appropriate column.

4. Explain to youngsters that in addition to eating nutritious foods, there are other ways to keep their teeth healthy. Share the Background Information on page 209.

5. Give each student a copy of page 211. Read the directions and Word Bank with youngsters.

6. Read each sentence with students and have each youngster complete it on his sheet. Then read the directions at the bottom of the page and have each student solve the riddle.

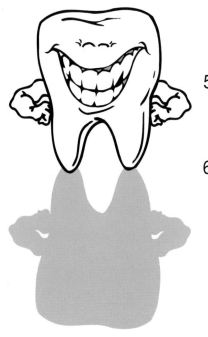

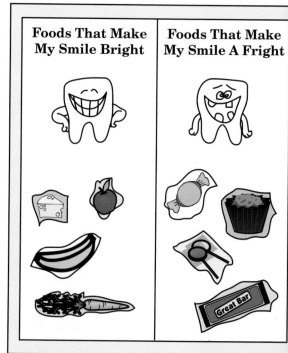

Foods That Make My Smile Bright	Foods That Make My Smile A Fright

7. Challenge students to complete the Bonus Box activity.

Name _____

Tooth Wisdom

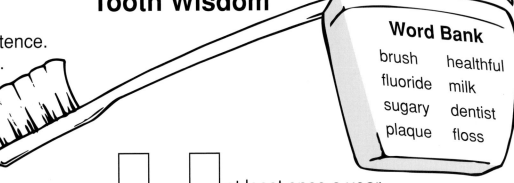

Complete each sentence.
Use the Word Bank.

Word Bank

brush   healthful
fluoride   milk
sugary   dentist
plaque   floss

1. Visit your ___ ___ ___ ___ [4] ___ [7] at least once a year.

2. [2] ___ ___ ___ ___ your teeth after every meal.

3. If you don't brush well, ___ ___ [1] ___ ___ [12] will form on your teeth.

4. Clean between your teeth with ___ ___ ___ [8] ___ .

5. Eat [6] ___ ___ ___ ___ ___ ___ ___ [11] foods.

6. Water and toothpaste with ___ ___ ___ ___ [3] [10] ___ ___ help prevent cavities.

7. [9] ___ ___ ___ keeps teeth strong.

8. ___ ___ [5] ___ ___ ___ treats can cause cavities.

What do you get when you cross good dental habits with a smart student?
Write the letter from each numbered box below to find the answer!

___   ___ ___ ___ ___ ___ ___   ___ ___ ___ ___ ___ !
1   2   3   4   5   6   7   8   9   10 11 12

Bonus Box: On the back of this sheet, draw and label three foods that are good for your teeth.

How To Extend The Lesson:

- Brush up on math and critical-thinking skills with this "tooth-errific" graphing activity! On chart paper, draw and label a graph for a question related to dental health, such as "What color is your toothbrush?" or "How many toothbrushes are in your bathroom?" Have each student respond to the question by personalizing and taping a tooth or toothbrush cutout to the graph in the appropriate location. Then analyze the results with youngsters. Now that's an idea that you can count on!

- Give students practice flossing with this fun simulation. Give each pair of students a 12-inch length of yarn. Instruct one student in each pair to hold up his hands and put them together, palm to palm. Then have him slightly spread apart his fingers to represent teeth. Direct his partner to guide his yarn between the first set of fingers and pull it up and down, "cleaning" the sides of the "teeth." Have him repeat this step with the remaining "teeth." Then ask each youngster to switch roles with his partner. Encourage each student to put his flossing skills into practice with real floss at home.

- Your young book lovers will have something to smile about with this project! Duplicate on tagboard a class supply of the bookmark below. Give each student a copy; then have her personalize her bookmark and cut it out. Review the listed titles with youngsters and encourage them to use their bookmarks as they enjoy these books. At the end of your dental-health study, give each student a tooth-shaped or gold-star sticker to place beside her favorite "toothy" title.

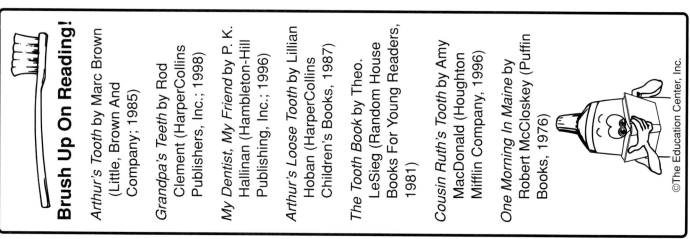

Brush Up On Reading!

Arthur's Tooth by Marc Brown (Little, Brown And Company; 1985)

Grandpa's Teeth by Rod Clement (HarperCollins Publishers, Inc.; 1998)

My Dentist, My Friend by P. K. Hallinan (Hambleton-Hill Publishing, Inc.; 1996)

Arthur's Loose Tooth by Lillian Hoban (HarperCollins Children's Books, 1987)

The Tooth Book by Theo. LeSieg (Random House Books For Young Readers, 1981)

Cousin Ruth's Tooth by Amy MacDonald (Houghton Mifflin Company, 1996)

One Morning In Maine by Robert McCloskey (Puffin Books, 1976)

©The Education Center, Inc.

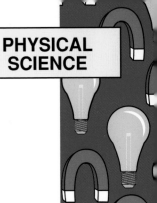

Delectable Desserts

*Cook up a little classification practice
with this appetizing lesson about attributes.*

Skill: Classifying solids by attributes

Estimated Lesson Time: 30 minutes

Teacher Preparation:
1. Duplicate page 215 for each student.
2. Duplicate enough dessert patterns from the bottom of page 215 for each student to have one pattern.

Materials:
1 copy of page 215 per student
1 dessert pattern from page 215 per student
crayons
scissors
glue
tape

Background Information:
- *Matter* has weight and takes up space. It can be touched or held. All objects consist of matter and occupy space.
- Matter can be described by naming its properties. Some properties of matter are size, shape, texture, color, and temperature.
- Matter can exist in three states: *solid, liquid,* or *gas.*
  — A solid has a distinct shape and resists change in shape.
  — A liquid has no shape of its own and takes the shape of the container that holds it.
  — A gas has no definite shape and can expand indefinitely. Gases are not usually visible.

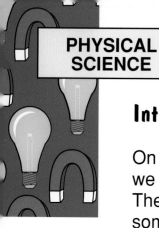

Introducing The Lesson:

On the chalkboard, draw a large triangle, circle, and square. Explain that we often sort things using *attributes,* or special features that an object has. Then tell students that they will use the figures on the chalkboard to sort some bakery items.

Steps:

1. Distribute crayons, scissors, and a copy of one of the dessert patterns (page 215) to each student. Provide time for each student to color his pattern.

2. Ask one student at a time to come to the chalkboard and tape his dessert pattern in the figure that most resembles his dessert. Inform students that they just used the attribute of shape to sort objects.

3. Ask students to name other ways they could sort their dessert patterns. List their responses on the chalkboard. If desired, have students retrieve their dessert patterns and play another round of sorting using a different attribute.

4. Distribute glue and a copy of page 215 to each student. Have each student color and cut out his patterns. Announce a way for students to sort their desserts onto the bakery counters, such as square or not square. (See the list on this page for additional ideas.) Quickly verify students' papers; then ask them to clear their bakery counters. Repeat the activity for a desired number of times. Then ask each student to sort his dessert patterns into two categories. Finally, have him write his sorting rules on the lines and glue the dessert patterns to the corresponding bakery counters.

5. Challenge students to complete the Bonus Box activity.

Different Ways To Classify Desserts

circle / not a circle
square / not a square
triangle / not a triangle
chocolate / not chocolate
hard (crunchy) / soft
topping / no topping
fruit / no fruit

Classifying solids

Delectable Desserts

Color and cut out the bakery treats.
Follow your teacher's directions.

category: _____

Desserts For Sale!

category: _____

Desserts For Sale!

Bonus Box: On the back of this paper, list ways you could sort candy bars.

candy apple

frosted brownie

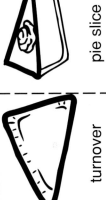

pie slice

turnover

cake slice

ice-cream cone

cookie

donut

215

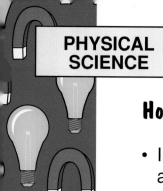

How To Extend The Lesson:

- Introduce another tasty classification activity by having each student fill a small, resealable plastic bag with cereal pieces from home. Arrange the bags for easy viewing, and then have your students suggest ways of classifying the cereal pieces. List the attributes given in response; then mix the cereal pieces and distribute a cupful to each student. Conclude the activity by inviting students to munch on their cereal pieces!

- Sharpen your students' creative-thinking skills with an exercise in comparing and contrasting. Display two solids for the class to observe. Challenge each student to think of two ways that the objects are alike and two ways that they are different. For an added incentive, use objects that your students have brought from home.

- Shape up your youngsters' classification skills with this nifty idea. Cut out large shapes from bulletin-board paper and place them on the classroom floor. Divide students into as many groups as there are shapes, then assign each group a shape. At your signal, have each group search the classroom for solids that are the same shape as its designated shape. When a student finds a solid with a matching shape, she places it on the large paper shape. After a predetermined amount of time, gather students around the paper shapes to share the solids they found.

What's The Source?

Work a little science magic with this lesson on the sources of heat, light, and sound. It's as fun as pulling a rabbit out of a hat!

Skill: Classifying sources of heat, light, and sound

Estimated Lesson Time: 30 minutes

Teacher Preparation:
1. Duplicate page 219 for each student.
2. On the chalkboard, draw and label a picture of each of the following items: a lightbulb, a microwave, and a drum.

Materials:
1 copy of page 219 per student

Background Information:
Heat, light, and sound are just a few of the many kinds of energy.
- Anything that gives off heat is a source of heat. There are two main sources of heat: *natural* and *man-made.* Natural sources include sunshine, volcanoes, hot springs, and lightning. Man-made sources include heat caused by friction (striking a match, running a car engine) and heat harnessed from the flow of electrons (almost all electrical appliances).
- Light sources can be classified as *natural* or *artificial.* Natural light comes from sources that cannot be controlled, such as the Sun and the stars. Artificial light comes from sources that can be controlled, such as candles and flashlights.
- Every sound is produced by the vibrations of an object. Some ways sounds may be classified are loud or soft, high or low, noise or music, sustained sounds or short sounds.

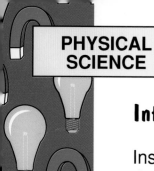

Introducing The Lesson:

Instruct students to imagine each of the following scenarios. Then ask them to describe each one.
• They are standing near a heater.
• They are looking at a lamp turned on.
• They are listening to a band play music.
Tell students that in each scenario, they experienced a type of energy—heat, light, or sound. Challenge students to match each type of energy with the corresponding scenario.

Steps:

1. Share the Background Information on page 217 with students.

2. Ask students to name sources of each type of energy: heat, light, and sound. Write their responses on the chalkboard. (See the examples below as needed.)

3. Distribute a copy of page 219 to each student. Read the directions and the words in the Word Bank with students; then provide time for students to complete the reproducible.

4. Challenge students to complete the Bonus Box activity.

Sources Of Heat	Sources Of Light	Sources Of Sound
geyser (hot spring)	lamp	drum
Sun	Sun	piano
toaster	flashlight	airplane
dryer	laser	radio
oven	street light	telephone
		alarm clock

Name _____   *Classifying energy sources*

What's The Source?

Read the energy sources in the Word Bank.
Write each word in the correct column to show
   the type of energy for which it is a source.
Some words may fit in more than one column.

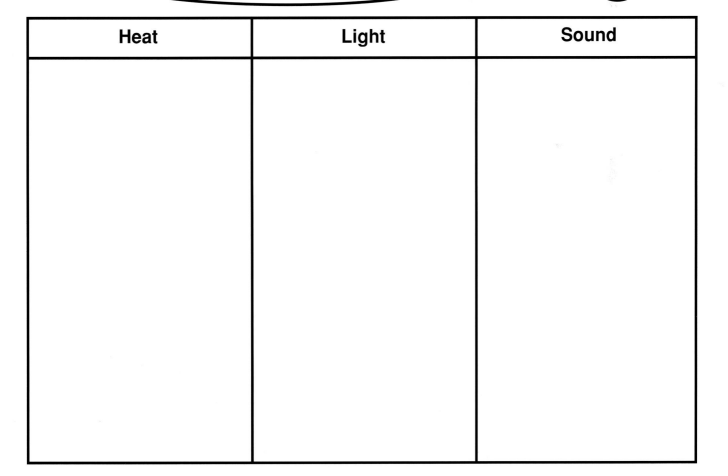

Word Bank

horn	Sun	lamp
oven	laser	drum
geyser	bell	heater
firefly	headlight	telephone
toaster	radio	flashlight

Heat	Light	Sound

Bonus Box: On the back of this paper, write one more energy source for each type of energy: heat, light, and sound.

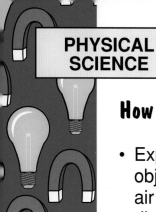
How To Extend The Lesson:

• Explain to students that every sound is produced by the vibrations of an object. When an object vibrates, the object causes the molecules in the air to start vibrating. The *vibrations* (or sound waves) move outward in all directions from the object. The vibrations enter your ears, and your ears convert them to nerve impulses. The nerve impulses are then relayed to the brain, where they are interpreted as sounds. After presenting this information, share *Science Magic With Sound* by Chris Oxlade (Barron's Educational Series, Inc.; 1994). Students are sure to enjoy trying the entertaining magic tricks that use sound as the trickster. Each trick includes directions for preparing and performing the trick as well as a scientific explanation.

• Remind students that there are two main sources of heat: natural and man-made. Explain that both sources of heat are important to man, for without harnessed heat, we would not have the convenience of modern appliances. Without natural heat, we would really be in trouble—we depend on the Sun to keep our planet warm enough to live on! After sharing this information, challenge students to think about the many types of heat they use each day. Assign each student a room of a house and have him list the different types of heat found in that room. Enlist students' help in compiling the findings onto a chart labeled "Heat In Our Homes."

• Review with students the two ways light sources can be classified—as natural or artificial. Then have each student write a letter to his parents explaining the importance of light. Encourage students to also name examples of both types of light sources.

• Present each student with a personalized copy of the award shown.

_____ is a *source* of great science knowledge!

©The Education Center, Inc. • *Ready-to-Go Lessons* • TEC1115

Simple-Machine Match

Gear up students' classification skills with this machine matching game!

Skill: Classifying simple machines

Estimated Lesson Time: 45 minutes

Teacher Preparation:

1. Duplicate page 223 onto tagboard for each student.
2. Gather items to demonstrate each simple machine listed in the Background Information. (See Step 1 on page 222.)

Materials:

1 tagboard copy of page 223 per student
scissors
materials used to demonstrate each of the six types
    of simple machines

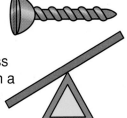

Background Information:

There are six types of simple machines that help people work. All machines are based on one or more of these simple machines.

- An **inclined plane** helps move an object upward with less effort than it would take to lift it directly. The longer the slope, the smaller the effort required. One type of inclined plane is a ramp.

- A **pulley** is a grooved wheel with a rope or cable around it. It moves things up, down, or across.

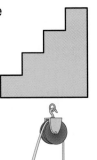

- A **wheel and an axle** work together to disperse force. A wheel can move a great distance with little effort.
- A **wedge** is an object with at least one slanting side that ends in a sharp edge. It cuts or splits an object apart.
- A **screw** is an inclined plane wrapped around in a spiral. It holds things together or lifts.
- A **lever** helps lift a load with less effort. The lever is positioned on a pivot called a fulcrum. Seesaws and crowbars are levers.

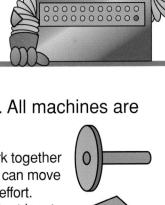

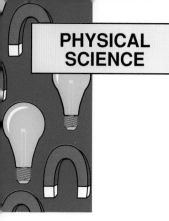

Introducing The Lesson:

Tell students that machines make work easier. Explain that a machine does not have to be a complicated contraption with many parts powered by electricity. Actually, all complex machines are based in some way on six types of simple machines.

Steps:

1. Use the following objects (or similar ones) and the Background Information on page 221 to explain and demonstrate how each type of simple machine works.
   —toy car (wheel and axle)
   —ramp and toy car (inclined plane)
   —balance scale (lever)
   —window blinds (pulley)
   —plastic knife (wedge)
   —jar lid (screw)

2. Take students on a walk around the school in search of simple machines. Back in the classroom, write a student-generated list of simple machines they saw.

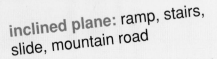

inclined plane: ramp, stairs, slide, mountain road

wedge: knife, razor, chisel, pin, axe, fork

screw: jar lid, water faucet, bolt, base of a lightbulb

pulley: flagpole, window blinds, fishing reel

wheel and axle: wagon, rolling pin, bicycle, pencil sharpener

lever: seesaw, hammer claw, shovel

3. Next give students additional practice classifying simple machines with this Concentration-type game. Have each student cut out a copy of the cards on page 223. Pair students and have each twosome combine its cards, then shuffle them and place them facedown. In turn each student flips over two cards, trying to match a simple-machine name with a corresponding picture. If a match is made, the student keeps the cards and takes another turn. If the cards do not match, the student returns them to their positions, facedown, and her partner takes a turn. Play continues until all cards have been matched. The student with the most cards wins!

inclined plane	pulley	pulley
wedge	wedge	screw
lever	lever	wheel and axle

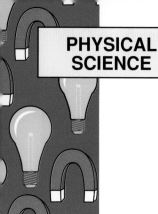

How To Extend The Lesson:

- Try this activity to demonstrate how common simple machines are in our world. Place students in small groups. In a designated amount of time, challenge each group to find and cut out as many magazine pictures as possible of each type of simple machine. While students are working, label a sheet of poster board for each simple machine. At the end of the designated time, have each group sort its findings by type of simple machine, then glue the pictures onto the corresponding poster. Display the completed posters on a classroom wall for everyone to see!

- Ask each student to bring a toy to school. Display the toys on a table. Then, for each toy, challenge students to identify any simple machines within it.

- Sharpen students' critical-thinking skills with this activity. Write simple-machine word problems (similar to the ones shown below) on separate paper cards. Program the back of each card for self-checking; then laminate the cards and store them in a decorated container at a center. A student selects a card, answers the question, and flips the card to check her work. She continues in this manner until she answers each simple-machine question.

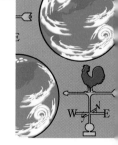

Oh, The Weather Outside...

Fun is in the forecast with this weather identification activity!

Skill: Identifying types of weather

Estimated Lesson Time: 25 minutes

Teacher Preparation:
Duplicate page 227 for each student.

Materials:
1 copy of page 227 per student
scissors
glue

Background Information:
Weather—the condition of the atmosphere around us—affects everyone in some manner, from wardrobe selections to the growth of crops. Information about several different types of weather is provided below.

- **Sunny:** All of the Earth's energy comes from the Sun. Because the Earth is round, the Sun's rays strike its surface at different angles, resulting in an uneven distribution of heat.
- **Windy:** Some parts of the Earth are warmed more than others, which results in wind—moving air.
- **Cloudy:** Clouds are made of millions of water droplets or ice crystals. They are named for their shape and height.
- **Precipitation:** Precipitation is any form of water that falls from the atmosphere and reaches the ground. Rain and snow are the most common types.
  - **Rain:** When water droplets become so heavy that they fall from clouds, rain is produced.
  - **Snow:** Snow is formed when ice crystals in a cloud cling together.
  - **Sleet:** Sleet is partly melted snow or a mixture of snow and rain.
- **Extreme Weather**
  - **Thunderstorm:** A thunderstorm produces lightning and thunder. Lightning is a huge electric spark. Thunder is the sound of air quickly expanding as lightning heats it.
  - **Tornado:** A tornado is a dangerous and powerful funnel-shaped whirlwind of spinning, rising air.
  - **Hurricane:** A hurricane is a strong, whirling storm that measures 200 to 300 miles in diameter and has winds of 74 miles per hour or more.
  - **Blizzard:** A blizzard is a heavy snowstorm with strong winds and low temperatures.

Introducing The Lesson:

Write the words "windy," "rainy," and "snowy" on the chalkboard. Ask youngsters to determine what these words have in common. Lead students to the conclusion that each word is a type of weather. Challenge students to brainstorm other types of weather as you record their responses on the chalkboard. Then discuss with youngsters how each of these weather conditions affects our lives.

Steps:

1. Use the Background Information on page 225 to define the term *weather* and provide details about several different weather conditions.

2. Explain that weather influences our lives in many respects, including clothing and activity choices. Name a weather condition and invite students to identify clothing and activities that would be appropriate for it. (Be sure to caution students that outside activities are not safe during severe weather.) Continue this discussion in a like manner with other types of weather.

3. Then give each student a copy of page 227. Read the chart with students and review the picture cards at the bottom of the page.

4. Have each youngster cut apart his picture cards. Then have him use the information provided on his chart and glue each card in the correct space.

5. Instruct each student to use information from the discussion to write appropriate facts and activities in the remaining spaces on his sheet.

6. Challenge youngsters to complete the Bonus Box activity.

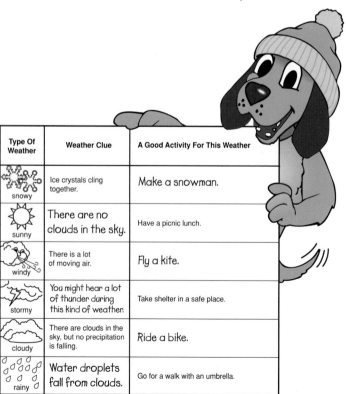

Type Of Weather	Weather Clue	A Good Activity For This Weather
snowy	Ice crystals cling together.	Make a snowman.
sunny	There are no clouds in the sky.	Have a picnic lunch.
windy	There is a lot of moving air.	Fly a kite.
stormy	You might hear a lot of thunder during this kind of weather.	Take shelter in a safe place.
cloudy	There are clouds in the sky, but no precipitation is falling.	Ride a bike.
rainy	Water droplets fall from clouds.	Go for a walk with an umbrella.

Name _____

Oh, The Weather Outside...

Cut.
Glue and write to complete the chart.

Type Of Weather	Weather Clue	A Good Activity For This Weather
	Ice crystals cling together.	
		Have a picnic lunch.
	There is a lot of moving air.	
		Take shelter in a safe place.
	There are clouds in the sky, but no precipitation is falling.	
		Go for a walk with an umbrella.

Bonus Box: What is your favorite type of weather? Write about it on the back of this sheet. Add a picture.

sunny   cloudy   rainy   snowy   stormy   windy

How To Extend The Lesson:

- Try this class bulletin-board activity for a seasonal approach to weather! Cover a bulletin board with brightly colored paper. Use a marker or yarn to divide it into quarters, and label each section with the name of a season. Then have youngsters create seasonal collages by cutting out pictures from discarded magazines and mounting them on the bulletin board in the appropriate sections. After everyone has contributed to the display, invite students to describe the types of weather depicted for each season. Record their responses for each time of year on a small separate sheet of chart paper, and mount the paper beside the corresponding section of the display.

- Long ago, many people used weather legends and sayings to help them remember natural signs of weather changes. Share with youngsters several of these sayings, such as the ones below.
    - When dew is on the grass, rain will never come to pass.
    - Flies will swarm before a storm.
    - Red sky at night, sailors' delight; red sky in the morning, sailors take warning.

  Engage students in a discussion about these sayings. Do youngsters believe that they accurately forecast the weather? How could they find out? No doubt your young meteorologists will be eager to put these legends to the test!

- Have each student record her weather observations in a weather log! Instruct her to staple a desired number of sheets of paper between two construction-paper covers and to personalize the cover. Direct her to make daily entries in her log by drawing and writing about the day's weather conditions. Also have her draw in a corner of each page the corresponding international weather symbol (refer to the chart shown). For added learning fun, have each youngster

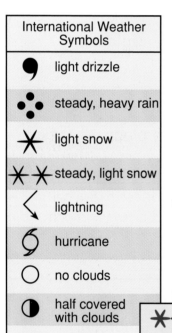

International Weather Symbols	
❟	light drizzle
⦂•	steady, heavy rain
✳	light snow
✳✳	steady, light snow
⦦	lightning
၆	hurricane
◯	no clouds
◐	half covered with clouds
●	completely overcast

✳✳ December 16

It snowed all day.
I made a snowman!

Seasonal Search

Creativity springs forth as youngsters explore the seasons!

Skill: Identifying seasonal attributes

Estimated Lesson Time: 40 minutes

Teacher Preparation:
1. On the chalkboard, write the four lists shown at the bottom of page 230. Be sure to write the words in the exact order shown.
2. Duplicate page 231 for each student.

Materials:
1 copy of page 231 per student
crayons

Background Information:
An area's typical weather pattern is known as its *climate.* The area near the equator has a tropical climate, and the Arctic and Antarctic have a polar climate. Neither of these climates changes much during the year. In contrast, the areas that have a temperate climate (located between the equator and the poles) experience noticeable weather changes throughout the year. They usually have warm, dry summers and cold, wet winters. These seasonal changes are caused by the Earth's tilting toward or away from the Sun. When it is summer in the Northern Hemisphere, it is winter in the Southern Hemisphere. Some of the characteristics of each season in the Northern Hemisphere are described below.

Spring: This season begins about March 21. Increasing temperatures, new leaves and flowers, and animals coming out of hibernation are evident during spring.
Summer: This is the warmest season, and it begins about June 21. Flowers and plants flourish and fruit ripens during the summer.
Autumn: This season begins about September 21. In autumn the weather cools; deciduous trees change color and lose their leaves.
Winter: This is the coldest season, and it begins about December 21. Most plants rest during the winter months, causing many landscapes to look bare.

Introducing The Lesson:

Read with students the words listed on the chalkboard. Challenge youngsters to determine how the words are grouped in columns. Help students reach the conclusion that the words are grouped by season—autumn, winter, spring, and summer, respectively. Invite students to identify listed words that could belong in more than one seasonal category, and have them explain their reasoning.

Steps:

1. Use the Background Information on page 229 to explain where and why seasonal changes occur.

2. Describe some of the attributes of each season. Invite youngsters to name additional characteristics.

3. Tell students that each of them will use this information to create a seasonal word search for a classmate to solve.

4. Give each student a copy of page 231. Instruct her to use her favorite season for the activity. Each youngster completes the sentences by writing an appropriate answer in each blank on her sheet. Then she writes each of these words either horizontally or vertically in the grid at the bottom. (If a student has a two-word answer, instruct her not to leave a blank between the two words.) She fills in the remaining squares with random letters.

5. Have each youngster trade her completed puzzle with a classmate and ask him to solve it by lightly coloring or circling with crayons the featured words.

6. Ask students to return their papers to the owners and have the creator of each word search verify her classmate's solution.

7. For an added challenge, have students complete the Bonus Box activity.

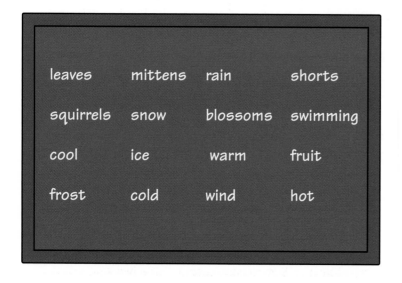

leaves	mittens	rain	shorts
squirrels	snow	blossoms	swimming
cool	ice	warm	fruit
frost	cold	wind	hot

Seasonal Search

Choose a season.
Complete each sentence to tell about it.

1. The name of the season is _____.

2. The temperature during this season is usually _____.

3. The weather during this season is usually _____.

4. _____ is a month in this season.

5. During this season you can _____ and _____.

6. Two types of clothing for this season are _____ and _____.

7. In this season you will see _____ and _____.

Write each answer on the grid below.
Fill in the rest of the squares with different letters.
Trade papers with a classmate and have him or her find the words.

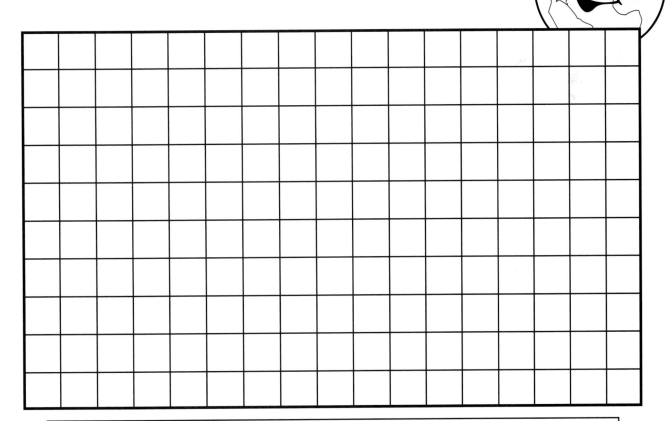

Bonus Box: On the back of this sheet, list the four seasons. Beside each season, write two words that tell about its weather.

How To Extend The Lesson:

• For a fun science-based writing activity, have youngsters create seasonal flip books. To make a booklet cover, a student folds a sheet of 9" x 12" construction paper in half, keeping the fold at the top. Next she folds in half two or three sheets of blank paper. She slides the folded paper inside the booklet cover and staples the resulting 9" x 6" booklet near the fold. On one cover she writes the name of her favorite season. Then she lifts the cover and writes about this season on the front of each booklet page. Encourage her to include information from her word search, such as the typical temperature and weather. Next have each student turn over her booklet and write the name of her least favorite season on the other cover. Instruct her to lift this cover and write about the corresponding time of year. (This story will be written on the back of her first story.) Give students an opportunity to share their completed books before showcasing them in the classroom library. Youngsters will surely flip over these creative-writing projects!

• A love of literature will blossom any time of year with these seasonal selections!
  — *Ox-Cart Man* by Donald Hall (Puffin Books, 1983)
  — *What A Wonderful Day To Be A Cow* by Carolyn Lesser (Alfred A. Knopf Books For Young Readers, 1995)
  — *The Seasons And Someone* by Virginia Kroll (Harcourt Brace & Company, 1994)
  — *The Reasons For Seasons* by Gail Gibbons (Holiday House, Inc.; 1996)

Winter

Weather	Clothing	Animals & Plants	Activities
cold	jackets	bears hibernate	skiing
icy	hats		sledding
snowy	mittens	thicker fur	making snowmen
stormy		bare trees	
frosty			

• Reinforce students' understanding of seasons with this vocabulary-building activity! Write the four seasons on separate sheets of bulletin-board paper. Divide each sheet into four columns and label each column with a different category as shown. Then focusing on one season per day, have youngsters brainstorm words for each category as you record their ideas in the corresponding columns. Display the lists in an accessible area of your classroom. As you continue to explore the topic of weather with students, record additional information. Encourage youngsters to refer to these growing vocabulary lists throughout the year.

Fall For Temperature

*This red-hot lesson teaches students that
reading thermometers is really cool!*

Skill: Reading and interpreting Fahrenheit thermometers

Estimated Lesson Time: 45 minutes

Teacher Preparation:

1. On the chalkboard, draw four simple thermometer shapes without scales. Shade the thermometers to represent the following temperatures: hot, warm, cool, and cold.
2. Cut one 1 1/2" x 12" strip of red paper for each student.
3. Write a different temperature on each of ten or more index cards.
4. Duplicate page 235 for each student.

Materials:

1 copy of page 235 per student
one 1 1/2" x 12" strip of red paper per student
ten or more index cards, each programmed with a different temperature
stapler
scissors

Background Information:

- Thermometers—the most common type of weather instrument—not only help people determine appropriate clothing for each day, but also provide information about variations in weather patterns. Temperatures are usually lowest just before dawn. They peak in the afternoon, then fall. Any discrepancies in this pattern indicate that the weather is about to change.

- In 1612 Galileo made the first thermometer with colored alcohol and a glass tube. He based this invention on his discovery that liquids expand when warmed. During the next 200 years, scientists experimented with the design of thermometers by using many different liquids, including wine. Mercury is now the most commonly used substance for thermometers because it results in the most accurate readings. Thermometer readings were standardized in 1714, when Gabriel Daniel Fahrenheit created the first widely used thermometer scale. On this scale, the freezing point of water is 32° and its boiling point is 212°.

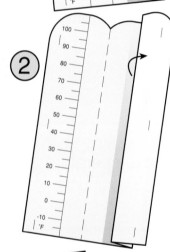

Introducing The Lesson:

Direct students' attention to the thermometers on the chalkboard. Ask them to identify the thermometer that represents a hot temperature; then write the word *hot* below it. Continue in a like manner with *cold,* then *warm* and *cool.* Discuss with youngsters the subjectivity of these terms. Explain that this lesson will teach each of them how to read a thermometer with a standard numerical scale.

Steps:

1. Share the Background Information on page 233 with students.

2. On one of the thermometers on the chalkboard, add a scale with marks at five- and ten-degree intervals and labels at ten-degree intervals. Help students use the scale to determine the temperature shown.

3. Give students additional practice reading a thermometer by increasing or decreasing the shaded area on this thermometer and having them identify the corresponding temperature. With students' help, write the new temperature below the thermometer.

4. Tell youngsters that each of them will make a thermometer. Distribute a copy of page 235, a strip of red paper, and scissors to each student.

5. Each child cuts his pattern on the heavy dark lines. Then, on one of the dotted lines, he folds the paper toward the middle. Next he folds back the resulting flap on the solid line. (See the illustrations.) He repeats these steps with the other dotted and solid lines.

6. Have each youngster staple his folded paper on the staple lines and insert his paper strip between the two folded sections as shown.

7. Announce that students will represent different temperatures with the resulting thermometers. Display a programmed index card; then have a volunteer read it aloud and describe the temperature as hot, warm, cool, or cold. Have each student move his paper strip up or down to correspond with this temperature; then verify youngsters' responses.

8. Repeat this activity in a similar manner with the remaining index cards and different student volunteers.

Pattern

Use with Steps 4, 5, 6, 7, and 8 on page 234.

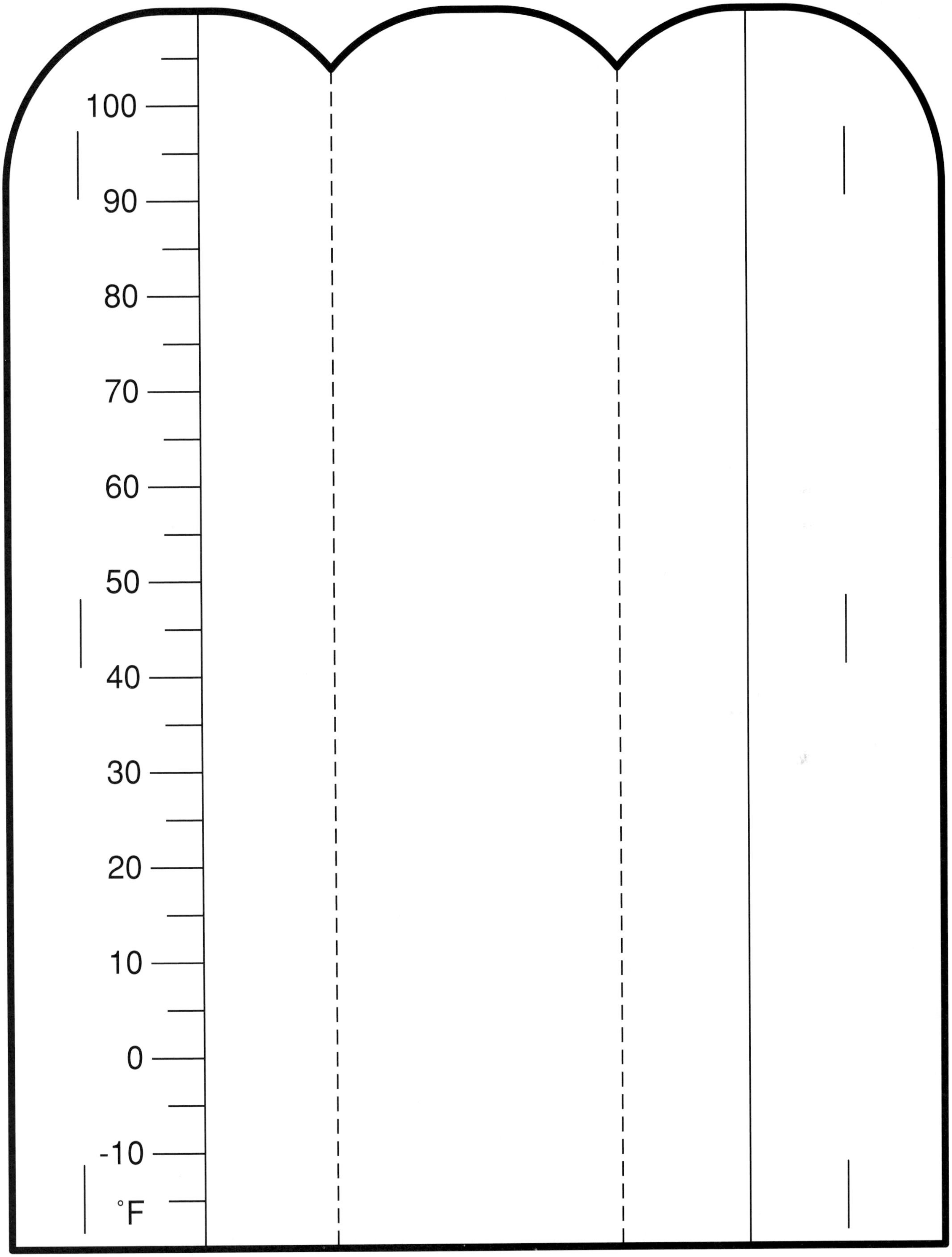

100
90
80
70
60
50
40
30
20
10
0
-10
°F

100 —
90 —
80 —
70 —
60 —
50 —
40 —
30 —
20 —
10 —
0 —
-10 —
°F

How To Extend The Lesson:

• Have youngsters use their paper thermometers for this weather-wise activity! Give each youngster a paper card that has been programmed with a different temperature. Have him adjust the paper strip of his thermometer to correspond with this temperature. Next direct him to fold a sheet of white paper in half and then unfold it. Have him cut out and shade a copy of the thermometer pattern shown and then glue it onto one side of his paper. On the other side, instruct him to draw an activity or outdoor scene that is appropriate for the temperature shown. Then have students group and sequence their completed drawings by temperature (from coldest to hottest) and mount them on a classroom or hall wall to create an eye-catching display.

• Incorporate addition and subtraction into your study of thermometers. To prepare for this activity, place an outdoor thermometer in an easily accessible location on your school grounds. Each morning select a student at random to read the thermometer and record the temperature on a class chart or bar graph. Ask another youngster to read and record the temperature in the afternoon. Then challenge students to determine the difference. After several days, have youngsters analyze the data that they have collected and invite them to make predictions based on this information. Remind students that any variations in the typical temperature pattern indicate upcoming changes in the weather.

• Students will love this nifty center activity! Program each of several index cards with a different temperature. Color a copy of the thermometer pattern shown to correspond with each temperature; then cut it out and glue it onto a blank index card. Code the back of each temperature and thermometer card for self-checking. Shuffle the prepared cards and place them in a container in a center. A student reads each temperature card and pairs it with the corresponding thermometer card. He then flips the cards to check his work. After completing the center, he prepares it for the next student by shuffling the cards and returning them to the container.

Planets On Parade

Send your students into orbit with an out-of-this-world lesson on planet order!

Skill: Identifying planet order

Estimated Lesson Time: 25 minutes

Teacher Preparation:
1. Duplicate page 239 for each student.
2. On the chalkboard, draw a solar system illustration similar to the one shown on page 238. Exclude the planet names.
3. Make a list of the nine planets on the chalkboard.

Materials:
1 copy of page 239 per student
glue
scissors

Background Information:
- All the planets move around the Sun in the same direction.
- The Sun's gravitational pull keeps the planets in a path around itself.
- Each planet spins, or *rotates,* as it revolves around the Sun. The farther a planet is from the Sun, the longer it takes to complete the orbital path around it and the longer the year. The planets' rotation periods (the time required to spin around once) range from less than ten hours for Jupiter to 243 days for Venus. Earth rotates once every 24 hours.
- The list at the right gives a short description of each planet. (Planets are listed in order going outward from the Sun.)

Mercury—second-smallest planet
Venus—hottest planet
Earth—our home planet
Mars—known as the "red planet"
Jupiter—largest planet
Saturn—known for its bright rings
Uranus—orbits on its side
Neptune—dark and icy planet
Pluto—smallest and most distant planet

Introducing The Lesson:

Tell students the word *planet* comes from a Greek word meaning *to wander*. Ask your class to guess why ancient people might have chosen that name for the planets. Lead students to realize that the planets wander by moving in paths, or *orbits,* around the Sun.

Steps:

1. Refer to the illustration on the chalkboard as you share the information from the first three items of Background Information on page 237.

2. Next tell students that the illustration shows the location of each of the nine planets from the Sun. Then point to the planet closest to the Sun, Mercury, and share its short description with students. Ask a student volunteer to find the word *Mercury* on the list (located on the chalkboard). Then have him copy the planet's name on the corresponding drawing.

3. Continue in this same manner with the remaining planets.

4. Distribute glue, scissors, and a copy of page 239 to each student. Instruct her to complete the page by cutting out and gluing each planet to its correct orbit.

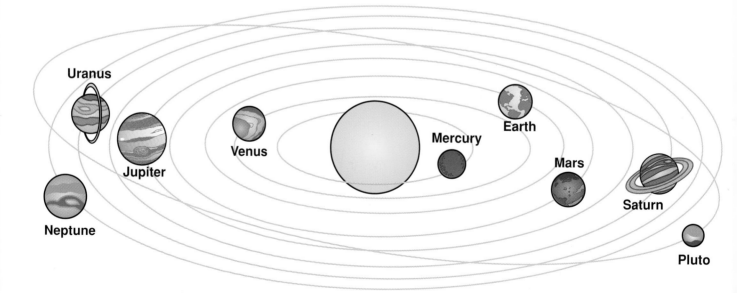

Planets On Parade

Cut out the planets. Glue them in the correct order.

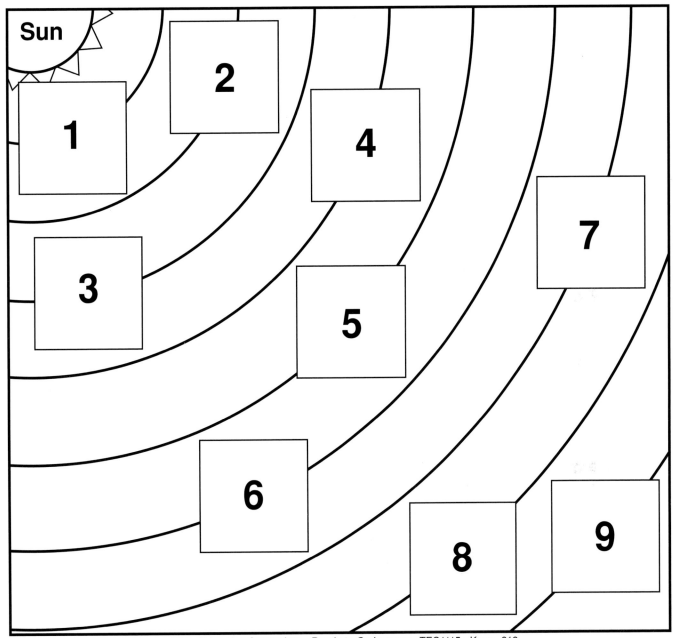

How To Extend The Lesson:

• Display the sentence "**M**y **V**ery **E**nergetic **M**other **J**ust **S**ewed **U**s **N**ine **P**illows!" Show students that the first letter of each word corresponds with the first letter of each planet in the solar system. Also explain that the words are arranged in the planets' correct order from the Sun. After your students become familiar with the learning device, encourage them to make up other sentences using the first letter of each planet in the correct sequence. Provide time for students to share their solar sentences with the class.

• Have your students work in small groups to create an out-of this-world display. Challenge each group to use modeling clay to create a model of the solar system. Challenge students to show the planets roughly to scale. To display the planets, have each group arrange its planets in the correct order in a large shallow box.

• Use this nifty idea to display an eye-catching reproduction of the solar system on your playground. Label poster-board cutouts to represent the Sun and each of the nine planets. Also label a resealable plastic bag for each planet. Cut string lengths using the chart below, and place each length of string in its corresponding bag. On the playground, position the Sun cutout in an open area. Seat students near the Sun cutout. Then, for each planet, have student volunteers tape one end of its corresponding length of string to the Sun cutout and walk away from the Sun. When the string's end is reached, tape the corresponding planet cutout to it.

Planet	Distance From The Sun	String Length
Mercury	36 million miles	1 foot
Venus	67 million miles	approx. 2 feet
Earth	93 million miles	approx. 2.5 feet
Mars	142 million miles	approx. 4 feet
Jupiter	484 million miles	approx. 13.5 feet
Saturn	885 million miles	approx. 24.5 feet
Uranus	1,780 million miles	approx. 49.5 feet
Neptune	2,790 million miles	approx. 77.5 feet
Pluto	3,660 million miles	approx. 101.5 feet

Our Sunny Neighbor

Get ready for a "sun-sational" lesson about our source of heat, light, and energy.

Skill: Recognizing the Sun's importance

Estimated Lesson Time: 30 minutes

Teacher Preparation:
Duplicate page 243 for each student.

Materials:
1 copy of page 243 per student
one 6" x 20" strip of
   bulletin-board paper
scissors
glue
crayons
colored chalk

Background Information:
Want the scoop on the Sun? Then share the following bright facts with your students:

- The Sun is a medium-sized star—a bright, big ball of burning gas.
- Although the Sun's average distance from Earth is about 93 million miles, it is closer than any other star.
- It weighs 2 billion billion billion tons (that's 2 with 27 zeros after it).
- The Sun's gravity is 28 times greater than Earth's. If you weigh 100 pounds on Earth, you'd weigh almost 1.5 tons on the Sun.
- Its surface temperature is 11,000° F. Things are hotter in the core; temperatures there reach 27,000,000° F.
- Light takes only 8 minutes and 20 seconds to zoom from the Sun to Earth. The fastest jet on Earth would take a million times that long. Some stars you see at night are so far away that their light takes 4,000 years to reach Earth.

Introducing The Lesson:

Use colored chalk to draw a picture of the Sun on the chalkboard. Ask students why they think the Sun is important to us. Accept reasonable responses; then confirm that the Sun is an important source of heat, light, and energy.

Steps:

1. Explain to students that the Sun's light and heat make life possible on Earth. Plants make their food with photosynthesis, which is dependent on the Sun. All other life is dependent on plants or plant eaters. For example, plants give us food to eat and oxygen to breathe. Tell students that they are going to help you illustrate an example of how important the Sun is to our planet.

2. To create the example shown below, draw a line to represent the ground under the drawing of the Sun. Also draw a small kernel of corn planted below the ground. Tell the class that the Sun's heat and light will help the seed to sprout. Ask a student volunteer to draw the seed sprouting (to the right of the seed drawing). Then, in turn, explain each of the following stages and have a volunteer draw the provided symbol (of the stage) on the chalkboard.
   — The Sun's heat and light help the corn plant grow (mature corn plant).
   — After the corn is harvested, it is used in many ways (a bag of corn feed).
   — Corn is used in some chicken feed (chicken).
   — Chickens provide us with eggs (a carton of eggs).
   — People sometimes eat eggs for breakfast (a plate of eggs).

3. Connect the pictures with arrows as shown below. Remind students that without the Sun, we would not be alive. There also would not be any plants, animals that eat plants, or products we get from those animals.

4. Distribute scissors, glue, crayons, paper strips, and a copy of page 243 to each student. Explain that each student will complete a diagram showing how the Sun helps our planet. To make a diagram (similar in style to the one shown), a student colors and cuts out the pictures, then cuts out the labels. Next he matches the pictures with their corresponding labels, then glues the picture-word pairs to the drawing paper to indicate how the Sun indirectly provides milk for people to drink.

The Sun gives off heat and light.	The cow produces milk.	Grass and plants grow.
	The child drinks the milk.	A cow eats the grass.

How To Extend The Lesson:

• On the next sunny day, use this experiment to show students why some things get hotter in the Sun than others. Place an ice cube in the center of a sheet of construction paper in each of the following colors: black, white, red, blue, and yellow. Then enlist students' help in timing how long it takes each ice cube to melt. Lead students to realize that light colors reflect heat, so they stay cooler, and dark colors absorb heat, so they stay warmer. For an added challenge, enlist students' help in demonstrating that shiny, smooth surfaces also reflect heat, whereas rough, dull surfaces keep heat in.

• To show your students how Earth revolves around the Sun, follow the shadows! Early in the day, use chalk to trace the shadow of a permanent fixture that is cast upon a sidewalk or paved area. Follow the changing shape throughout the day by having students visit the sight to observe the shadow's movement. If desired, retrace the shadow as it moves throughout the day and record the time by each tracing. No doubt students will be impressed with this visible account of our planet's journey around the Sun.

Bright Ideas About The Sun

The Sun gives us heat.

• Review with students how important the Sun is with this illuminating bulletin-board display. Cover a bulletin board with blue bulletin-board paper; then mount a large yellow circle in the center of the board. Give each student a small yellow construction-paper triangle. (Be sure the triangles are equilateral). On his triangle, have him write one way that we depend on the Sun. Provide time for each child to share his information with the class. Then staple the triangles to the board as shown to create the Sun's rays. To complete the display, add facial features and sunglasses on the sun and mount the title.

Our Marvelous Moon

*Is it made of green cheese? Did a cow really jump over it?
Uncover the real facts about the Moon with this far-out activity!*

Skill: Learning about the Moon

Estimated Lesson Time: 30 minutes

Teacher Preparation:
1. Duplicate page 247 onto tagboard for each student. Use an X-acto® knife to slit the dotted lines on each moon.
2. Write "Hey diddle diddle, the cat and the fiddle, the cow…" on the chalkboard.

Materials:
1 tagboard copy of page 247 per student
1 sheet of writing paper per student
crayons
scissors
glue
X-acto® knife

Background Information:
Share a little lunar learning with these fascinating facts about the Moon.
- The Moon is a huge rock.
- It is the Earth's nearest neighbor in space. If you could walk to the moon, it would take almost ten years to get there. A rocket trip to the Moon and back takes about six days.
- The Moon is wide enough to cover Australia.
- It is over 4 1/2 billion years old.
- The Moon weighs 81 million trillion tons (81,000,000,000,000,000,000). Earth is 80 times heavier.
- If the Moon were seen next to the Earth, it would look like a tennis ball next to a basketball.

1. The Earth has more than one moon.

2. The Moon makes and gives off its own light.

3. The sky is always black on the Moon.

4. Objects weigh less on the Moon than they do on Earth.

5. The Moon has just a few craters.

Fact Or Fiction?

8. There is no air, wind, water, or weather on the Moon.

10. There is no noise on the Moon.

11. Astronauts on the Moon must carry air to breathe.

12. The Moon travels around the Earth in a path called an orbit.

13. It takes the Moon a year to travel around the Earth once.

14. The Moon changes shape throughout the month.

15. Each Moon shape you see is called a phase.

16. Astronauts have walked on the Moon.

17. Astronauts on the Moon must wear space suits.

18. The surface of the Moon changes constantly.

Introducing The Lesson:

Direct students' attention to the nursery rhyme phrase on the chalkboard. Ask your students to supply the ending to the rhyme *("…jumped over the moon.")*. Inform your class that there are two images in that sentence that could not be true—a cat playing a fiddle and a cow jumping over the Moon.

Steps:

1. Explain to your class that there are several *myths,* or untrue beliefs, about the Moon. One is that the moon is made of green cheese. This myth was probably created because the *craters,* or holes, on the Moon's surface make it look like Swiss cheese. Another myth is that there is a man in the Moon. This myth probably comes from the fact that the Moon has dark markings on it that form a pattern like a face.

2. Share the Background Information on page 245 with your students. Then tell them that they will review additional information about the Moon as they create the following project.

3. Distribute crayons, glue, a pair of scissors, and a copy of page 247 to each student. To make a moon tachistoscope, a student colors his moon pattern; then he cuts out the moon and the strips. Next he cuts the moon pattern on the dotted lines, glues the three strips together where indicated, and inserts the resulting strip into the moon.

4. Have each student number a sheet of paper from 1 to 18. Then, to use the tachistoscope, each student positions the strip so he can view the first question. He reads the statement, then indicates on his paper if the statement is "true" or "false." The student continues in this manner with the remaining statements.

5. After students have responded to each question, use the answer key on page 320 to review the answers. If desired, have each student also write "T" (true) or "F" (false) beside each fact on the strip. Encourage students to share these nifty moon facts with their families.

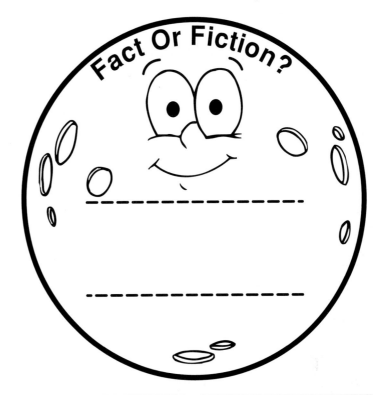

Fact Or Fiction?

_ _ _ _ _ _ _ _ _ _ _ _ _ _ _ _ _

_ _ _ _ _ _ _ _ _ _ _ _ _ _ _ _ _

1. The Earth has more than one moon.

2. The Moon makes and gives off its own light.

3. The sky is always black on the Moon.

4. Objects weigh less on the Moon than they do on Earth.

5. The Moon has just a few craters.

6. The Moon's craters were caused by spaceships.

7. Craters can be as tiny as pinholes or as large as cities.

8. There is no air, wind, water, or weather on the Moon.

9. There are many living things on the Moon.

Glue here.

10. There is no noise on the Moon.

11. Astronauts on the Moon must carry air to breathe.

12. The Moon travels around the Earth in a path called an orbit.

13. It takes the Moon a year to travel around the Earth once.

14. The Moon changes shape throughout the month.

Glue here.

15. Each Moon shape you see is called a phase.

16. Astronauts have walked on the Moon.

17. Astronauts on the Moon must wear space suits.

18. The surface of the Moon changes constantly.

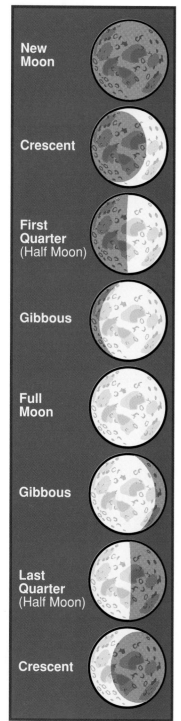

New
Moon

Crescent

First
Quarter
(Half Moon)

Gibbous

Full
Moon

Gibbous

Last
Quarter
(Half Moon)

Crescent

How To Extend The Lesson:

• Demonstrate how the Moon shines with this experiment. Have students observe a reflector or a mirror in a dark room or a box so that no light can reach it. Then shine a flashlight on the object. Students will observe that the object does not create its own light; it only reflects the beam from the flashlight. This is similar to the way the Moon reflects the light of the Sun.

• Students will discover how craters are made with this activity. Fill a large container with sand and gather a variety of round objects such as tennis balls, golf balls, marbles, and Ping-Pong® balls. Ask a student to drop an object on the sand. Carefully remove the object and have students talk about what they see. Invite additional students to repeat the activity using the remaining objects. Encourage students to share ideas about the differences in the size of the craters created with each drop.

• Explain to students that some people use the Moon to predict the weather. Share the weather sayings below; then encourage students to watch the Moon and the weather to determine if these sayings are believable.
  —A full moon on Saturday means rain on Sunday.
  —Thunderstorms will happen two days after you see a new moon.
  —A pale moon means rain is coming.
  —A halo around the Moon means rain or snow.

• Turn your students on to Moon watching with this appealing activity. In advance create a construction-paper model of each Moon phase (see the illustration). Also write the name of each Moon phase on a separate index card. Code the back of each matching pair for self-checking. To begin, explain to students that although from Earth the Moon seems to change shape, it really doesn't. The appearance of the Moon depends on how much of it is lit by the Sun. Use the Moon phase models to show students each phase of the Moon. (The lighted part is what is seen from Earth.) Also explain that the whole process takes about a month. Then place the models and labels at a center. A student matches each word card to its matching Moon, then flips the pieces to check his work.

Taking Care Of The Community

Introduce your students to the people who take care of their community with these class-created cards.

Skill: Analyzing the roles of different community helpers

Estimated Lesson Time: 45 minutes

Teacher Preparation:
Duplicate one copy of page 251 onto white construction paper for each student.

Materials:
1 white construction-paper copy of page 251 for each student
glue
crayons

Background Information:
- A *community* is any group living in the same area or having interests and work in common.
- Communities provide services for the people who live in them.
- Community governments make sure that community services run smoothly.
- Communities choose people to run different services in the community.
- The police and fire departments are examples of two types of community service.
- Some examples of community helpers include
  —firefighter
  —police officer
  —teacher
  —nurse
  —doctor
  —paramedic
  —sanitation worker
  —bus driver
  —veterinarian
  —construction worker

Introducing The Lesson:

Write "community helper" on the chalkboard. Have students name several community helpers. List students' responses on the board. Then challenge the class to name the different jobs each community helper performs.

Steps:

1. Remind students that community helpers perform different jobs to take care of the community. Then share the Background Information on page 249.

2. Distribute a copy of page 251 to each child.

3. Assign each child a different community helper from the list on page 249. (Some helpers may be assigned to more than one student.)

4. Instruct each student to write the name of his community helper on the provided line on page 251. Then have him draw a picture of his helper in the box.

5. Next direct each youngster to complete the information about his community helper on the right side of his paper.

6. Then, to complete the project, instruct each student to fold his paper along the dotted line and glue the two sides together.

7. Invite students to share their community helper cards with their classmates. Then collect the cards and place them at a center for further investigation.

Name:____________________

Community Helper:

____

©The Education Center, Inc. • *Ready-to-Go Lessons* • TEC1115

This community helper is ______________________________.

This community helper works to

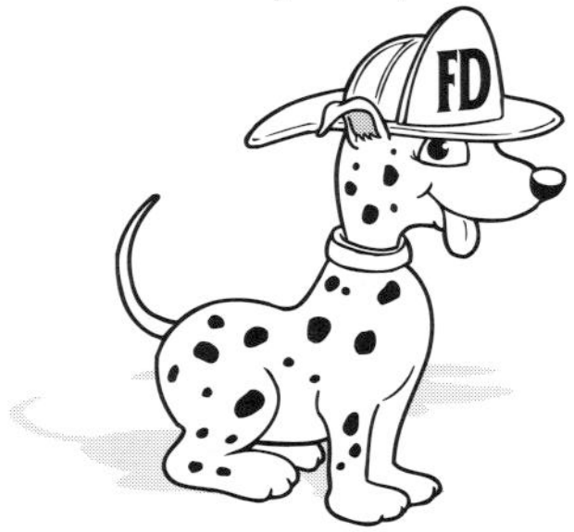

- ____ keep us healthy.
- ____ keep us safe.
- ____ give us transportation.
- ____ help us learn.
- ____ give us goods.
- ____ provide us with a service.

This community helper works

- ____ inside only.
- ____ outside only.
- ____ both inside and outside.

This community helper works

- ____ in the daytime only.
- ____ at night only.
- ____ both day and night.

The place where this community helper works is ______________________________.

The special equipment this community helper uses is ______________________________.

This community helper is important to the community because ______________________________.

How To Extend The Lesson:

- Distribute a different community helper card to each student. Ask youngsters to group the helpers by types of jobs, places of work, or people they help.

- Invite some helpers in your community to your classroom to tell about their jobs. Before each visit, challenge each youngster to write five questions to ask the helper about her job. Then have the students ask the community helper their questions during her visit.

- Take a walking field trip or a bus ride around your community. Encourage students to take note of all the helpers found throughout the trip. If desired, have students keep a tally of the helpers found in each workplace. Then compile the information into a bar graph after the trip.

- Have each student think of which community helper's job she might like to have as a career in the future. Challenge the student to draw a picture of herself working as her selected community helper. Then ask the student to write about the jobs she would perform for the community. Invite students to share their creations with the class. Then, if desired, display the papers on a bulletin board titled "Future Community Helpers."

When I am grown-up, I will be a teacher. I will teach grade school. I will help students be better learners.

I am going to be a great doctor when I grow up. I will make sick people well. I will take care of sick children.

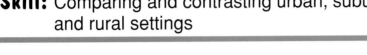

What's It Like?

*Have your students visit three types of communities
and discover the importance of each one.*

Skill: Comparing and contrasting urban, suburban,
and rural settings

Estimated Lesson Time: 45 minutes

Teacher Preparation:

1. Duplicate page 255 for each student.
2. Divide a sheet of chart paper into three columns. Label the first column "Urban," the middle column "Suburban," and the last column "Rural." Post the chart in a prominent location.
3. Cut three pictures from a magazine—an urban, a suburban, and a rural setting.

Materials:

1 copy of page 255 per student
labeled chart
3 magazine pictures
crayons
scissors
glue

Background Information:

- Urban setting—a large city community
- Suburban setting—a community that is near a city
- Rural setting—a community that is near forests or farms
- Many people live in cities (urban settings). There are a lot of schools, stores, and different kinds of jobs. Cities can be very crowded and noisy. Sometimes there is a lot of traffic in a city.
- Suburbs are communities near large cities. They have their own schools and business centers. People often move to the suburbs because they do not want to live in large cities.
- Most of the people who live in rural settings know one another. These community members may farm or raise animals for food.

Introducing The Lesson:

Share the three magazine pictures with students. Ask students to point out the picture that most looks like their community and tell why.

Steps:

1. Point to the picture of the urban setting and ask students to name things they may find in this type of community. Record their responses on the chart under the column labeled "Urban." (See the examples below.)

2. Repeat the process with each of the remaining magazine pictures, recording student responses in the appropriate columns.

3. Discuss with students the Background Information on page 253. Then review the students' community responses on the chart paper. Referring to each item on the list of responses, have students verify that each is in the appropriate column.

4. Distribute a copy of page 255 to each student. Read the directions together and have students complete the page independently. Challenge students to complete the Bonus Box activity.

Urban	Suburban	Rural
crowded streets	houses in neighborhoods	lots of land
tall buildings	people mowing yards	farms
many people	children at school	trees
lots of cars	shopping mall	few cars
traffic		country roads
many stores		

Name _____

What's It Like?

Color and cut out the pictures. Glue each picture in the correct box.
Then write about each setting on the lines.

1. Urban

_____

_____

_____

2. Suburban

_____

_____

_____

3. Rural

_____

_____

_____

Bonus Box: In which place would you most like to live? On the back of this paper, write why you would live in that type of setting.

How To Extend The Lesson:

- Put creative talents to work as students make a class chapter book of urban, suburban, and rural areas. Have each student cut out a picture of either an urban, suburban, or rural setting from a discarded magazine. (You may wish to assign settings so that the areas are evenly distributed.) Direct him to glue his picture to a sheet of construction paper. Instruct him to write a few sentences to accompany his picture. Then have students help categorize the completed pictures into urban, suburban, or rural settings. Place a labeled divider page ("Urban," "Suburban," or "Rural") between each section before binding the pages into a class booklet.

- Have students work in small groups to develop a community newsletter. To begin, provide each group with a description of a real or imaginary community (in an urban, suburban, or rural setting). Instruct students to design newsletters featuring articles related to their assigned communities. Challenge each group to include items such as upcoming community events, sales ads, school activities, and housing information. Encourage students to include headlines, illustrations, and captions for each article. Display the completed news-letters for all to enjoy!

- Have each student select the kind of community in which she would prefer to live—an urban, suburban, or rural area. Provide students with a supply of discarded magazines. Direct each youngster to cut out pictures that represent the type of community she chose. Then have the student glue her pictures to a tagboard house shape to make a collage. Provide time for each student to share her reasons for choosing her selected area. Then display the projects on a bulletin board titled "Home, Sweet Homes."

Best Neighborhood Behaviors

What's the word around the neighborhood? Conduct counts!
Review the shoulds and shouldn'ts of neighborly behavior.

Skill: Identifying neighborhood rules

Estimated Lesson Time: 30 minutes

Teacher Preparation:
Duplicate page 259 onto white construction paper for each student.

Materials:
1 white construction-paper copy
   of page 259 per student
1 additional sheet of white
   construction paper per student
scissors
glue
crayons

Background Information:
A neighborhood has many kinds
of rules. For example, parks have
rules to help us get along. Schools
have rules that keep order, so
that everyone can learn. There
are even rules to protect us
when we cross the street. Rules
help keep a neighborhood safe,
healthy, and free from problems.

Introducing The Lesson:

Tell students that instead of having a lesson, they are going to play a game. Ask a student volunteer to come to the board and play a game of tic-tac-toe with you. Invite the student to make the first move. As she begins to take her turn, take your turn at the same time. Continue playing the game, making several mistakes, such as taking two turns in a row, erasing one of the student's marks, and changing one of your marks from *X* to *O*.

Steps:

1. After the game, ask students to explain why things didn't go smoothly. Confirm that there is a set of rules that both players should follow to ensure that the game is played fairly.

2. Next ask students to identify some other instances in which there are rules to follow. Reinforce answers such as fire drills, library visits, bike riding, and crossing streets.

3. Inform students that there are also certain rules that we follow in our neighborhoods. Share the Background Information on page 257 with your students. Then ask them to identify several neighborhood rules and explain the reasons for them.

4. Distribute a copy of page 259 and one sheet of white construction paper to each student. Instruct each youngster to color the picture and trim the pattern along the bold lines. Next have him cut his pattern along the dotted lines to create doors that open outward. Then direct the student to draw a line of glue around the border of the pattern page and place it atop the sheet of white construction paper, making sure the doors are not glued down. (See the illustration below.)

5. Instruct each child to list five neighborhood rules on the white paper behind his doors. Then have him decorate the back of each door with illustrations of people in his neighborhood.

6. Collect the projects and display them on a bulletin board titled "Best Neighborhood Behaviors!"

Best Neighborhood Behaviors by Jake

1. Walk on the sidewalks.
2. Put litter in the trash.
3. Walk your pets on a leash.
4. Look both ways before you cross the street.
5. Keep your grass cut short.

©1999 The Education Center, Inc.

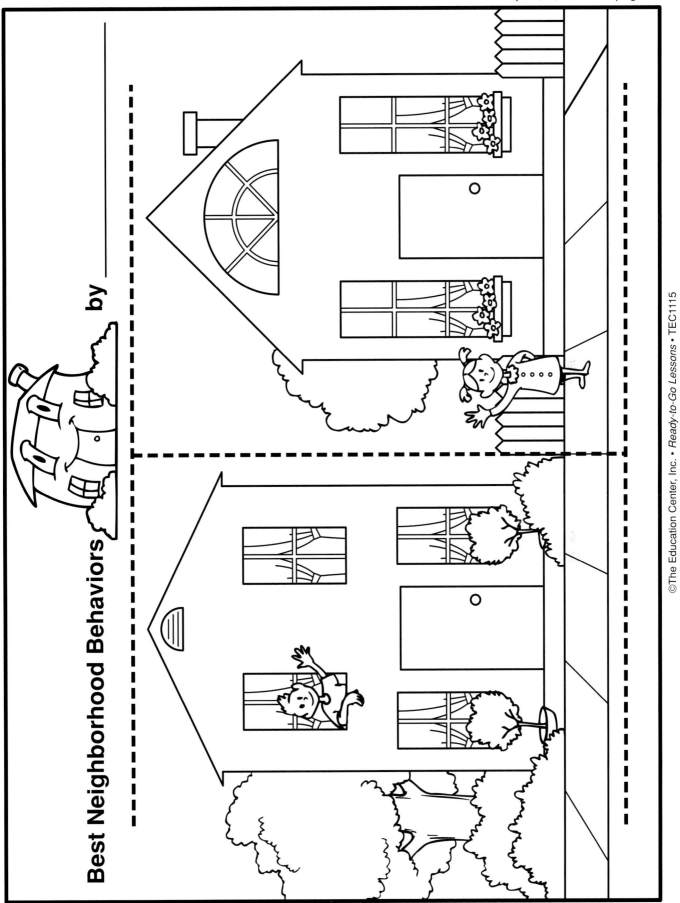

Best Neighborhood Behaviors

by

How To Extend The Lesson:

- Have students evaluate the existing rules for school activities such as going to the library, eating in the cafeteria, handling science equipment, or playing on the playground. Ask them to discuss the reasons for the current rules, whether or not they seem fair, and if additional rules need to be enforced. If desired, challenge each student to write and then illustrate another rule for the activity.

- Personalize the importance of rules by asking each child to imagine that he is going to entertain a small child in his room while his parents have visitors. Ask him to make a list of rules for playing in his room and with his toys. Remind him that rules need to be fair as well as protective!

- Have students illustrate important neighborhood rules by having each child create a minibook. Provide each student with five unlined index cards and crayons. Instruct her to use four of the cards to draw and label pictures that reinforce neighborhood rules. Next have her create a cover from the remaining index card. Help the student staple her completed cards together to make a minibook. Then display the completed projects in your reading center to reinforce appropriate neighborhood behavior.

- Share with your students the book *Officer Buckle And Gloria* by Peggy Rathmann (Scholastic Inc., 1995). In this tale, a police officer with a wealth of safety tips finds a perfect (and four-legged!) partner to interest children in his safety campaign. After the story, invite a police officer to speak to your students about neighborhood safety. Wrap up his visit by challenging small groups of students to each make a poster showing safety both during and after school.

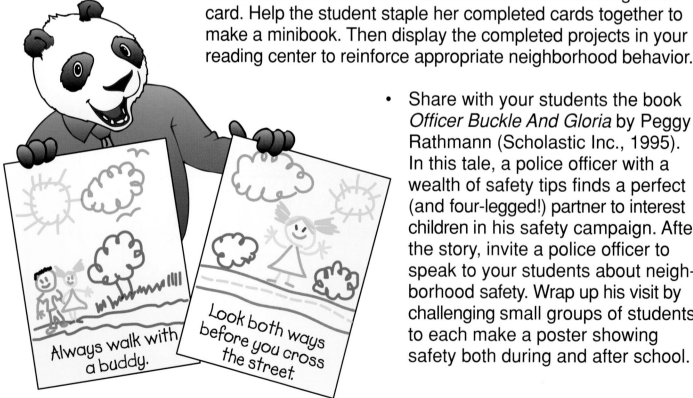

Always walk with a buddy.

Look both ways before you cross the street.

Hello, Good Neighbor!

Explore good citizenship with these neighborly activities.

Skill: Identifying characteristics of neighborhood citizenship

Estimated Lesson Time: 45 minutes

Teacher Preparation:
1. Duplicate page 263 onto white construction paper for each student.
2. Program a set of index cards for role-playing. (See page 262 for examples.)

Materials:
1 white construction-paper copy of page 263 for each student
programmed index cards
scissors
glue

Howdy, neighbor!

Background Information:

Good citizens are people who

- respect others
- respect property
- obey rules and laws
- help others
- work together

Introducing The Lesson:

Tell students that they will work together in groups to role-play some situations that might happen in a neighborhood. Explain that you will give each group a card telling about the situation. The group members will discuss what good neighbors would say and do in that situation; then they will act it out in front of the class.

Steps:

1. Organize students into groups of two or three. Distribute a programmed card to each group. (Examples are shown below.) Allow time for students to discuss and plan their role-play situation. Then have students return to their seats to watch each group act out good neighborhood citizenship.

2. Next discuss the scene performed by each group. Have students point out the examples of good citizenship shown by each group. Then review the characteristics of good citizenship listed in the Background Information shown on page 261.

3. Distribute a copy of page 263 to each student. Review the directions; then have each child complete her page independently.

4. Invite students to display their projects on a countertop in the classroom.

A young child falls off his bike. He is crying for his mother.

A neighbor is sick in bed. You know it is her birthday.

A neighbor has a large sack of groceries. She can't open the door to her house.

A neighbor has gone on a trip. The wind blows over the flowerpots on his porch.

Two children see another child at the park. He is writing his name on a bench.

You see a strange car in the neighborhood. It keeps driving slowly up and down your street.

Name _____

Hello, Good Neighbor!

Color the cards and the houses.
Cut out the houses on the bold line and the picture cards on the dotted lines.
Read each card and glue to the correct house in the shaded area.
Then draw two more pictures for each house. Write about each picture.
Fold the completed project along the center line.

Good Neighbors Don't...   ## Good Neighbors Do...

fold

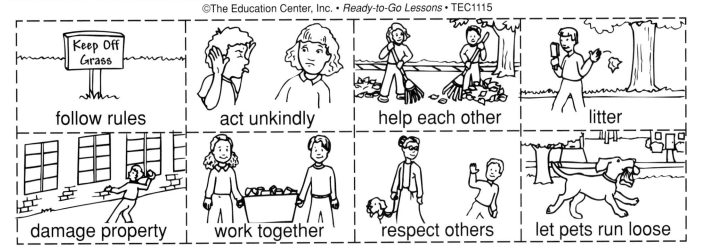

Keep Off Grass

follow rules | act unkindly | help each other | litter

damage property | work together | respect others | let pets run loose

How To Extend The Lesson:

- Have each student interview family members to find out how they show good neighborhood citizenship. Provide time for students to share their findings. Then have each student draw and label an illustration of her family demonstrating good neighborhood citizenship. Compile the completed drawings into a class booklet titled "Hello, Good Neighbor!"

- Challenge students to cut out examples from discarded magazines of different types of neighborhoods and people showing neighborly acts. Have students glue their pictures in collage fashion to a large piece of bulletin-board paper. Mount the completed collage to a large wall; then add the title "Welcome To The Neighborhood!"

- Reinforce neighborly relations with this thank-you note project. Invite each child to tell about a person in the community who has demonstrated neighborhood citizenship. Then instruct each youngster to fold a sheet of construction paper in half to make a card. Next have him write a note of gratitude to this person. Then invite him to decorate his card as desired. Encourage each child to hand-deliver his note of appreciation.

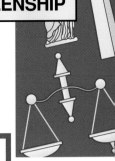

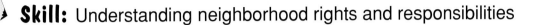

Neighborhood Know-How!

*Help your students learn to be good neighbors
and use their rights responsibly.*

Skill: Understanding neighborhood rights and responsibilities

Estimated Lesson Time: 30 minutes

Teacher Preparation:
Duplicate page 267 for each student.

Materials:
1 copy of page 267 for each student
crayons

Background Information:
Neighborhood responsibilities include the following:
• helping to keep the neighborhood clean
• keeping noise at an appropriate level
• following safety rules
• being considerate of other people's feelings
• respecting other people's privacy
• respecting other people's property

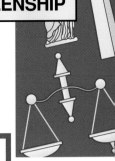

Understanding neighborhood rights and responsibilities   265

Introducing The Lesson:

Write the word *neighbor* on the chalkboard. Ask each student to think of a good neighbor who lives near him. Challenge him to think about the characteristics that make this person a good neighbor.

Steps:

1. Encourage each student to talk about the characteristics of a good neighbor. Write students' responses on the chalkboard.

2. Explain that all neighbors have rights and with these rights come responsibilities. For example, neighbors have the right to live in a clean community, so all neighbors are responsible for putting their trash in its proper place. Another example is that people have the right to be safe, so all neighbors need to be responsible and follow safety rules.

3. Ask students to give more examples of neighborhood rights and responsibilities. Guide students to include the responsibilities listed in the Background Information on page 265.

4. Distribute crayons and a copy of page 267 to each student. Instruct him to illustrate and write about a responsible neighborhood behavior.

5. Invite each student to share his completed work with the class.

6. If desired, display their work on a bulletin board or compile them into a class booklet.

He is stopping his car at a stop sign. This is responsible because he is being careful of others.

He is playing his boombox quietly. He is being responsible by not disturbing his neighbors with loud music.

Name _____

Neighborhood Know-How!

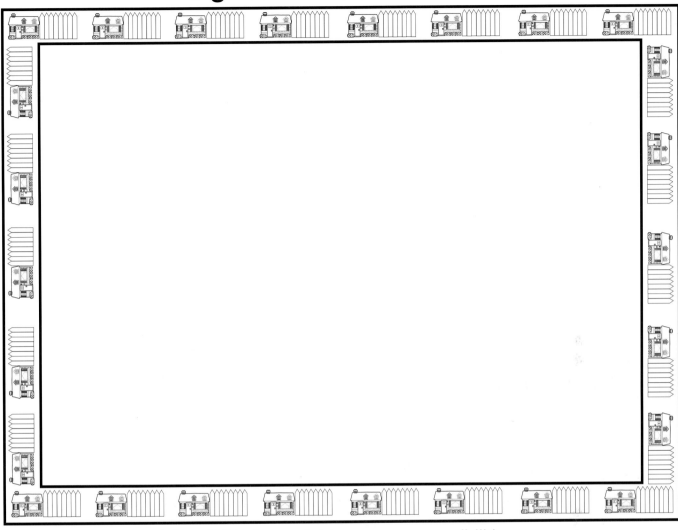

All neighbors have rights. With these rights come responsibilities.
Draw a picture of a responsible neighbor.

This neighbor is being responsible because _____

_____

_____

_____

_____

_____

_____

How To Extend The Lesson:

- Provide time for students to share examples of how they have been responsible neighbors and the rights that they protect by their actions. Create a newspaper titled "The Neighborhood News." Have students write or dictate articles about protecting rights in the neighborhood through responsible actions.

- Incorporate writing skills by having each youngster describe the rights and responsibilities that are evident in his neighborhood. If some responsibilities are not met, encourage each student to think of ways that he could improve the situation.

- For a truly hands-on activity, have students make these helping hand puppets. Have each youngster trace his hand on a piece of construction paper and cut the pattern out. Next have him draw a small self-portrait on the palm of his cutout. Then, on each finger, have him write a different way that he acts responsibly in his neighborhood. To complete the project, have each youngster glue his cutout to a craft stick as shown. Invite students to sit in a circle and use their puppets to describe neighborhood rights and responsibilities.

Let's Vote!

Youngsters will cast votes of approval for this democratic activity!

Skill: Participating in the democratic process

Estimated Lesson Time: 30 minutes

Teacher Preparation:
1. Duplicate page 271 for each student.
2. Determine issues to be put to a vote. (See list of suggestions below.)

Materials:
1 copy of page 271 for each student
chalk or dry-erase markers in
    assorted colors

Background Information:
Registration is the process by which a person has his or her name added to a list of qualified voters. When a person wants to vote, an official checks the voter's name against the list of qualified voters.

Possible Classroom Voting Issues
- The signal to be used for asking a question
- The method of lining up for the day
- The game to play at recess
- The color of crayon to be used in checking papers

Introducing The Lesson:

Ask students to think of a time when they may have had to make a decision at home—like what to eat for dinner or what program to watch on television. Then ask each student to think of how her decision might have been affected if another family member did not make the same decision.

Steps:

1. Inform students that each person has a chance to make her opinion known by putting an issue to a vote. The choice with the most votes—the *majority*—wins.

2. Tell students that you would like to use a different color of chalk (or dry-erase marker) during the lesson. Display three different colors of chalk. Ask each student to raise her hand to vote for the color of her choice. Tally students' votes on the board.

3. Ask students to determine which color wins the election.

4. Explain the practice of voter registration (see Background Information on page 269) and distribute a copy of page 271 to each student. Have her cut out the voter registration card (the top portion of the page), setting aside the tally sheet (the bottom portion of the page). Then direct the student to fill in the information on her registration card.

5. Announce the topic of the next election. Write the choices to be voted upon at the top of the chalkboard. Then have each student cut out her tally sheet and fill in the information.

6. Have each student, in turn, show you her voter registration card and cast a vote by putting her initials beneath her choice on the chalkboard.

7. Have each youngster tally the results on her sheet as you do the same on the board. Then tell which choice gets the majority of votes and announce the winner of the election.

Voter Registration Card

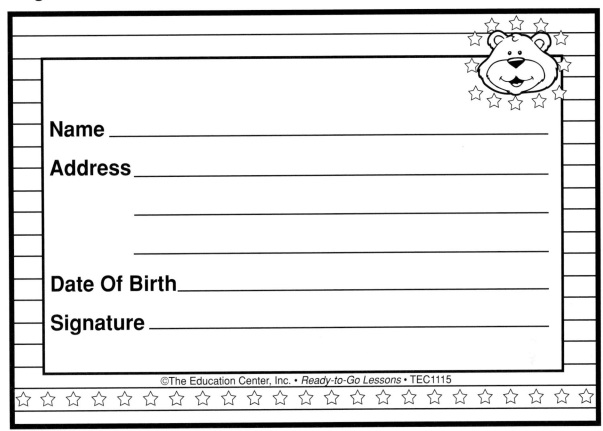

Name _____

Address _____

_____

_____

Date Of Birth _____

Signature _____

©The Education Center, Inc. • *Ready-to-Go Lessons* • TEC1115

Tally Sheet

Election Time

Topic: _____

Choices: **Tally:**

1. _____

2. _____

3. _____

4. _____

The majority voted for _____ .

©The Education Center, Inc. • *Ready-to-Go Lessons* • TEC1115

How To Extend The Lesson:

- Integrate a little graphing practice into your election results. After tallying the results of each election, draw a reusable bar graph on the chalkboard or a sheet of chart paper. Have each child place a mark on the graph to show how she voted. Then ask student volunteers to make observations about the resulting information.

- Arrange for a guest speaker from the voter registration office to visit your classroom. Have the speaker explain the registration process, including the use of ballots. If possible, have her show examples of ballots that have been used in previous elections. Then invite her to hold a mock election for students to participate in.

- Use the democratic process to create an interest in literature. At the beginning of the week, place three or four books in your reading center. Explain that you will read one of the books to the class on Friday. Invite the students to examine the books throughout the week. On Friday, write the title of each book on the chalkboard. Instruct each student to make a campaign poster or button to promote her preference. After displaying the projects, distribute a slip of paper to each student. Have her vote for one book by writing its title on her slip of paper. Collect the slips. Count each vote by making a tally mark on the chalkboard beside the corresponding title. Conclude the election by reading the winning book to the class.

A Treasure Of Maps And Globes

Yo-ho-ho! This treasure of an idea will help students discover the likenesses and differences between maps and globes.

Skill: Comparing and contrasting maps and globes

Estimated Lesson Time: 45 minutes

Teacher Preparation:

1. Duplicate page 275 for each student.
2. Copy each map and globe fact listed below onto a different yellow construction-paper circle (to represent a coin).
3. Place the coins into an empty box.

Materials:

1 copy of page 275 per student
11 labeled yellow construction-paper circles
1 United States map
1 globe
1 empty box (to be used as a treasure box)
tape
scissors
crayons
glue

Background Information:

- *Cartographers* are people who make and study maps.
- *Maps and globes* help us find things and places in our world.

Maps	Globes	Both
are flat	are round	have a compass rose, a key or legend, and a scale
are flattened, stretched-out pictures of the earth	show mostly oceans and land	become out-of-date (because of new things being built or name and boundary changes)
show many different kinds of places	show the entire earth	
are drawings or pictures of the earth	show the true shape of the earth	
	are models of the earth	

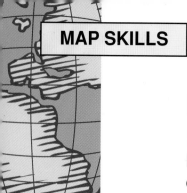

Introducing The Lesson:

Explain to students that long ago pirates traveled the seven seas, hiding their treasures. Show students the construction-paper coins, explaining that they are from a pirate's treasure chest. Ask your students to brainstorm how pirates would have found the treasure they had hidden. Then inform them that many people, including pirates, used maps or globes to find places or things.

Steps:

1. Show students a map and a globe. Have them tell some things they know about each one. List their responses on the chalkboard. Then share the Background Information on page 273.

2. Display the treasure box that contains the construction-paper coins. Draw a large Venn diagram on the board. Label the diagram as shown below. Then invite a volunteer to select a coin from the box. Direct him to read aloud the fact on the coin. Then challenge him to tape the coin to the appropriate place on the diagram. Repeat the process with additional volunteers. When every coin has been placed on the diagram, discuss how maps and globes are the same and different. Remove the coins from the board before beginning Step 3.

3. Distribute one copy of page 275 to each student. Discuss the directions with the students. Then have youngsters complete the page independently.

4. Challenge students to complete the Bonus Box activity.

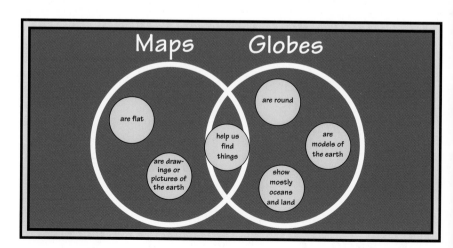

A Treasure Of Maps
And Globes

Read each fact on the coins below.
If the fact is about a **map,** color it **gray.**
If the fact is about a **globe,** color it **yellow.**
Then cut out each coin and glue it to the
   correct treasure chest.

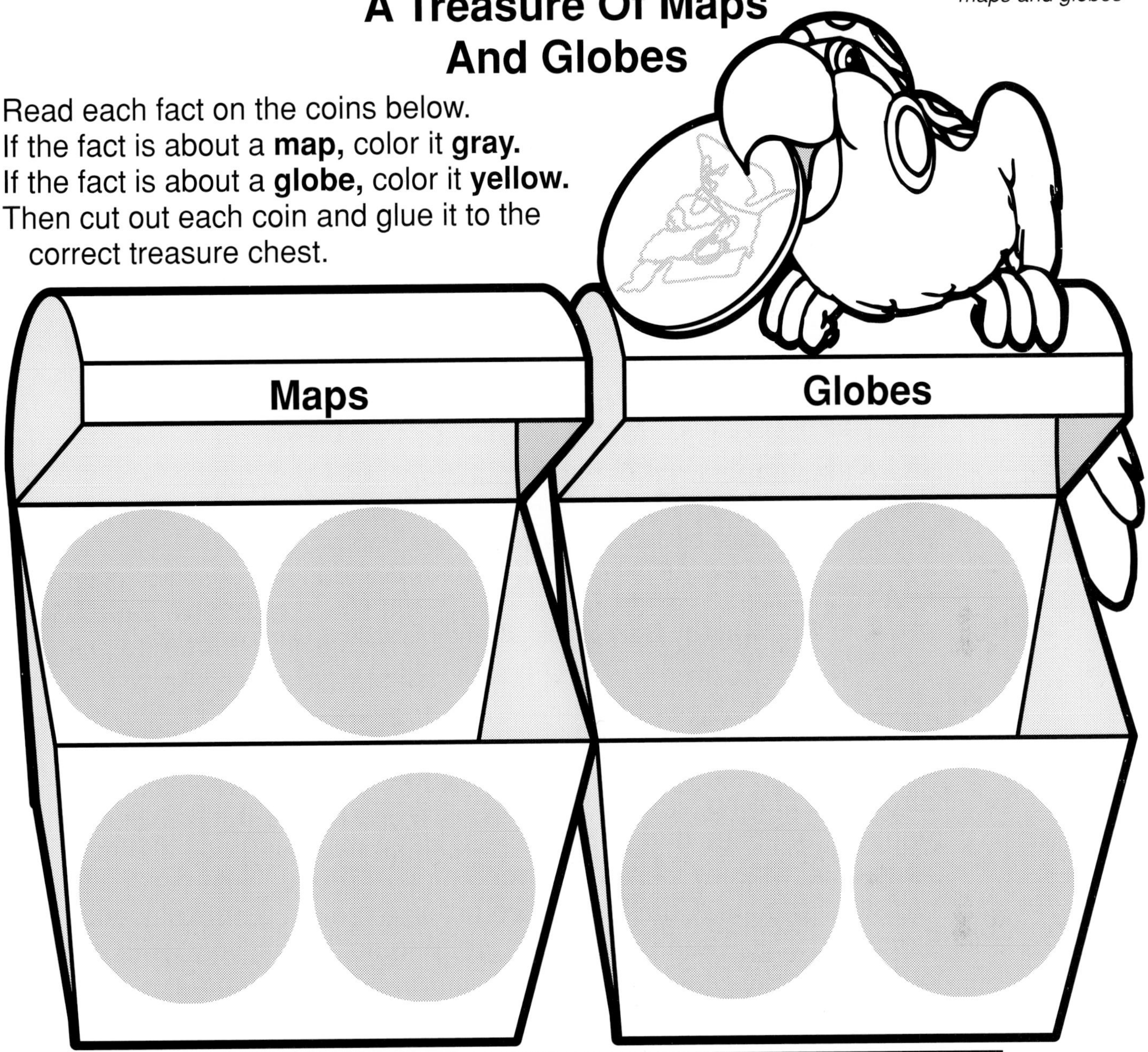

Maps

Globes

Bonus Box: On the back of this paper, write a story about a pirate looking for his lost
treasure. Include at least five facts about maps and globes in your story.

are flat

are models
of the earth

show
mostly land
and oceans

stretch the
shape of the
earth

show the
true shape
of the
earth

show
different
kinds of
places

are round

are
drawings
of places

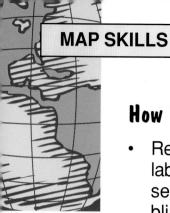

How To Extend The Lesson:

- Reinforce map and globe skills with this treasure hunt game. In advance, label your classroom "North," "South," "East," and "West." To play the game, select a student to be the "pirate." Send the pirate out of the room, or blindfold her so that she cannot see. Next choose another child to hide an object, or "treasure," somewhere in the classroom. Challenge the students to give the pirate cardinal directions to the place where the treasure is hidden. When the pirate finds the treasure, have her pick a new student to search for hidden treasure.

- Share these treasured books about maps and globes!
  —*Me On The Map* by Joan Sweeney (Crown Publishers, 1996)
  —*Maps And Globes* by Jack Knowlton (HarperTrophy®, 1986)
  —*As The Crow Flies: A First Book Of Maps* by Gail Hartman (Aladdin Paperbacks, 1993)
  —*Around The World* by Gary Hincks (Rand McNally & Company, 1997)
  —*Chester The Worldly Pig* by Bill Peet (Houghton Mifflin Company, 1980)

- Share the story *Flat Stanley* by Jeff Brown (HarperTrophy®, 1996). Flat Stanley is a young boy who has the misfortune of having a bulletin board fall on him, making him flat. He is sent in a letter all over the world, having many experiences during his travels. Have your students locate the places Flat Stanley visits on a world map or globe. Next divide students into small groups. Challenge each group to select a new place for Flat Stanley to visit. Then direct each group to collaboratively write a story to describe Flat Stanley's new adventure. Next instruct each group to cut a large rectangle from a large paper grocery bag or a large piece of brown bulletin-board paper. Then instruct each group to color the rectangle to look like a map of where Flat Stanley's new adventure takes place. To make its map look more authentic, have each group fold and then unfold it. Then direct each group to tape its story to the bottom of its map. If desired, collect the stories and staple them to a bulletin board titled "Flat Stanley, World Traveler."

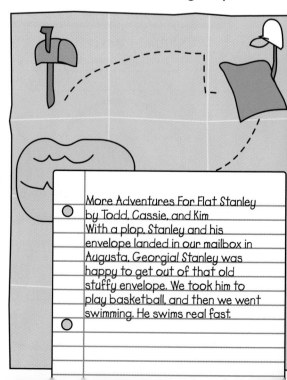

More Adventures For Flat Stanley
by Todd, Cassie, and Kim
With a plop, Stanley and his envelope landed in our mailbox in Augusta, Georgia! Stanley was happy to get out of that old stuffy envelope. We took him to play basketball, and then we went swimming. He swims real fast.

North, South, East, And West!

Keep your students headed in the right direction with this review of cardinal directions!

Skill: Using cardinal directions

Estimated Lesson Time: 30 minutes

Teacher Preparation:
1. Duplicate page 279 for each student.
2. Label each of four sheets of construction paper with a different cardinal direction: "N" for north, "S" for south, "E" for east, and "W" for west.

Materials:
1 copy of page 279 per student
labeled cardinal direction signs

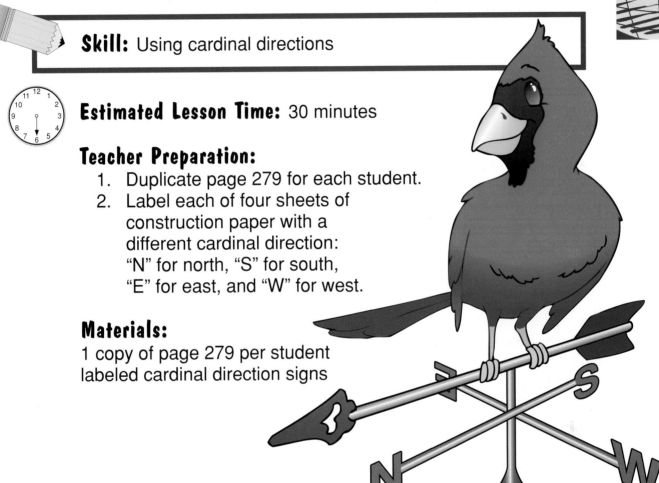

Background Information:

• A *compass rose* tells you directions, or which way to go.

• The compass rose was so named because, on paper, the drawing looked something like the petals of a rose.

• Each of the four main arrows on the compass rose points to a different direction. These directions are *north, south, east* and *west.*

• The "N" on the compass rose means *north,* the "S" means *south,* the "E" means *east,* and the "W" means *west.*

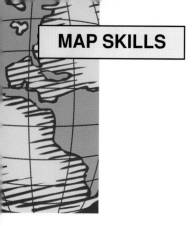
Introducing The Lesson:

Begin the lesson by posting each prepared cardinal direction sign on the appropriate wall of the classroom. Then ask a student volunteer to stand in the middle of the room. Have him follow simple directions, such as "Walk two steps north. Now turn and walk one step east."

Steps:

1. Share the background information on page 277. Tell students that they will be playing a game of I Spy using cardinal directions as clues.

2. Select a volunteer to be the Spy. Instruct the student to secretly think of one object in the room.

3. Direct the Spy to announce, "I spy an object by the [north, south, east, west] wall." Then have him call on another student to identify the object. If the student guesses correctly, he becomes the next Spy. If the student's guess is incorrect, the Spy must give other clues until the object is identified.

4. Play several rounds of I Spy until students exhibit an understanding of using cardinal directions.

5. Distribute a copy of page 279 to each student.

6. Review the directions with the class. Complete the first problem with students; then have youngsters complete the rest of the problems independently.

Which way to go?

Name _____

North, South, East, And West!

Help Mr. Cardinal find the objects on the map.
Follow the clues to find the object.
Draw the object you land on in the box.

N

W   **E**

S

---

1. Start at the butterfly.
Go east 2 boxes.
Then go south 3 boxes.
Draw a picture of the object you landed on.

5. Start at the footprint.
Go east 4 boxes and north 3 boxes.
Then go west 5 boxes and north 3 boxes.
Draw a picture of the object you landed on.

2. Start at the turtle.
Go north 2 boxes.
Then go west 2 boxes.
Draw a picture of the object you landed on.

6. Start at the compass rose.
Go south 1 box and west 5 boxes.
Then go south 2 boxes and west 3 boxes.
Draw a picture of the object you landed on.

3. Start at the whistle.
Go north 5 boxes.
Then go east 3 boxes and north 1 box.
Draw a picture of the object you landed on.

7. Start at the turtle.
Go east 2 boxes and south 4 boxes.
Then go east 7 boxes and north 2 boxes.
Draw a picture of the object you landed on.

4. Start at the spider.
Go west 4 boxes.
Then go north 4 boxes and east 2 boxes.
Draw a picture of the object you landed on.

8. Start at the heart.
Go south 5 boxes.
Then go west 3 boxes.
Draw a picture of the object you landed on.

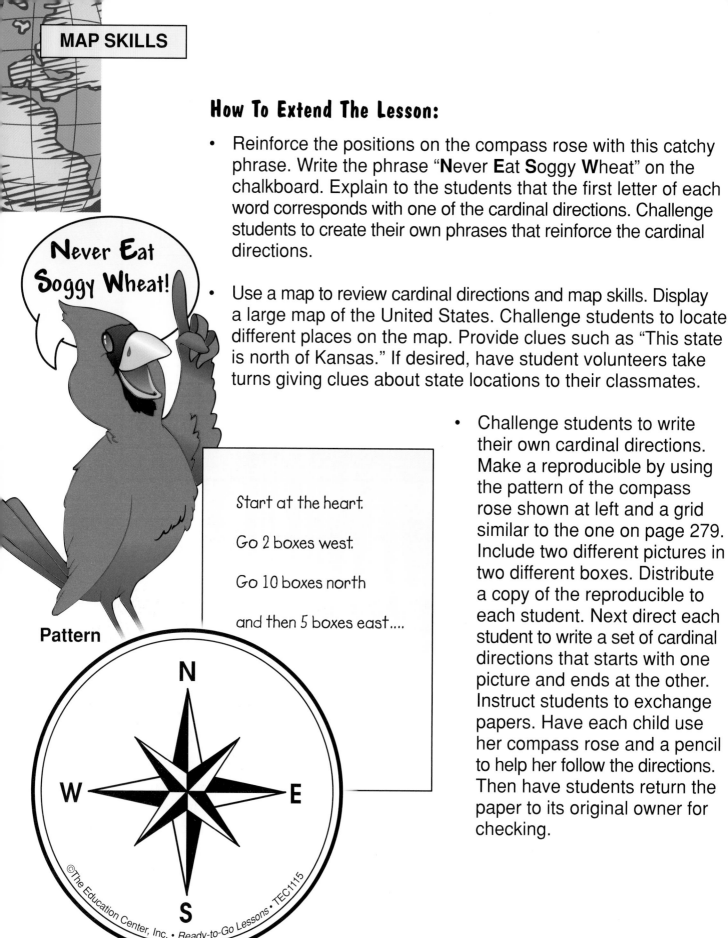

How To Extend The Lesson:

- Reinforce the positions on the compass rose with this catchy phrase. Write the phrase "**N**ever **E**at **S**oggy **W**heat" on the chalkboard. Explain to the students that the first letter of each word corresponds with one of the cardinal directions. Challenge students to create their own phrases that reinforce the cardinal directions.

- Use a map to review cardinal directions and map skills. Display a large map of the United States. Challenge students to locate different places on the map. Provide clues such as "This state is north of Kansas." If desired, have student volunteers take turns giving clues about state locations to their classmates.

- Challenge students to write their own cardinal directions. Make a reproducible by using the pattern of the compass rose shown at left and a grid similar to the one on page 279. Include two different pictures in two different boxes. Distribute a copy of the reproducible to each student. Next direct each student to write a set of cardinal directions that starts with one picture and ends at the other. Instruct students to exchange papers. Have each child use her compass rose and a pencil to help her follow the directions. Then have students return the paper to its original owner for checking.

Never Eat Soggy Wheat!

Start at the heart.

Go 2 boxes west.

Go 10 boxes north

and then 5 boxes east....

Pattern

©The Education Center, Inc. • Ready-to-Go Lessons • TEC1115

Welcome To The Neighborhood!

Get to know the neighborhood with the use of a map key.

Skill: Using a map key

Estimated Lesson Time: 30 minutes

Teacher Preparation:
1. Duplicate page 283 for each student.
2. Draw a simple map on a sheet of poster board. (See the example on page 282.)

Materials:
1 copy of page 283 for each student
simple poster board map

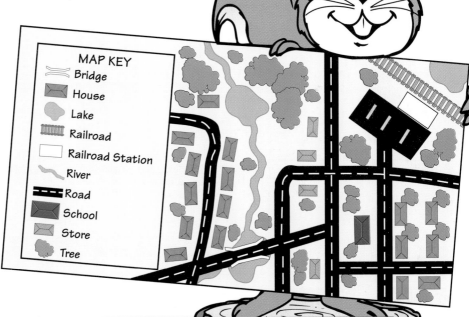

Background Information:
A *map* is a special drawing of a place or area.
A *symbol* is a picture that represents an object.
A *map key* explains what each symbol found on the map means.
A *compass rose* is a symbol that shows direction on a map.

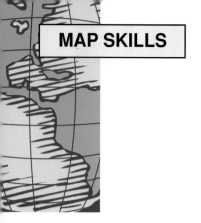

Introducing The Lesson:

Begin the lesson by drawing a simple house shape on the chalk-board. Ask students if they can identify the object you have drawn. Then draw a simple tree shape and repeat the question.

Steps:

1. Explain that the shapes you have drawn are *symbols,* or pictures that represent objects. Tell students that you will show them symbols, like the ones you have drawn, on a map. The symbols on the map will be explained in a map key.

2. Display the prepared map in a prominent location. Ask students to refer to the map key as they answer questions such as
   —How many houses are on the map?
   —How many trees are on the map?
   —What is near the lake?

3. Next explain the use of a compass rose. Review cardinal directions by asking questions such as
   —Is there a house south or north of the lake?
   —What is east of the lake?
   —Are there more houses in the east or in the west?

4. Distribute a copy of page 283 to each student. Review the directions and have each child complete the page independently.

5. Challenge students to complete the Bonus Box activity.

MAP KEY
House
Lake
Tree

N
W E
S

Name _____

Welcome To The Neighborhood!

Answer the questions.
Use the map key to help you.

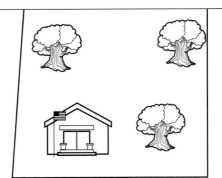

Acorn Avenue

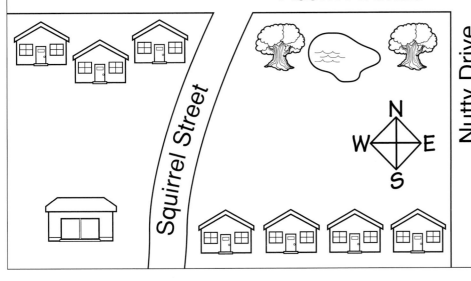

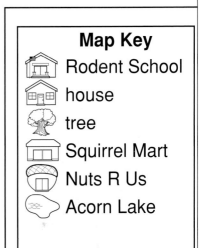

Map Key
Rodent School
house
tree
Squirrel Mart
Nuts R Us
Acorn Lake

Squirrel Street

Nutty Drive

N W E S

1. How many houses are on the map? _____

2. How many trees are on the map? _____

3. How many trees are north of Acorn Avenue? _____

4. How many houses are west of Squirrel Street? _____

5. Is Rodent School north or south of Acorn Lake? _____

6. How many houses are south of Squirrel Mart? _____

7. What is the name of the store on the east side? _____

Bonus Box: Add an airport to the map. Add an airport symbol to the map key.

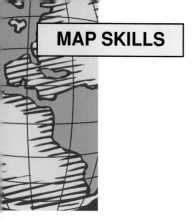

How To Extend The Lesson:

- Have students create a floor map of the area surrounding their school. Take students on a walk around the school. When you return to the room, have the class name the landmarks seen on the walk. With the students' help, use masking tape to map out the area on the carpet or floor in the classroom. Invite small groups of students to design a map key and symbols for the map.

- For an added challenge to the activity described above, have each student write a question that can be answered by looking at the map. Collect the questions. Review map skills by challenging students to answer the questions you read aloud.

- Invite your youngsters to compare the map keys of different maps. Ask each student to bring a map to school. When all the maps have been collected, have students discuss the similarities and differences among the map keys. Then challenge each student to design another symbol for his map key.

- Have each student design a map and map key for a park. Instruct her to include at least five symbols in her map key. For added fun, pair students; then have each pair swap maps. Challenge each youngster to ask her partner questions that can be answered by using the map key.

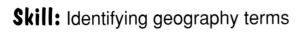

Land Ho!

Set your youngsters afloat with this booklet-making activity that reviews geography terms!

Skill: Identifying geography terms

Estimated Lesson Time: 30 minutes

Teacher Preparation:
1. Duplicate one copy of page 287 for each student.
2. For every two students, program one index card with an outdoor activity. (See the listed suggestions.)

Materials:
1 copy of page 287 per student
programmed index cards
crayons
scissors
glue

skiing
skating
sledding
swimming
fishing
running
boating
hiking
canoeing
walking
gardening
biking
camping

Background Information:

hill—a raised area of land that is lower than a mountain

lake—a body of water surrounded by land

mountain—a very high piece of land with steep sides

plain—a large, flat area of land

river—a large stream of freshwater that flows into a larger body of water

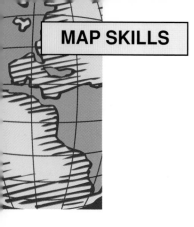

Introducing The Lesson:

Explain to students that they will be pantomiming some outdoor activities. Pair students; then distribute one programmed index card to each pair. Challenge each pair to act out the activity stated on its card. Encourage youngsters to guess the pantomimed activity. Write the name of each activity on the chalkboard as it is correctly identified.

Steps:

1. Share the Background Information on page 285. Ask students to decide where each activity listed on the sign could take place. Lead youngsters to the conclusion that some of the activities could take place on *landforms*—such as hills, islands, mountains, and plains—or in *bodies of water,* such as lakes or rivers.

2. Next distribute one copy of page 287 to each student.

3. Read aloud the title and have the student write her name on the provided line.

4. Then read aloud the definition on booklet page 1. Direct each student to illustrate the hill. Then challenge her to read and illustrate the definition on each remaining page.

5. To complete the booklet, have each student cut apart her pages along the bold lines. Direct her to glue the pages together where indicated. Then, starting with the title page, have her accordion-fold her pages along the dotted lines.

6. Invite students to take their booklets home to share with family members.

Glue page 3 here.

lake—a body of water surrounded by land

2

river—a large stream of fresh-water that flows into a larger body of water

5

hill—a raised area of land that is lower than a mountain

1

©The Education Center, Inc.

plain—a large, flat area of land

4

Land Ho!

And water, too!

Name _____

©The Education Center, Inc.

mountain—a very high piece of land with steep sides

3

©The Education Center, Inc. • *Ready-to-Go Lessons* • TEC1115

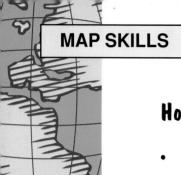

How To Extend The Lesson:

- Challenge your students to work creatively as they design a classroom country that includes landforms and bodies of water. Place a large, sturdy piece of cardboard and a supply of modeling clay in a learning center. Invite each student to visit the center to construct and label a landform or body of water out of the clay. Have him place his creation on the cardboard. Once every student has visited the center, invite the class to vote on a name for the country. Then place the completed project in a prominent location for all to enjoy.

- Impress your students with the geographical record holders listed below. Prompt a class discussion after sharing the information. Challenge students to find each location on a world map. Next have small groups of students illustrate a different record holder on a large sheet of construction paper. Then compile the completed pages into a class booklet titled "Record-Holding Wonders!"

  - Largest Sea—Coral Sea (1,850,200 square miles)
  - Largest Island—Greenland (840,004 square miles)
  - Largest Desert—Sahara in North Africa (3,320,000 square miles)
  - Highest Mountain—Mount Everest in China-Nepal (8,850 miles)
  - Highest Waterfall—Angel Falls in Venezuela (807 miles)
  - Deepest Cave—Jean Bernard in France (1,494 miles)
  - Longest River—Nile in Africa (4,160 miles)
  - Longest Lake—Caspian Sea, north of Iran (143,240 square miles

- Have your students create a wall mural that shows different landforms and bodies of water. Tape a large piece of bulletin-board paper to a classroom wall. Encourage students to draw and label the different landforms and bodies of water they have learned about. Display the completed mural throughout your study of geography terms.

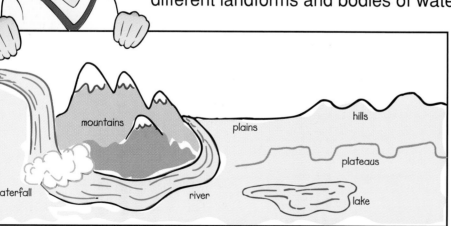

Down To Basics

*Help your youngsters understand that what they want
is not always what they need!*

Skill: Comparing and contrasting wants and needs

Estimated Lesson Time: 25 minutes

Teacher Preparation:
Duplicate page 291 for each student.

Materials:
1 copy of page 291 for each student
1 sheet of drawing paper for each student
glue
crayons
scissors

Background Information:
- **Needs**—things a person must have to live. The three basic needs are *food, clothing,* and *shelter.* People also need love and care.

- **Wants**—things people would like to have but do not need.

- In the past, most people worked with their families to grow or make the things they wanted and needed. They would grow fruits, grain, and vegetables; raise animals; sew clothes; and build their own homes. Today it is easier for most people to buy what they want and need at stores. Much has changed over time, but people's basic needs remain the same.

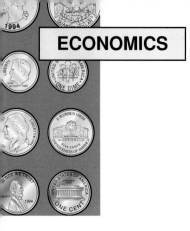

ECONOMICS

Introducing The Lesson:

Distribute one sheet of drawing paper to each student. Give each student 3–5 minutes to illustrate as many items in his home as he can. Then have him draw a star beside the three most important items on his paper.

Steps:

1. Share the Background Information on page 289. Explain that a *need* is something you must have to live, and a *want* is something that you would like to have, but do not need. Basic needs include food, shelter, and clothing.

2. Have each student revisit his paper. Direct him to circle all his *needs* with one color crayon; then have him circle all his *wants* in another color.

3. Instruct each youngster to share his paper with a partner. Challenge each student to compare and contrast his wants and needs with his classmate's.

4. Distribute a copy of page 291 to each student. Review the directions together. Then remind students that although each item on the page can be used for camping, Rodney Raccoon may only bring those things which are considered basic needs. Then have students complete the page independently.

5. Challenge students to complete the Bonus Box activity.

Comparing and contrasting
wants and needs

Down To Basics

Rodney Raccoon is shopping for his camping trip.
He only has room to pack his basic needs.
Color and cut out each picture.
Glue Rodney's basic needs to the appropriate shopping bags.

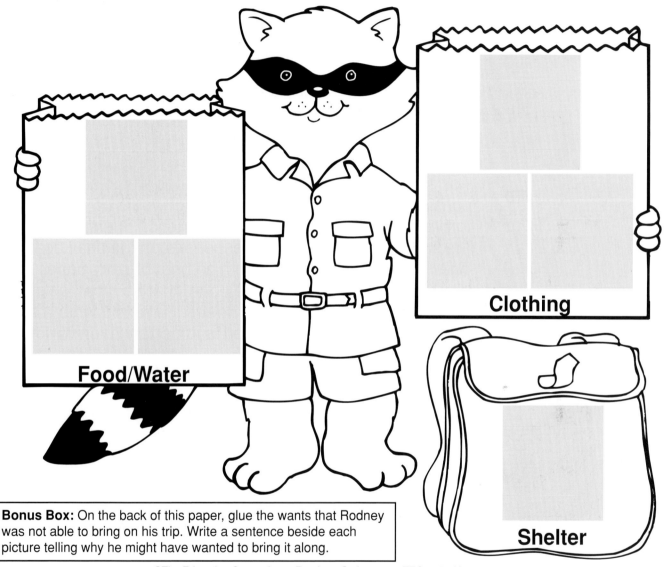

Bonus Box: On the back of this paper, glue the wants that Rodney was not able to bring on his trip. Write a sentence beside each picture telling why he might have wanted to bring it along.

©The Education Center, Inc. • *Ready-to-Go Lessons* • TEC1115 • Key p. 320

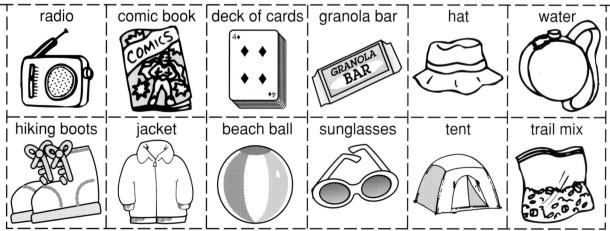

| radio | comic book | deck of cards | granola bar | hat | water |
| hiking boots | jacket | beach ball | sunglasses | tent | trail mix |

How To Extend The Lesson:

- Use this simple activity to ensure that each student in your class can distinguish between wants and needs. Provide each child with an index card. Instruct each student to write the word "Needs" on one side of his card, and "Wants" on the other side. Then call out assorted items—such as apple, video game, apartment, and pencil—one at a time. After each item is named, have students show you the corresponding side of their cards.

- Ask students to generate a list of things which are not considered the three basic needs, but would be very difficult to live without—like money, transportation, friendship, or medicine. List the students' responses on the chalkboard. Then provide each student with a sheet of story paper. Ask him to choose the item on the board that he most feels should be included among the basic needs. Have him write a paragraph explaining why this need is important; then direct him to illustrate it as desired.

- Reinforce wants and needs with this activity. Enlarge and duplicate one copy of the suitcase pattern below for each student. Direct each student to label one side of his suitcase "Wants" and the other side "Needs." Next have each student think of at least ten items he would like to take with him on an imaginary trip. Challenge him to include a balance of at least five wants and five needs. Then instruct him to list or illustrate each item on the appropriate side of his suitcase. Provide time for youngsters to compare their wants and needs to their classmates'.

Suitcase Pattern

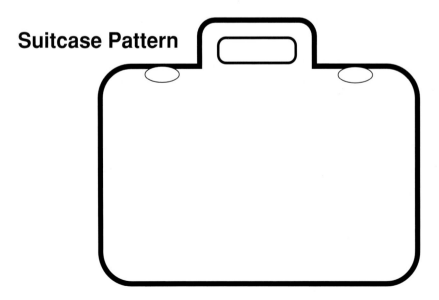

It's In Demand!

Strengthen students' understanding of supply and demand with this engaging game.

Skill: Understanding supply and demand

Estimated Lesson Time: 30 minutes

Teacher Preparation:
Duplicate page 295 for each student.

Materials:
1 copy of page 295 for each student
1 additional sheet of white paper
  per student
scissors
glue

Background Information:
- **Supply**—the number of items available
- **Demand**—the number of items wanted
- **Scarcity**—the lack of goods or resources as compared to what is wanted

When the *supply* is greater than the *demand,* store owners have too many items on their shelves. Sometimes owners drop prices so that it will be easier to sell the extra items.

When the *demand* is greater than the *supply,* the store owner may not be able to keep enough items in stock. The item becomes worth more because so many people want it, and the price may increase.

Things are considered more valuable when they are *scarce.*

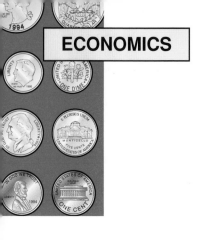

ECONOMICS

Introducing The Lesson:

Ask students to name items that have been popular and in demand. Reinforce examples such as beanbag toys, video games, newly released rental movies, and certain brands of sneakers. Help students to conclude that when these items are in demand, they can be hard to find and higher in price.

Steps:

1. Share the Background Information on page 293.

2. Distribute a copy of page 295 to each child. Then pair students. Distribute one pair of scissors to each twosome.

3. Ask students what the problem would be if you instructed them all to cut out their game cards. Guide students to understand that there are not enough scissors to go around. Inform students that this is an example of demand that is greater than supply.

4. Distribute additional scissors and instruct students to cut out their game cards. Explain that the cards will be used to play a game about supply and demand.

5. Explain the rules of the game as follows:
   —All players place their cards facedown in the center of their group.
   —Each student in the group takes a turn selecting two cards and placing them faceup. She reads the passages aloud and/or identifies the picture(s). If the cards make a match (a picture matches a passage), she keeps the cards and takes another turn. (Cards are coded for self-checking.) If the cards do not make a match, she returns them to their facedown position, and the next player takes his turn.
   —Play continues until all cards have been matched. The player who has the most cards wins!

6. When the game is over, have each student collect a complete set of cards. Direct him to glue the cards in matching pairs onto another sheet of paper.

There was a big storm.
Many houses were damaged.
What will be in demand?

The town is having a picnic.
People will buy food for the picnic.
What will be in demand? ●

The weather is getting colder.
Soon it will snow.
What will be in demand? ■

People are starting to think about spring.
They know that April can be a rainy month.
What will be in demand? ▲

 ●

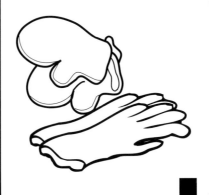 ■

 ▲

Something important has happened.
Everyone wants to know more about it.
What will be in demand? ♥

It's time for school to start.
Children will need supplies.
What will be in demand? ★

There was a big storm.
Many houses were damaged.
What will be in demand? ✗

 ♥

 ★

 ✗

How To Extend The Lesson:

- Ask students to discuss the concept of supply and demand with family members. Have each student bring to school a list of items that family members can recall being limited, and, if possible, the reasons why. Then discuss the completed lists in class.

- Have students think of how natural resources such as air, water, land, plants, and animals could be affected by scarcity. Discuss the importance of protecting the environment and our resources. Then have each student make a poster encouraging others to help take care of our planet.

- Have children consider the fact that the demand for services can exceed the supply. Discuss with your students services that can be affected by factors such as weather, or illness. Then have students role-play situations in which service workers must explain to customers why the services are not readily available.

- Encourage each student to draw a toy that would be in demand. Have her use her marketing skills to write an advertisement for her product, reminding her that her toy must have a special feature to make customers want to buy it. Provide time for each student to "advertise" her toy to the class. Encourage students to discuss what would happen if their products were popular and in demand.

Buy a Fuzzby!

It talks!
It sings!
It eats your broccoli!

Everyone loves Betsy!

The doll who tells you how to dress her.

All Around The Town

This activity will teach students that goods and services are provided all around the town.

Skill: Comparing and contrasting goods and services

Estimated Lesson Time: 45 minutes

Teacher Preparation:

1. Duplicate a copy of page 299 for each student.
2. Place an article of clothing, a can or box of food, and a toy in a shopping bag. (Substitute magazine pictures or drawings, if desired.)

Materials:

1 copy of page 299 per student
two 1" x 18" strips of black construction paper per student
one 1" x 12" strip of black construction paper per student
one 12" x 18" piece of green construction paper per student
crayons
scissors
glue
shopping bag filled with items described in "Teacher Preparation"

Background Information:

- **goods**—merchandise that people make or grow

- **service**—work that a person or company provides for others

- In the United States, people are able to own and run businesses without much government control. Each business tries to provide goods or services that are useful and well made. To succeed and compete with other businesses, these goods and services are offered at reasonable prices. This is the free enterprise system, upon which our country's economy is modeled.

Introducing The Lesson:

Begin the lesson by showing your students the prepared bag. Explain that you went to several shops in town and purchased a variety of goods. Write the word *goods* on the chalkboard.

Steps:

1. Remove one item from the bag. Ask students to guess the type of store in which it was purchased, and record reasonable responses under the word *goods.* Repeat this process for each item in the bag.

2. When the bag is empty, explain that you also spent some money on services, which could not be carried in a bag. Write the word *services* on the chalkboard.

3. Provide students with several scenarios, such as "I had my teeth cleaned," "I had the flat tire on my car repaired," or "I had my clothes cleaned." Ask students to guess where you'd been. Record reasonable responses under the word *services.*

4. Explain that money can be used to buy goods (merchandise) or services (work). Review the Background Information on page 297 with students.

5. Provide each student with the green and black construction paper and glue. Have each student glue the black strips onto his green construction paper as shown. Then direct each child to label one 18-inch strip "Goods Road," the other 18-inch strip "Service Street," and the 9-inch strip "[Student's name] Lane."

6. Distribute a copy of page 299 to each student. Ask each youngster to color and then cut out the buildings. Next have him glue each shop on the appropriate street, indicating whether goods or services are provided there.

7. Then have students exchange papers. Challenge youngsters to discuss why each building is placed in its location.

1ST PROMISE BANK

Bake-A-Cake Bakery

We Make Scents Florist

Cathy's CAR REPAIR

Fancy Fashions CLOTHING STORE

FUN FOR YOU TOY STORE

Bob's BARBER SHOP

SUPER FOOD GROCERY STORE

MILK 2¹⁹ GAL

Special! EGGS 99¢ DOZ

How To Extend The Lesson:

- Extend students' understanding of goods and services with this letter-writing activity. Ask students to think of a good or service they recently received and especially enjoyed or appreciated. (Perhaps a student is thankful for a new board game, a good dental checkup, or a nice haircut.) Have each youngster write a thank-you letter to the person, store, or company that provided the good or service. Encourage students to hand-deliver or send their thank-you notes.

- Explain to students that tax money is used to pay for services from the government. These services can be found in and outside of the local community. Elicit a student-generated list of government services on the board (such as a school, post office, police station, or library). Then provide each child with two 3-inch squares of white paper. Have each youngster draw and color a different community building on each square. Invite each student to cut out the buildings and glue them beside the others on Service Street.

- Tie your study of goods and services to a review of community helpers with this fun guessing game. Divide the class into two teams. Invite a student from the first team to come to the front of the room. Secretly assign her a career from the list shown. Ask the student to give three clues about her occupation to the class. If a member of her team can guess her occupation, the team earns one point. If the team can tell whether she provides a good or service, it earns an additional point. Play continues, alternating between the two teams, until each child has had a turn to give clues. The team with more points wins!

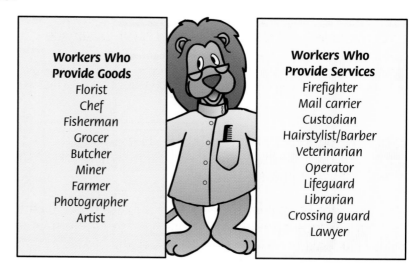

Workers Who Provide Goods	Workers Who Provide Services
Florist	Firefighter
Chef	Mail carrier
Fisherman	Custodian
Grocer	Hairstylist/Barber
Butcher	Veterinarian
Miner	Operator
Farmer	Lifeguard
Photographer	Librarian
Artist	Crossing guard
	Lawyer

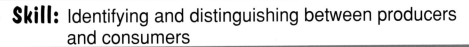

Producing Sharp Consumers

*Your young consumers are sure to profit when they complete
this lesson on producers and consumers.*

Skill: Identifying and distinguishing between producers
and consumers

Estimated Lesson Time: 40 minutes

Teacher Preparation:
1. Duplicate page 303 for each student.
2. Duplicate the response triangle pattern on page 304 for each
   student.
3. Collect several classroom items (such as a calculator, a box
   of crayons, a book, a box of tissues, a small article of clothing, and a food item) and place them in a shopping bag.

Materials:
1 copy of page 303 for each student
1 copy of the pattern on page 304 for each student
1 shopping bag
several small classroom items

Shop
till I drop!

Background Information:
- The United States produces (makes) and consumes (buys) goods and
  services to meet the wants and needs of its people.

- A *need* is something that is necessary for living. A *want* is something a
  person would like, but does not need in order to survive.

- *Goods* and *services* are things that can be bought and sold. Goods
  can be grown or made. Services are provided by people to help
  the public.

- *Producers* are people who provide goods or services that can be
  bought and sold. Examples of producers include cooks, farmers, bak-
  ers, and factory workers.

- *Consumers* are people who use goods and services. Examples of
  consumers include parents, moviegoers, video renters, restaurant
  patrons, students, mall shoppers, and bank customers.

Introducing The Lesson:

Display the prepacked shopping bag. Tell the students that you did a little shopping for school today. Unload the bag, one item at a time. Ask students to guess where each item was purchased. On the chalkboard, list students' responses, which may include guesses such as a *factory, store, farm, mall,* or specific store name. Explain that someone sold you each item, and before that, someone made it.

Steps:

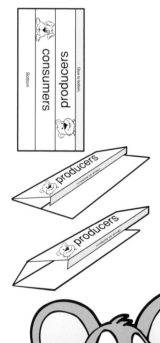

1. Share the Background Information on page 301. Explain to students that when you are shopping, you are a consumer. Encourage the class to brainstorm a list of other consumers and producers.

2. Next inform students that they are going to play a game to show their knowledge of producers and consumers. Distribute a copy of the pattern on page 304 to each student. Instruct each child to cut out the pattern along the dotted lines, fold it along the solid lines, and then glue the two outer flaps together as shown.

3. To play the game, announce a consumer or producer role. (See the Background Information on page 301 for examples.) Instruct each child to decide whether the role described names a producer or a consumer. Then have her display the correct side of the response triangle on her desk, facing you. Discuss the appropriate answer. Continue the activity until students appear confident in their responses.

4. Next give each student a copy of page 303. Review the directions with the class. Provide time for students to complete the activity independently.

5. Challenge students to complete the Bonus Box activity.

Name_____

Producing Sharp Consumers

Read the information in the box.
Decide which person below is a *producer* and which is a *consumer*.
Use the color code to color the symbol beside each item.
Write the reason for your choice on the blank.

Producers	Consumers
A producer is someone who provides goods or services that can be bought and sold.	A consumer is a person who buys the goods or services available for sale.
• The maker	• The customer

$$ 1. farmer _____

$$ 2. Mom and Dad _____

$$ 3. TV manufacturer _____

$$ 4. karate teacher _____

$$ 5. sports fan _____

$$ 6. shoe repairman _____

$$ 7. child in toy store _____

$$ 8. traveler _____

Bonus Box: On the back of this paper, list three things you would like to purchase as a *consumer*. For each one, write a sentence that tells what *producer* you would need to visit.

Color Code
green = consumer
purple = producer

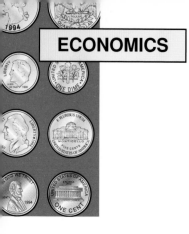

How To Extend The Lesson:

- Challenge youngsters to work together to create a mural depicting producers and consumers. Divide a large piece of bulletin-board paper into five sections. Label each section with a different heading: "Food," "Housing," "Clothing," "Transportation," and "Miscellaneous." Encourage the class to cut out advertisements from discarded magazines and circulars that fit into each category. Then have students glue their pictures to the appropriate section of the paper. Mount the completed mural and the heading "Second Grade Satisfies Consumers' Wants And Needs!" to a wall outside your classroom.

- Reinforce the concept of distinguishing between producers and consumers with this creative idea. Secretly assign each youngster a different producer or consumer. Then provide each student with a sheet of drawing paper and instruct her to illustrate her person. Then challenge her to show the class her picture and give clues until the identity of her person is guessed. Then collect the papers and display them on a bulletin board titled "Producer Or Consumer?"

Pattern
Use with Steps 2 and 3 on page 302.

Glue to bottom.

producers

consumers

Bottom

The World Of Work

Wants and needs, goods and services, buying and saving—
they're all part of the world of work!

Skill: Explaining uses of money as a means of exchange

Estimated Lesson Time: 30 minutes

Teacher Preparation:
Duplicate page 307 for each student.

Materials:
1 copy of page 307 per student

Background Information:
Wants are things a person or group wishes to have. *Needs* are things a person or group must have for its survival and well-being. *Goods* are items or products made or grown by people or companies. *Services* are jobs people do to help others. *Income* is the money people earn for the jobs they do. People use their income to buy the goods and services they want and need.

Introducing The Lesson:

Write "Wish List" on the chalkboard. Ask students if they know what type of items would appear on such a list. Confirm that wish lists name things that we would like to have. Then ask students to name things that they have wished for. Record responses on the chalkboard.

Steps:

1. After all students have had the opportunity to respond, ask them to identify ways to get the things they wish for. Acknowledge that sometimes we get these things as presents but that most often people work to earn money for the things they would like to have. Then share the Background Information on page 305.

2. Next write "Ways To Earn Money" on the chalkboard. Have students name chores or jobs they might do to earn money. List these responses on the chalkboard.

3. Distribute a copy of page 307 to each student. Explain that the newspaper pictured at the top contains information about an entertainment park. It also shows a list of jobs available.

4. Review the directions for completing the paper. Then have each child complete it independently.

5. Challenge students to complete the Bonus Box activity.

Wish List	Ways To Earn Money
skates	take out trash
video game	clean the garage
basketball	wash dishes
camera	do yard work

The World Of Work

Read the newspaper pages below.
Make a wish list of things you would like to do at Fun Town.
Then make another list of ways to earn the money.

Entertainment Section

Now Open **FUN TOWN!**
Come see us for fun!

Movie ticket	$3.00
Bowling	$3.00
Video tokens	$5.00
Face painting	$2.00
Pizza & soda	$4.00
Ice cream	$1.00

Help-Wanted Section

Now hiring part-time help.

Wash dishes	$1.00
Rake leaves	$5.00
Weed garden	$3.00
Sweep and mop ..	$4.00
Walk the dog	$2.00
Dust furniture	$1.00
Fold laundry	$2.00
Water plants	$2.00

My Wish List	Cost	Ways To Earn Money	Payment
_____	_____	_____	_____
_____	_____	_____	_____
_____	_____	_____	_____
_____	_____	_____	_____
_____	_____	_____	_____
_____	_____	_____	_____
Total	$ _____	**Total**	$ _____

Bonus Box: On the back of this paper, write about something you would like to have. Then explain how you could earn the money for it.

How To Extend The Lesson:

- Bring in an assortment of U.S. coins and currency for students to examine. Ask students to look for markings or features that make each denomination unique. Work as a class to make a chart listing each coin or bill, its value, and its distinguishing features. Then have students illustrate different coins and bills. (Some students may illustrate the same coin or bill.) Display the drawings and the chart on a bulletin board titled "Show Me The Money!"

- Send your students on a shopping trip without leaving the classroom. Organize the children into groups of four. Give each group a shopping list of five items and several sales circulars. Challenge each group to search the circulars for the best price on each item. After an appropriate amount of time, initiate a classroom discussion about the results of their bargain hunting.

- Reinforce students' understanding of making purchases with this activity. Give each student $20.00 in duplicated play money. Provide catalogs for students to look through for "purchases" they would like to make. Have each child write down what he would like to buy, why he wants it, and how much it will cost. Then have him total his purchases and attach the play money needed for his expenditures. Provide time for each student to discuss how much money he spent, the types of purchases he made, and what he plans to do with the remainder.

- Arrange a field trip to a bank to see how money is deposited and withdrawn, how it can be borrowed, and the different types of savings plans that are available. Also arrange for a bank employee to answer questions that students have prepared in advance. If possible, ask the bank to provide take-home information about savings programs for children.

I'd Like:	Why:	Cost:
toy dog	sister's b-day	$2.00
toy camera	take pictures	$3.00
gum	blowing bubbles	$1.00
soccer ball	playing soccer	$2.00
video game	give to brother	$10.00
	Total	$18.00

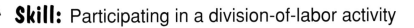
The Flower Factory

Student understanding of division of labor will bloom
with this cooperative activity!

Skill: Participating in a division-of-labor activity

Estimated Lesson Time: 30 minutes

Teacher Preparation:
Duplicate page 311 for each student.

Materials:
1 copy of page 311 per student
crayons
scissors
glue

Background Information:
People working together in communities help one another meet their needs for food, clothing, shelter, love, and safety. *Division of labor—* dividing work so that each person has a special job—produces more and better services for the same amount of work. With a division of labor, no one has to do all the work. For example, to make clothing we divide the labor. One group of people grows cotton, another makes thread out of the cotton, another turns the thread into fabric, and another fashions the fabric into a garment. People in communities share their work to save time.

Introducing The Lesson:

Begin the lesson by drawing a simple barn, chicken, and cornfield on the chalkboard. Ask students to name other items that can be found on a farm. List their responses on the chalkboard.

Steps:

1. After students have named several items, point out that a farm has almost everything a family needs to survive. Have students offer examples of needs that can be met with the resources on a farm.

2. Point out that many people no longer live on farms. Ask students how these people's needs are met. Reinforce that many people buy the things they need with money that they make from their jobs. Explain that instead of families working on farms to produce all their resources, we now have communities that divide the labor. Explain the Background Information on page 309.

3. Ask students to name different types of jobs in the community, such as a teacher, a baker, and a firefighter. Have the students identify the community's wants and needs that are met by having everyone contribute their skills to the workforce.

4. Tell students that they are going to work together to make a classroom bouquet. Each student in a group will be assigned one part of a flower to complete. Tell students that the labor will be divided so that each student can concentrate on his part of the job.

5. Place students in groups of four. Distribute a copy of page 311 to each child. Assign each group member a number that corresponds with one of the jobs listed on the page.

6. Provide time for each group to complete its flower. Allow time for discussion about how each group worked together to complete the job.

7. Collect the projects and display them as a classroom bouquet. If desired, present each student with a copy of the award pattern on page 312.

The Flower Factory

Your teacher will assign you a number.
Follow the directions for your number.

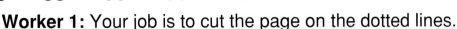

Worker 1: Your job is to cut the page on the dotted lines.
Give the piece with the **petals** to **Worker 2.**
Give the piece with the **stem** to **Worker 3.**
Give the piece with the **center** to **Worker 4.**
Make sure everyone is doing his job.

Worker 2: Your job is to color and cut out the petals. When you have completed your job, give the petals to **Worker 4.**

Worker 3: Your job is to color and cut out the stem. When you have completed your job, give the stem to **Worker 4.**

Worker 4: Your job is to color and cut out the center. When the other workers have passed their pieces to you, glue them together to make a flower.

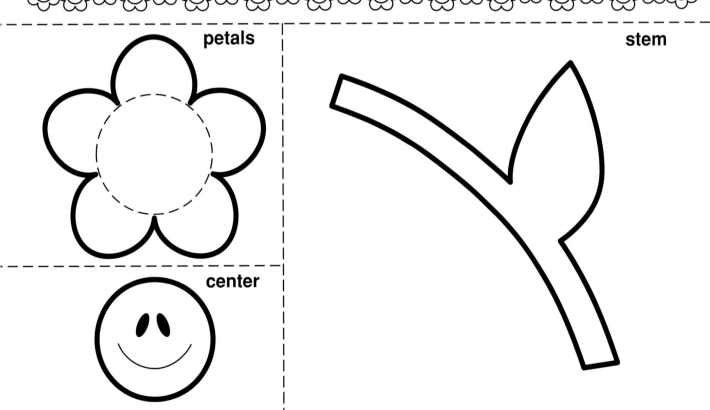

petals

stem

center

How To Extend The Lesson:

- Reinforce the concept that people in a community share work to help save time. Have each youngster illustrate one way people in his community share work, such as a farmer growing food that a grocer sells. Then instruct him to write a sentence or two that explains his illustration. Collect the papers and display them on a bulletin board titled "Sharing The Work!"

- Explain to students that keeping people safe in a community is a division of labor. Encourage youngsters to brainstorm emergency situations in which community members depend upon one another for help, such as when a rising river causes flooding or there is a widespread blackout. List student responses on the chalkboard. Then divide students into small groups. Have each group select a different situation from the list. Then instruct group members to determine how citizens work together to keep the community safe during its selected emergency.

- Invite parents or community members to visit the classroom and discuss their jobs. In advance, ask each guest to explain to students how they are part of a division of labor and how they need to count on others as well as be accountable to others. After each guest leaves, invite students to role-play some of the community workers at their jobs.

Award

Many Thanks
to you and your team
for a
job well done!

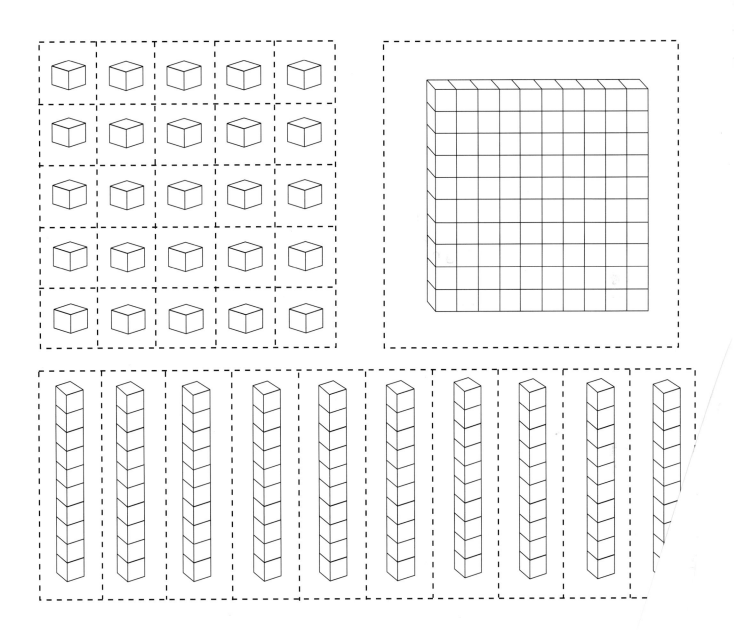

Clock Pattern
Use with the activity on page 145.

hour hand

minute hand

_____
(month)

Sunday	Monday	Tuesday	Wednesday	Thursday	Friday	Saturday

Note To The Teacher: Use with the fourth extension activity on page 152.

Patterns

Use with "Introducing The Lesson" on page 166 and with the fourth extension activity on page 168.

Answer Keys

Page 7

oo as in good
cook
look
took
foot
stood

oo as in food
choose
scoop
balloon
too
soon

Page 11

(The order of the answers will vary.)
long *a*
day, eight, rain, steak

long *e*
be, piece, seed, team

long *i*
buy, fly, nice, right

long *o*
hope, road, snow, toe

Page 15

(The order of the answers will vary.)
scr-
scrub, scratch, screen, scrape

spr-
sprout, sprinkle, spread, sprint

str-
stripe, straw, streak, street

Page 19

(The order of the answers will vary.)
synonyms
happy/glad
big/large
quick/fast
angry/mad
kind/nice

antonyms
hot/cold
open/close
day/night
in/out
up/down

Page 23

2. It's = It is
3. don't = do not
4. wouldn't = would not
5. I'd = I would
6. It's = It is
7. I've = I have
8. You'll = You will
9. you've = you have
10. You're = You are

Page 27

(The order of the answers will vary.)
1. doorbell
   doorknob

2. playhouse
   playground

3. goldfish
   starfish

4. sunrise
   sunshine

5. snowball
   snowflake

Page 31

cereal, chips, corn, crackers

pasta, peas, pickles, popcorn

salt, soup, stew, sugar

Page 35

cake—funny	game—juggle
candy	grape
cowboy	hero
desk	horse
doll	ice
eagle	insect
farm	jelly
fish	joke

Page 59

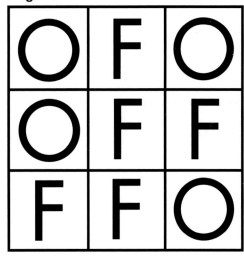

Who won the game? **F**

Who won the game? **O**

Page 71

1. period
2. period
3. question mark
4. period
5. question mark
6. question mark
7. period
8. question mark
9. period
10. question mark
11. period
12. period

Page 95

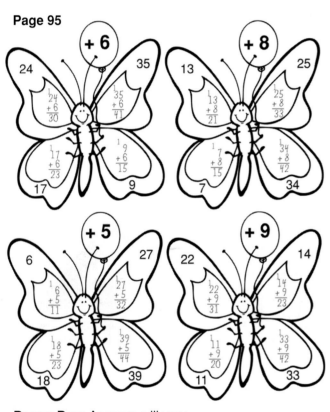

Bonus Box: Answers will vary.

Page 111

1. 853
2. 358
3. 385 or 583
4. 538 or 835
5. 972
6. 279
7. 792 or 297
8. 729 or 927
9. 641
10. 146
11. 164 or 461
12. 614 or 416

Bonus Box: Answers will vary.

Page 159

 1. I see 2 cars and 5 trucks. Sam sees 4 cars. How many cars are there?

2 + 4 = 6 cars

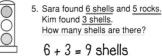 5. Sara found 6 shells and 5 rocks. Kim found 3 shells. How many shells are there?

6 + 3 = 9 shells

 2. Jan's garden has 6 flowers. Mike's garden has 2 flowers and 3 trees. How many flowers are there?

6 + 2 = 8 flowers

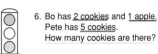 6. Bo has 2 cookies and 1 apple. Pete has 5 cookies. How many cookies are there?

2 + 5 = 7 cookies

 3. Bill has 5 frogs and 2 turtles. Jim has 3 frogs. How many frogs are there?

5 + 3 = 8 frogs

 7. Dave has 7 hats and 3 ties. Eva has 2 hats. How many hats are there?

7 + 2 = 9 hats

 4. Tom has 2 pennies and 4 dimes. John has 3 pennies. How many pennies are there?

2 + 3 = 5 pennies

 8. Jose has 4 sisters and 2 brothers. Alice has 3 sisters. How many sisters are there?

4 + 3 = 7 sisters

Bonus Box: Answers will vary.

Page 163

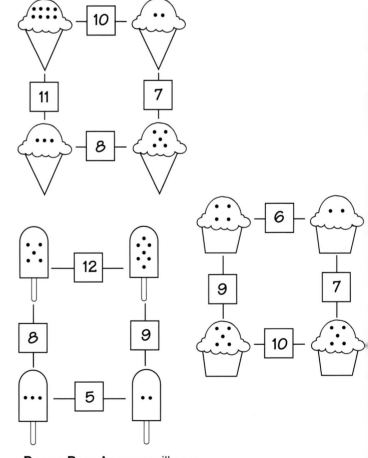

Bonus Box: Answers will vary.

318

Page 179
1. pistil
2. petals
3. stamens
4. stigma
5. anther
6. pollen

Bonus Box: Accept all reasonable responses.

Page 183
1. shade
2. fruits
3. roots
4. homes
5. soap
6. yards

Bonus Box: Accept all reasonable responses.

Page 187
1. mountain goat
2. camel
3. polar bear
4. elephant
5. chimpanzee
6. owl
7. dolphin

Page 191
fur: cat, giraffe, dog, bear, fox, mouse
feathers: owl, duck, parrot, chicken
scales: snake, turtle, crocodile
1. fur
2. 9
3. 7
4. mammals
5. birds
6. reptiles

Page 199
1. apatosaurus
2. ammosaurus
3. allosaurus
4. tyrannosaurus
5. stegosaurus
6. ankylosaurus
7. triceratops
8. brachiosaurus

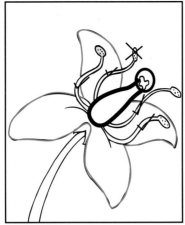

Page 239
1. Mercury
2. Venus
3. Earth
4. Mars
5. Jupiter
6. Saturn
7. Uranus
8. Neptune
9. Pluto

Page 243

The Sun gives off heat and light.

Grass and plants grow.

A cow eats the grass.

The cow produces milk.

The child drinks the milk.

Page 211
1. dentist
2. brush
3. plaque
4. floss
5. healthful
6. fluoride
7. milk
8. sugary

A bright smile!

Page 219
Heat: oven, geyser, toaster, heater, Sun
Light: firefly, laser, headlight, lamp, flashlight, Sun
Sound: horn, bell, radio, drum, telephone

Page 247

1. False—Earth only has one moon. There are other planets that have multiple moons.
2. False—Light from the Sun bounces off the Moon.
3. True—There is no atmosphere to scatter the light to see the colors in it.
4. True—The force of gravity on the Moon's surface is six times weaker than that on the surface of Earth.
5. False—You can see more than 30,000 craters from Earth.
6. False—They were caused by meteorites hitting the Moon's surface.
7. True—There are many sizes of craters on the Moon.
8. True—The Moon has no atmosphere.
9. False—There is no air or water, and the temperature is not suitable for living things.
10. True—There is no air for sound to travel through.
11. True—There is no atmosphere, which means there is no oxygen to breathe.
12. True—The path is oval shaped.
13. False—It takes almost one month.
14. False—As it moves around Earth, you see only the parts of the Moon that are lit by the Sun.
15. True—The phases follow the same pattern every four weeks.
16. True—In 1969, the Moon was the first object in space to be visited by humans.
17. True—The surface of the Moon gets much hotter and colder than any place on Earth.
18. False—Because there is no wind or rain on the Moon, its surface has changed little over billions of years.

Page 291
Food/Water:
granola bar
water
trail mix

Clothing:
hat
hiking boots
jacket

Shelter:
tent

Bonus Box: Answers will vary.

Page 303
(Reasons will vary.)
1. purple   A farmer sells his crops.
2. green   Parents buy household items.
3. purple   He is a person who makes and sells TVs.
4. purple   She provides a service.
5. green   She buys game tickets and sports equipment.
6. purple   He provides a service.
7. green   He is a shopper.
8. green   She buys airline tickets, souvenirs, and meals.

Bonus Box: Answers will vary.